Making MUG RUGS *& Cool Coasters*

Easy-to-Learn Techniques for Quilting and Sewing

Debi Schmitz Noriega

Landauer Publishing

Making Mug Rugs and Cool Coasters

Landauer Publishing, *https://landauer.foxchapelpublishing.com*, is an imprint of Fox Chapel Publishing Company, Inc.

Project Team
Editorial Director: Brian Hurley
Acquisitions Editor: Amelia Johanson
Editor: Christa Oestreich
Designer: Wendy Reynolds
Photographer: Mike Mihalo
Illustrator: Sue Friend
Proofreader & Indexer: Jean Bissell

ISBN 978-1-63981-157-1

Library of Congress Control Number: 2026943559

To learn more about the other great books from Fox Chapel Publishing, or to find a retailer near you, call toll-free at 800-457-9112 or visit us at www.FoxChapelPublishing.com.
We are always looking for talented authors.
To submit an idea, please send a brief inquiry to acquisitions@foxchapelpublishing.com.
Or write to:
Fox Chapel Publishing
903 Square Street
Mount Joy, PA 17552

Printed in China
First printing

FSC www.fsc.org MIX Paper | Supporting responsible forestry FSC® C147414

Coaster or Mug Rug?

The history of coasters started in 18th-century Europe as a functional tool and a badge of sophistication. Coasters are protective accessories, but they also reflect design, environmental ideas, advertising, and social interaction. Being slightly larger than the bottom of a glass, the main purpose of the coaster is to avoid water rings on surfaces.

Mug rugs are larger than coasters, most often 4" x 6" (10.2 to 15.2cm) to 10" x 12" (25.4 x 30.5cm). They are larger than coasters because mug rugs not only protect the surface from drink rings but also supply space for cookies or pastries. Furthermore, the larger size means they can be used under plants, to hold snacks, and displayed as decorative table mats. Mug rugs can be used in family rooms, living rooms, kitchens, offices, and many more areas.

Whether mug rug or coaster, these decorative table savers are fun to make, perfect for gifts, and a terrific way to try out different soft craft techniques without investing a lot of time, money, or effort. Since a set is the way to go, you'll have learned and mastered a new technique by the time you complete all four. I've included more than a dozen different techniques in this book: patchwork, paper piecing, *kawandi*, weaving, rope sewing, fabric folding, and more. Make identical sets or change each coaster/rug up a bit for a coordinated appeal—it's your choice. Start with your favorite technique or try something completely new!

This is the perfect book for creatives looking to land on a crafting technique that suits their style, taste, and skill level, letting you dabble before jumping in with both feet.

Contents

Basic Techniques & Tools

Please keep in mind that throughout this book I am using basic or beginning techniques and terms; however, I occasionally make mistakes when making quilt projects, just like you. Don't panic! Everything can be fixed in one way or another. Relax and enjoy the process.

Tools & Materials

Notes About Thread

I like to use Coats Dual Duty threads, although there are lots of options available to quilters. I have tried other threads, and this is just at my comfort level. Things to take into consideration when purchasing thread for your sewing machine:

- **Read the instructions** with your sewing machine and follow its guidance.
- **"All purpose" thread is safe** for most sewing projects. It is often a cotton blend.
- **Use strong thread.** Keep in mind that you will be sewing through several layers of fabrics and batting.
- **A cotton or poly-cotton blend** is usually the best thread for this type of quilting.
- **Evaluate threads on scraps** of fabric before and during the quilting process. Scraps of fabric are perfect for testing tension, stitch appearance, and the quality of the thread.
- **Keep care instructions in mind** for the fabric, batting, and thread. They need to be compatible.
- **Keep the threads clipped** throughout the project to keep them out of the seams.

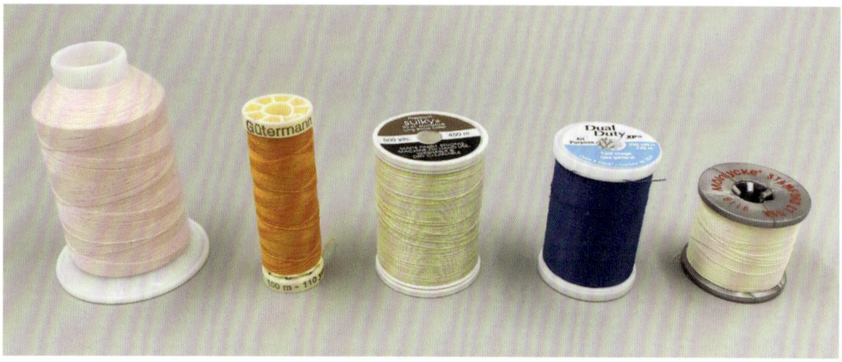

There are a lot of thread options out there; choose the one you feel comfortable with.

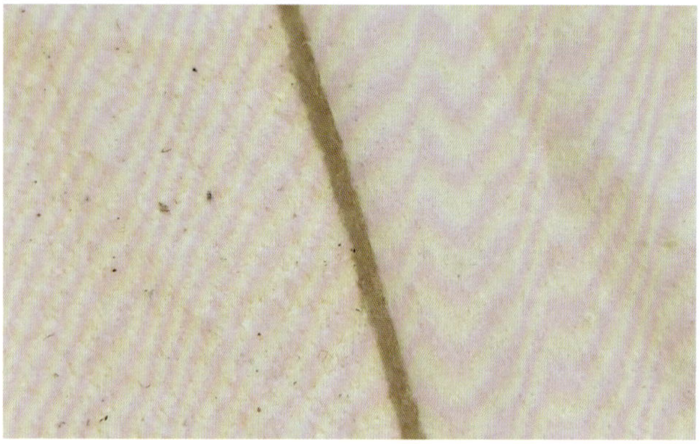

Needled cotton batting is a good choice for all the projects in this book.

Notes About Batting

I love working with Warm & Natural Needled Cotton Batting, but there are many different batting choices. Let me break it down a little:

- **Cotton batting** is lightweight and breathes well. I prefer needle-punched batting because it is felted with thousands of needle punches, so it holds together and does not pull apart easily.
- **Microwave batting** is fun when making mug rugs designed to be warm, such as trivets and coffee mug mats. Be sure to read all manufacturer's instructions before using.
- **Fusible batting** is a great alternative if you are worried about movement of your fabric pieces when quilting. I prefer to use basting spray as needed.
- **Polyester batting** is thicker but lighter weight. It does not breathe well but is usually warmer.
- **Wool batting** is lightweight and very warm. Another wonderful thing about wool batting is that it never shows creases or folds.
- **Bamboo batting** is a blend of 50% bamboo and 50% organic cotton. This batting is "green," meaning it is processed using pollution-free techniques. Bamboo is more expensive, but it drapes beautifully and dries quickly after washing. This is a great batting for an heirloom project.
- **Test your battings** for the appropriate iron temperature. Use a pressing cloth if necessary.

Bright colors and bold prints can turn any mug rug or coaster into a statement piece.

Notes About Fabrics

I prefer cotton fabrics but have used cotton/poly blends in this book as well. There is something beautiful in the feel of quality cotton.

- **Cotton** is tightly woven, easy to cut and sew, durable, and breathable. This fabric is the most popular among quilters.
- **Batik** is handmade and dyed to be great for adding color and texture to a project.
- **Linen** is used for an elegant appearance, but it has many characteristics to consider like washability and strength.
- **Felt** is a nonwoven polyester fabric. The felt that I use most often is Eco-fi® from Kunin®, which is made of recycled drink bottles.
- **The fabrics in this book are 44"–45"** (111.8–114.3cm) **wide.** If using different widths, keep this in mind when purchasing the fabrics and adjust accordingly.
- **Keep track of the laundering instructions** for the fabrics you choose. Make sure they are compatible. Test scraps for appropriate iron temperature.
- **Cut conservatively** from one end to the other when cutting fabrics. Never waste fabric by cutting from the center.
- **When sewing with a directional pattern fabric**, be mindful of the front and back as you create.
- **Keep a swatch for sewing.** I like to have a swatch of fabric that I can start the needle in and then stitch on the fabrics on which I am working. I use another swatch at the other end of the seam to end the threads.
- **Buy quality.** Color, strength, durability, feel, and appearance are worth the price.
- **Buy extra.** I always recommend buying a little more fabric than the pattern requires, in case you make a cutting mistake. Also, make sure the dye lot is consistent.

Basic Tools

- **Rotary Cutter** and **Extra Blades**—I would be lost without my rotary cutter. You may create all the projects in this book with simple fabric scissors, but why? If you have not tried a rotary cutter, give it a whirl. You will be so glad you did!
- **Cutting Mat**—This is a companion to the rotary cutter and comes in all sizes and colors. Choose what speaks to you. Mine is a basic one that is dark gray on one side and light gray on the other so I can flip it with different fabric colors in mind.
- **Acrylic Ruler**—Another companion of the rotary cutter. I love using a clear acrylic ruler that allows me to see what I am working with under it. The rotary cutter glides along the edge without bubbling or cutting the end of my finger off.
- **Thin, Sharp Quilting Pins**—I used to pick up the cheapest pins I could find for work in my studio. Let us not do that. I discovered that by using high-quality quilting pins, I get much better results and they do not all end up in the garbage because they bend.
- **Fabric Scissors**—Keep special fabric scissors in your possession and lock them up when you are not using them—unless you live alone. I am serious.
- **Needles** and **Strong Thread (Hand Sewing)**—There is usually a little hand sewing required when quilting. Keep your spools available, orderly, and visible.
- **Seam Ripper**—This is one of my best friends. I find myself ripping seams all the time. Keep a sharp one that fits in your hand comfortably next to your workstation.
- **Sewing Machine**—I love my Brother Pacesetter PS500. That is just me. When purchasing a sewing machine, do not go for the cheapest nor buy the expensive one that does everything including your nails. Talk to several different quilters, store owners, and friends that sew. Also read reviews and recommendations of reputable outlets.

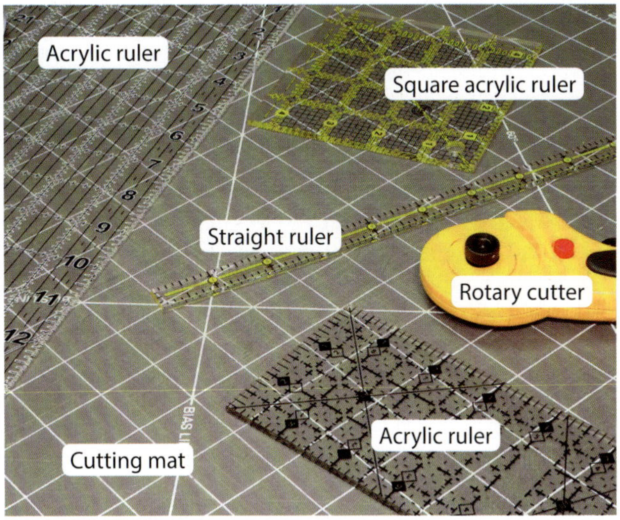

Make sure that you have a machine that is in fantastic working order and is up-to-date on maintenance. There is nothing worse than being ready to dive into a new project, and instead, ending up fighting with your machine.

- **Extra Needles for Piecing and Quilting**—Ask for the right needles for the job.
- **Machine Cleaning Tools**—A screwdriver and small brush are needed to periodically open the machine and remove lint.
- **Portable** or **Regular-Size Ironing Board and Iron**—I use both. My large iron and ironing board are great for large projects, but I love my wool ironing mat. It might smell like a wet sheep, but it works wonderfully.
- **Pressing Spray**—Love this. There is nothing like sewing pressed, firm fabrics. I just love the feel of the fabric in the sewing machine when it is not creased or holding fold lines.

Recommended Tools

- **Fabric Basting Spray**—I love this for a quick hold before sewing. Be sure to read all manufacturer's instructions before using.
- **Thimble** or **Finger Glove**—A thimble or finger glove is optional but helpful when doing hand stitching of bias tape and embellishment.
- **Chalk Pen** or **Fabric Marker**—I always have a pencil, water-erasable pen, chalk pen, or fabric marker in my toolbox. If nothing else, I can add to the grocery list next to me.
- **Walking Foot**—This foot is fantastic when you are sewing through multiple layers of fabrics.
- **Quarter-Inch Sewing Machine Foot**—When I started sewing, a long, long time ago, I was told that the presser foot will stitch a perfect ¼" (6.4mm) seam. Not anymore—look at your sewing machine tool kit. There are so many different types and sizes.
- **Seam Gauge Tool**—I love this tool. I have written several books with my sidekick, the seam gauge tool. It is the best for measuring small seams, stitches, or scraps of fabric.
- **Iron-On Adhesive**—This is a paper-feel product that has iron-on adhesive on one side. It is to be ironed to a piece of fabric, then that fabric is ironed to another like appliqué.

Optional Tools

- **Quilting Clips**—I love these for some applications, but I use the sharp quilting pins more. These would be safer for me.
- **Lint Brush** or **Roll**—Not only do I live in a house with pets, but I cannot stand all the tiny threads that collect on my projects and workspace. A lint roll is perfect for capturing all those cut threads. Also, when you rip out seams, this helps to remove that loose thread.
- **Pincushion** or **Container for Pins**—If you are like me, this is a necessity; otherwise, you will find yourself sitting on or stepping on those fantastic quilting pins. You do not want that.
- **Mini Iron** and **Pressing Mat**—Having these set up right next to your machine can make these projects go much more quickly.
- **Awl** or **Blunt-Point Instrument**—An awl isn't necessarily blunt, but whatever is chosen should help ease the fabric into the corners of a pillow without damaging the fabric.
- **Bias-Tape Maker**—This is a small metal or plastic tool. It folds the fabric strip in half as it is pulled through.
- **Grommet Template**—Grommet templates are clear pieces of plastic that have openings to draw through to mark the opening on the fabric. They come with the grommets.

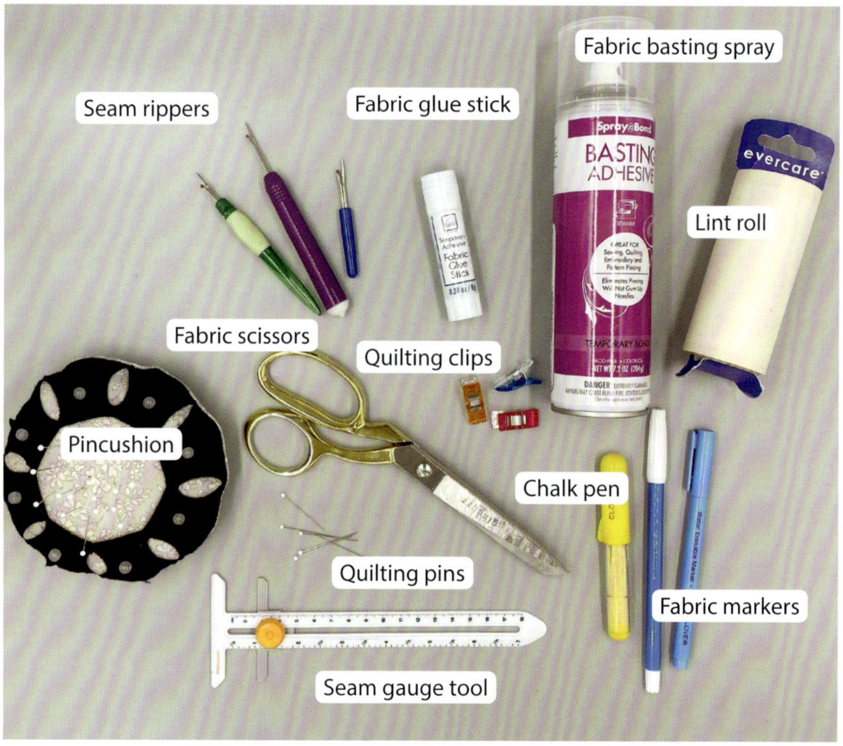

Finishing Techniques

Half-Inch Double-Fold Bias Tape

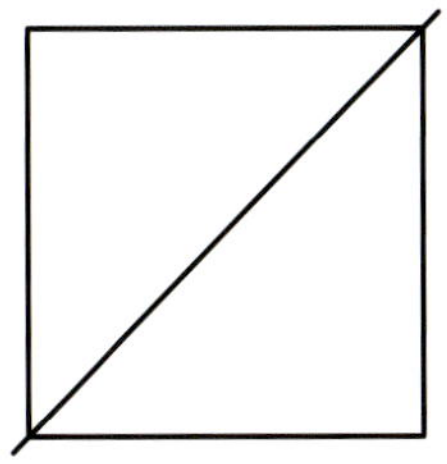

1. Cut the square of fabric across a corner, diagonally, for two triangular pieces.

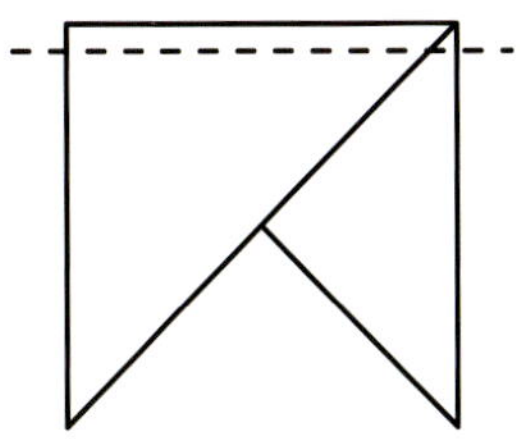

2. With right sides together and using a ¼" (6.4mm) seam allowance, sew the triangles together along one edge as shown. Press the seam allowance open.

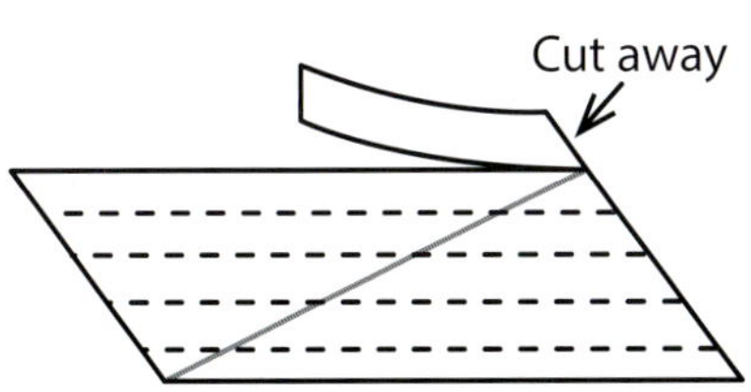

3. Draw lines 2" (5.1cm) apart from the bottom to the top of the fabric piece as shown. Cut off the excess fabric that is not a full 2" (5.1cm).

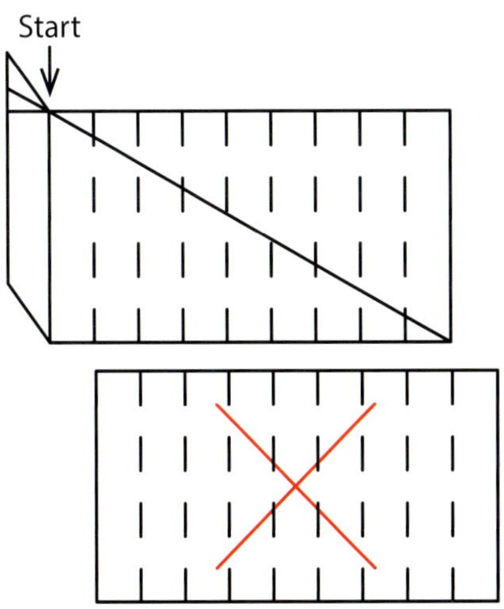

4. With the right sides (RS) on the inside, bring short edges together to form a tube. Offset the lines by one strip. **Do not line it up evenly.** Pin edges together by inserting pins ¼" (6.4mm) from cut edges through drawn lines. The lines should intersect at this ¼" (6.4mm) point. Sew edges together using a ¼" (6.4mm) seam allowance, and press open.

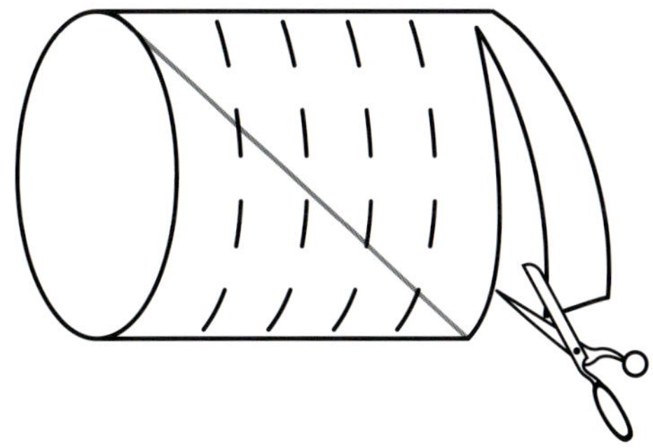

5. Cut along the pencil lines for a continuous 2" (5.1cm) strip of fabric, which is cut on bias.

> **One-Inch Single-Fold Bias Tape**
>
> Only follow step 6 if making a single-fold bias tape. Do not fold a second time. This will not be cut on the bias, just folded like bias tape.

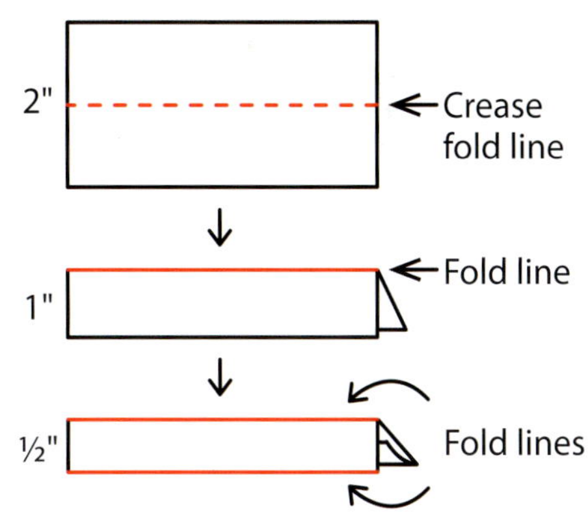

6. Use a bias-tape maker, if available, and follow the manufacturer's instructions. If no bias-tape maker is available, fold the fabric strip in half lengthwise and press. Open the strip, then fold the outside cut edges to the crease in the center of the fabric. Press these outside folds. Fold again to bring the outside folds together for the finished bias. Press folded edges.

How To Attach Double-Folded Bias Tape

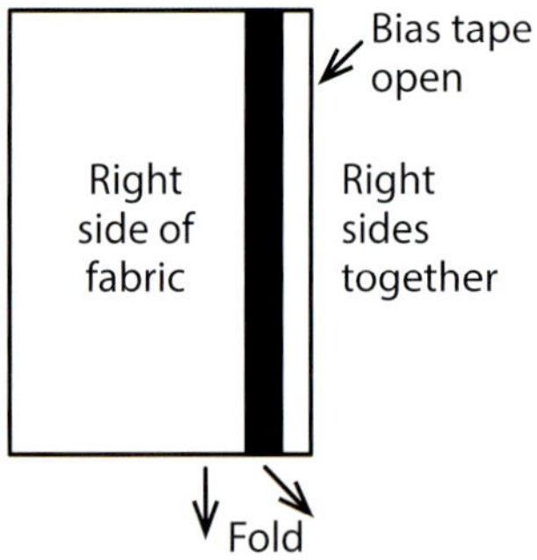

1. Line the raw edge of the bias tape with the raw edge of the quilted piece, right sides together (RST), and pin or clip. Sew a straight stitch along inside crease.

2. Fold the bias tape up and over the edge of the quilt to the back of the project. The center fold of the bias tape will line up with the raw edge of the quilt. Press and pin or clip on the back.

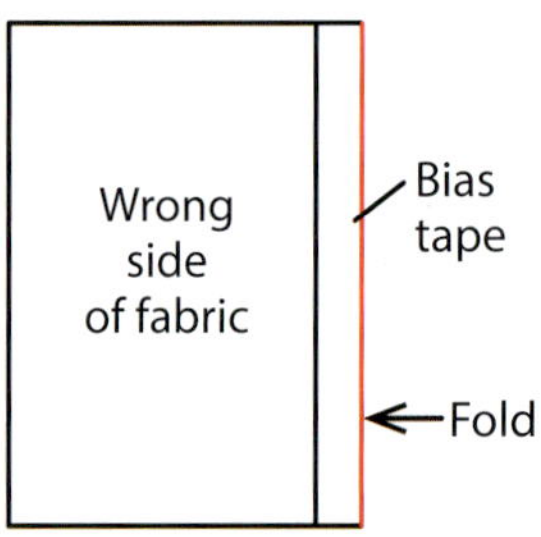

3. Sew along the bias tape from the RS, close to the folded edge.

4. To complete the corners, stitch up to ¼" (6.4mm) from corner. Pivot and stitch diagonally to the corner. Fold the bias tape back along the diagonal stitch line. Bring the fold up to the batting edge. Stitch from the batting edge to the next corner.

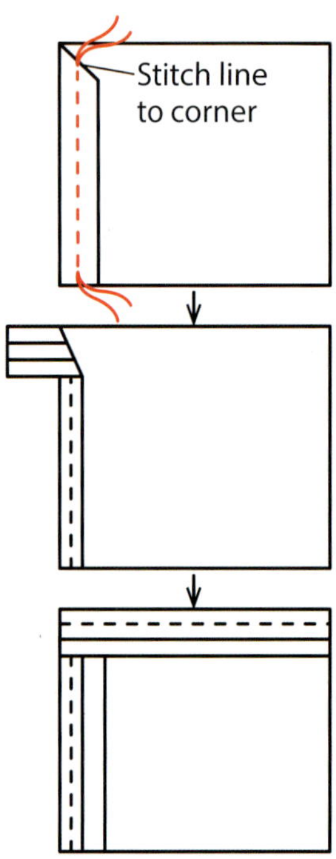

Straight Grain Binding

Binding with a Whipstitch Finish

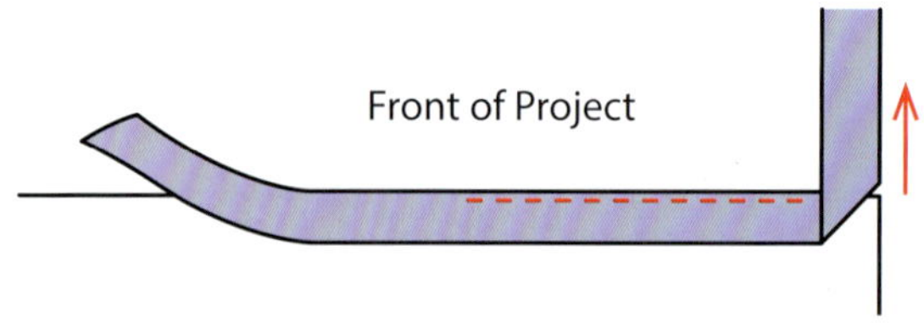

1. Fold the binding strip in half lengthwise, wrong sides together (WST). With raw edges aligned, start stitching your binding to the quilt edge, beginning on one side and leaving at least 5" (12.7cm) of unstitched binding as a tail. As you approach the corner, stop stitching ¼" (6mm) before you reach the edge. Fix (or lock) your stitching. Fold the binding up at a 90-degree angle.

2. Fold the binding back down so that the raw edge of the binding is flush with the raw edge of the quilt and the top fold is aligned with the original side. Begin stitching where you left off on the previous side, making sure to fix your stitch line at the starting point. Continue around the quilt, stopping approximately 7"–8" (17.8–20.3cm) from your starting point.

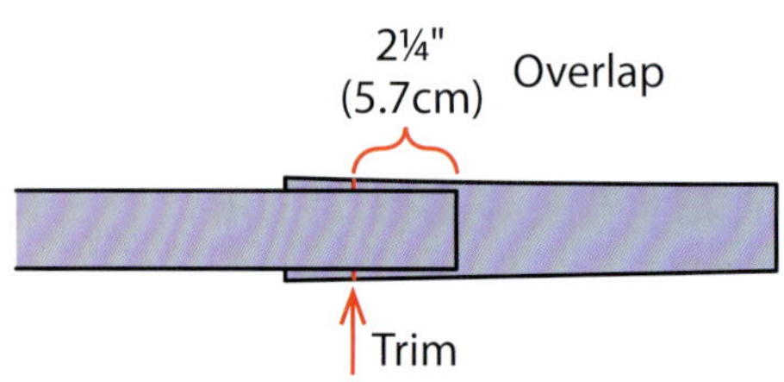

3. Place the tails smooth and flat along the quilt edge. The overlap will need to be the same amount as the width of your binding. For a 2¼" (5.7cm) binding, overlay 2¼" (5.7cm). Clip the excess ends of the tails perpendicular to the edge of the quilt.

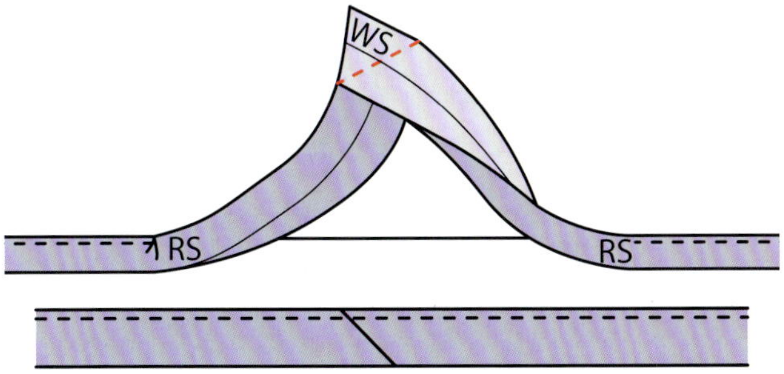

4. Place the ends RST at right angles. Stitch a diagonal line from corner to corner and trim off the corner, leaving a ¼" (6mm) seam allowance (top diagram). Now simply finger-press the binding into its original folded shape along the remaining raw edge of the quilt. Press, pin, and continue stitching to secure, fixing your stitch line as you start and stop (bottom diagram).

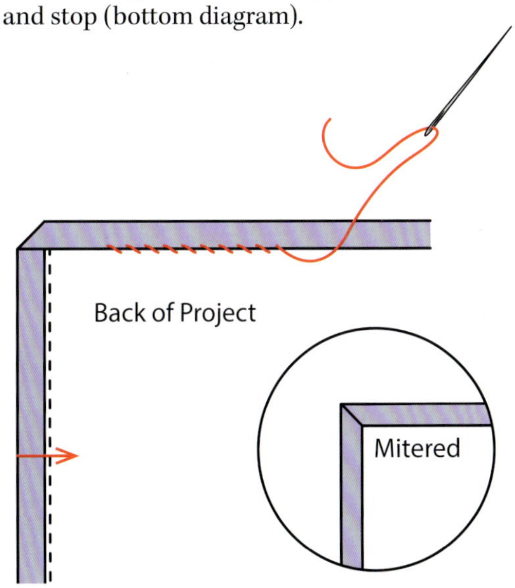

5. Press the binding away from the front edge and fold it over to the back of the quilt. Miter the binding at the corner and hand whipstitch into place with a single thread.

Binding with a Machine Edge Stitch Finish

Several of the projects in this book were bound in reverse; in other words, the double-fold binding was applied to the back side of the quilt first, wrapped around, and machine edge stitched through all layers to secure the binding to the front. To keep your binding in place for a machine finish, it helps to secure the binding to the quilt front with a fabric glue stick.

Embroidery Stitches

Sashiko Straight Stitch

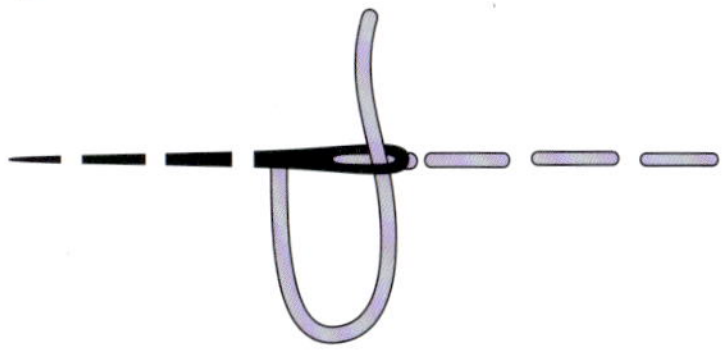

Blanket Stitch

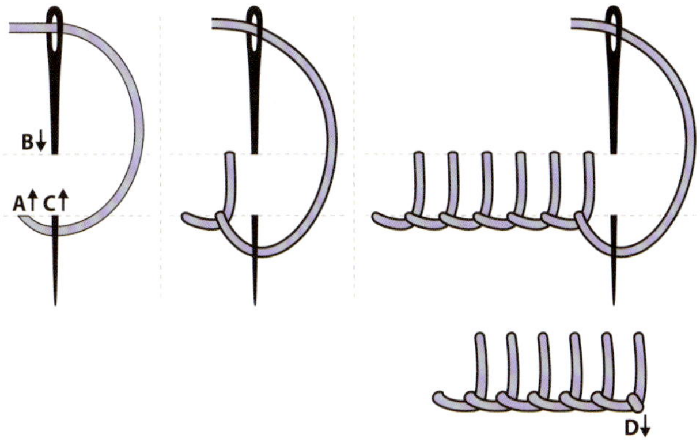

French Knot

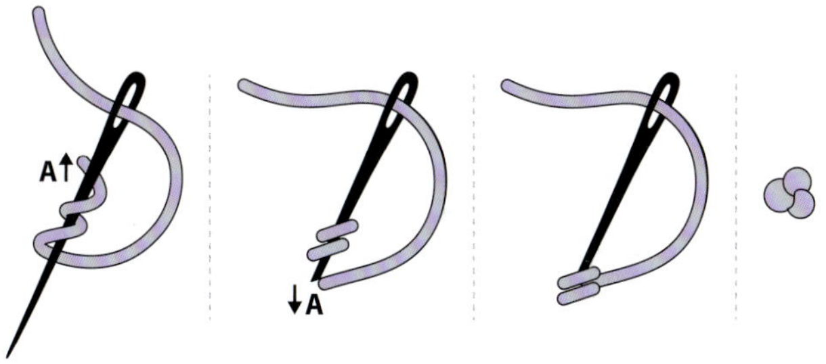

Lazy Daisy

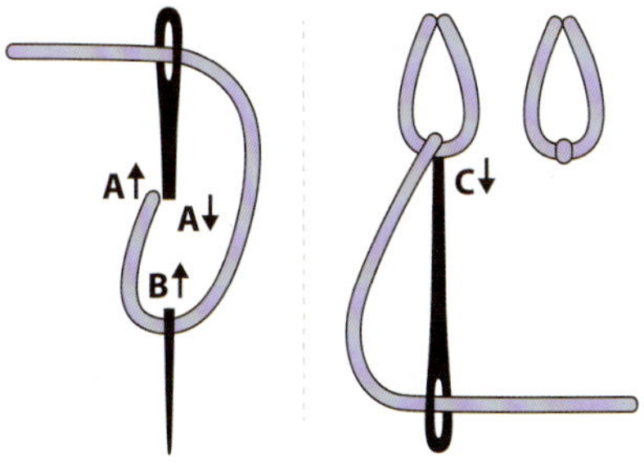

Whipstitch

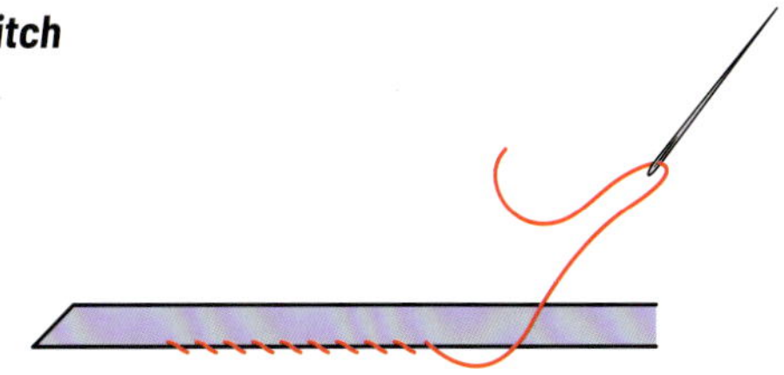

SCRAP PATCHWORK
Projects

The scrap patchwork technique means using fabric scraps to create new fabrics. Saving scraps of fabric in all colors, sizes, textures, and designs creates a treasure chest of possibilities. The scraps are most often used in string piecing, crumb piecing, or making traditional blocks.

My **Crumb Quilt Mug Rugs** are just that: "crumbs" of fabric joined to created six unique mug rugs.

The **Selvage-Edge Bias Mug Rugs** combine bias tape and unique fabric scraps. Saving the selvage edge of all fabrics used in the workroom provides opportunities for making unique mug rugs like these.

Crazy Quilt Tasseled Coasters are a fun way to use up fabric scraps and add embellishments for texture and color.

Crumb Quilt Mug Rugs

Finished Size: 5" x 7" (12.7 x 17.8cm)

Looking for a unique way to use up fabric scraps? Do you want to learn a new quilt technique that is extremely easy and relaxing? Crumb quilting is the art of creating fabric strips by stitching random scraps together. Long strips, chunky strips, blocks, and rectangles are used in crumb quilting. For these mug rugs, I created the crumb quilt strips and then incorporated them into patchwork designs.

Material Requirements

- Fat Quarter of rust print fabric
- Fat Quarter of lime green solid fabric
- (1) 18" x 44" (45.7 x 111.8cm) brown print fabric
- Fat Quarter of dark green print fabric
- Fat Quarter of light green print fabric
- Fat Quarter of orange print fabric
- Fat Quarter of yellow print fabric
- (6) 5" x 7" (12.7 x 17.8cm) batting
- Fabric scraps in colors: light green, white, blue, olive green, light yellow, rust, and purple
- Off-white thread
- Basic tools (page 7)

Cutting Requirements

Rust Print Fabric

- (2) 1¼" x 8" (3.2 x 20.3cm)
- (1) 5" x 7" (12.7 x 17.8cm)

Lime Green Solid Fabric

- (4) 1" x 8" (2.5 x 20.3cm)
- (3) 1" x 6" (2.5 x 15.2cm)
- (1) 5" x 7" (12.7 x 17.8cm)
- (1) 1½" x 6" (3.8 x 15.2cm)

Brown Print Fabric

- (2) 2" x 8" (5.1 x 20.3cm)
- (2) 1½" x 2¼" (3.8 x 5.7cm)
- (1) 20" x 20" (50.8 x 50.8cm) for bias tape
- (1) 5" x 7" (12.7 x 17.8cm)

Dark Green Print Fabric

- (1) 5" x 7" (12.7 x 17.8cm)

Light Green Print Fabric

- (1) 1½" x 6" (3.8 x 15.2cm)

Orange Print Fabric

- (1) 1" x 8" (2.5 x 20.3cm)
- (1) 5" x 7" (12.7 x 17.8cm)
- (1) 1½" x 6" (3.8 x 15.2cm)
- (1) 1" x 6" (2.5 x 15.2cm)

Yellow Print Fabric

- (1) 1½" x 10" (3.8 x 25.4cm)
- (1) 2½" x 2½" (6.4 x 6.4cm), cut in half diagonally for two triangles
- (1) 5" x 7" (12.7 x 17.8cm)
- (1) 1½" x 4" (3.8 x 10.2cm)
- (2) 1" x 8" (2.5 x 20.3cm)

Crumb Quilt Strip (For All Mug Rugs)

1. Organize the different fabric scraps into piles of matching colors.

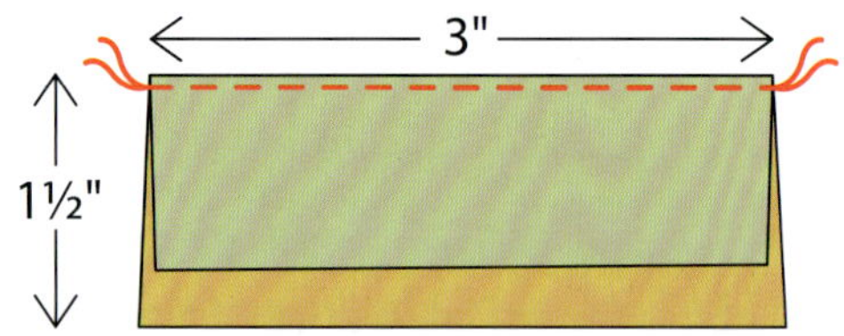

2. Start with (2) 3" (7.6cm) long scraps that are up to 1½" (3.8cm) wide. Sew them RST on one edge.

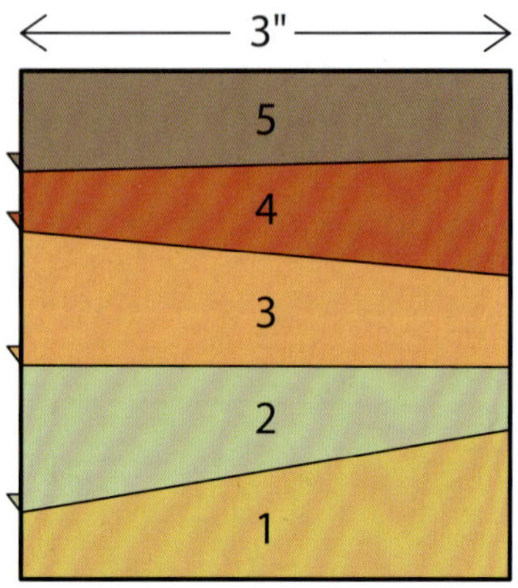

3. Repeat step 2, using all the fabric scrap colors listed in a random order. All scraps should be no more than 1½" (3.8cm) tall and no less than 3" (7.6cm) long. Because they are not perfectly rectangular, the scraps can be stitched diagonally if needed.

4. Press the seams to the darker fabric or where it naturally falls. Press after each piece is added.

5. Keep the strips of patchwork 3" (7.6cm) wide and stop when you reach 2½ yards (2.3m). Cut the finished patchwork into (11) 8" (20.3cm) strips.

Brown Horizontal Stripe Mug Rug

1. Trim (1) crumb strip to 2½" x 8" (6.4 x 20.3cm).

2. With RST, stitch (1) 2" x 8" (5.1 x 20.3cm) brown strip to the crumb strip. Press the seams.

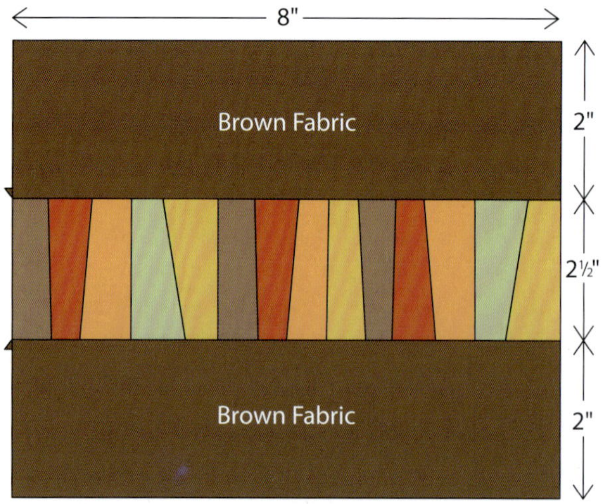

3. Stitch the other 2" x 8" (5.1 x 20.3cm) brown strip RST on the other side of the crumb strip.

4. Trim the mug rug front evenly from center out to 5" x 7" (12.8 x 17.8cm).

5. Make a quilt sandwich as follows: Lay (1) 5" x 7" (12.7 x 17.8cm) brown print fabric RS down. Lay (1) 5" x 7" (12.7 x 17.8cm) batting on top of the fabric. Lay the mug rug front on top of the batting RS up.

6. Stitch around the quilt sandwich as close to the edge as possible to keep all layers together.

7. Quilt as desired. I stitched straight lines from one short edge to another on the brown stripes.

8. Make ½" (1.3cm) double-fold bias tape from (1) 20" x 20" (50.8 x 50.8cm) brown fabric, as explained on page 9. Cut into (6) 30" (76.2cm) strips.

9. Fold the bias tape over the edge and hand sew to the back.

Yellow Diagonal Stripe Mug Rug

1. Lay (1) 1½" x 10" (3.8 x 25.4cm) yellow strip diagonally on (1) 5" x 7" (12.7 x 17.8cm) batting from the top-left corner. Place 1" (2.5cm) from the left edge and 1" (2.5cm) from the right edge. Trim to the batting.

2. Lay (1) 2" x 8" (5.1 x 20.3cm) crumb strip RST with the yellow diagonal, making sure it fits the batting. Sew the right edges to the batting. Flip the crumb strip back. Repeat with a second crumb strip on the left edge.

3. Sew (1) yellow triangle to the right edge of the right crumb strip, lining up with the top edge of the batting. Repeat for the other yellow triangle on the opposite corner.

4. Evenly trim the mug rug front to 5" x 7" (12.7 x 17.8cm), again using the batting as a template.

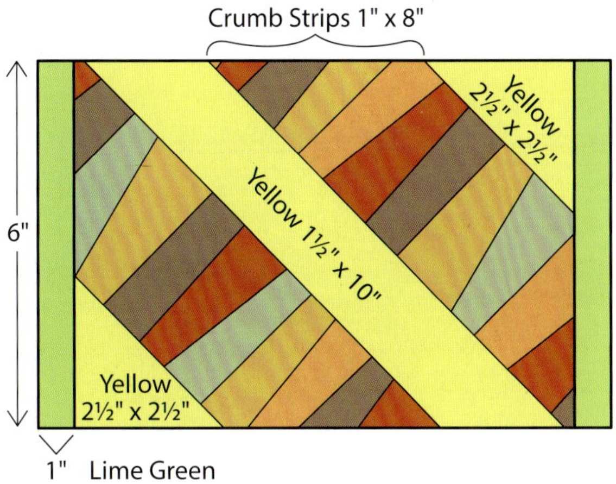

5. Stitch (2) 1" x 6" (2.5 x 15.2cm) lime green strips to the mug rug front, one on each end. Trim as needed.

6. Make a quilt sandwich as follows: Lay (1) 5" x 7" (12.7 x 17.8cm) yellow print fabric RS down. Lay (1) 5" x 7" (12.7 x 17.8cm) batting on top of the fabric. Lay the mug rug front on top of the batting RS up.

7. Stitch around the quilt sandwich as close to the edge as possible to keep all layers together. Quilt as desired.

8. Sew the bias tape to the front of the mug rug. Fold the bias tape over the edge and hand sew to the back.

Rust Horizontal Stripe Mug Rug

1. Cut (1) 3" x 8" (7.6 x 20.3cm) crumb strip into (2) 1½" x 8" (3.8 x 20.3cm) strips. Trim (1) 3" x 8" (7.6 x 20.3cm) crumb strip to (1) 2" x 8" (5.1 x 20.3cm) strip.

2. With RST, stitch (1) 1½" x 8" (3.8 x 20.3cm) crumb strip to (1) 1¼" x 8" (3.2 x 20.3cm) rust strip. Press to the rust fabric. Repeat with the other rust strip and 1½" x 8" (3.8 x 20.3cm) crumb strip.

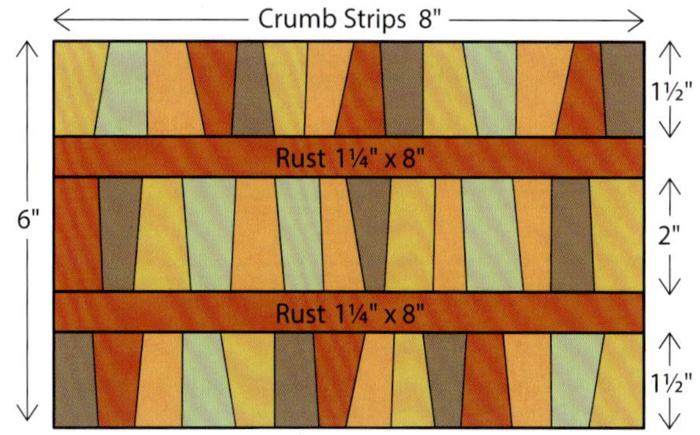

3. Using (1) crumb/rust strip, stitch the other side of the rust strip RST to (1) 2" x 8" (5.1 x 20.3cm) crumb strip. On the other side, repeat with the other crumb/rust strip. Trim to 5" x 7" (12.7 x 17.8cm).

4. Make a quilt sandwich as follows: Lay (1) 5" x 7" (12.7 x 17.8cm) dark green print fabric RS down. Lay (1) 5" x 7" (12.7 x 17.8cm) batting on top of the fabric. Lay the mug rug front on top of the batting RS up.

5. Stitch around the quilt sandwich as close to the edge as possible to keep all layers together. Quilt as desired.

6. Sew the bias tape to the front of the mug rug. Fold the bias tape over the edge and hand sew to the back.

Lime Green Horizontal Stripe Mug Rug

1. Trim (2) crumb strips to 1¾" x 8" (4.4 x 20.3cm).

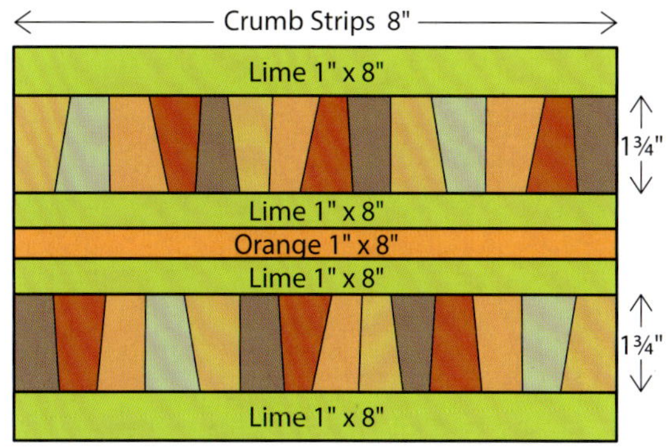

2. Stitch the stripes RST with the previous one. Press seams after every addition. From top to bottom, horizontally, stitch as follows:

- (1) 1" x 8" (2.5 x 20.3cm) lime green
- (1) 1¾" x 8" (4.4 x 20.3cm) crumb
- (1) 1" x 8" (2.5 x 20.3cm) lime green
- (1) 1" x 8" (2.5 x 20.3cm) orange
- (1) 1" x 8" (2.5 x 20.3cm) lime green
- (1) 1¾" x 8" (4.4 x 20.3cm) crumb
- (1) 1" x 8" (2.5 x 20.3cm) lime green

3. Trim the mug rug front evenly from center out to 5" x 7" (12.8 x 17.8cm).

4. Make a quilt sandwich as follows: Lay (1) 5" x 7" (12.7 x 17.8cm) orange print fabric RS down. Lay (1) 5" x 7" (12.7 x 17.8cm) batting on top of the fabric. Lay the mug rug front on top of the batting RS up.

5. Stitch around the quilt sandwich as close to the edge as possible to keep all layers together. Quilt as desired.

6. Sew the bias tape to the front of the mug rug. Fold the bias tape over the edge and hand sew to the back.

Yellow Horizontal Stripe Mug Rug

1. Trim (2) crumb strips to 2" x 8" (5.1 x 20.3cm).

2. Stitch (1) 1½" x 4" (3.8 x 10.2cm) yellow strip to (1) 1½" x 2¼" (3.8 x 5.7cm) brown strip. Stitch another 1½" x 2¼" (3.8 x 5.7cm) brown strip on the other end of the yellow strip.

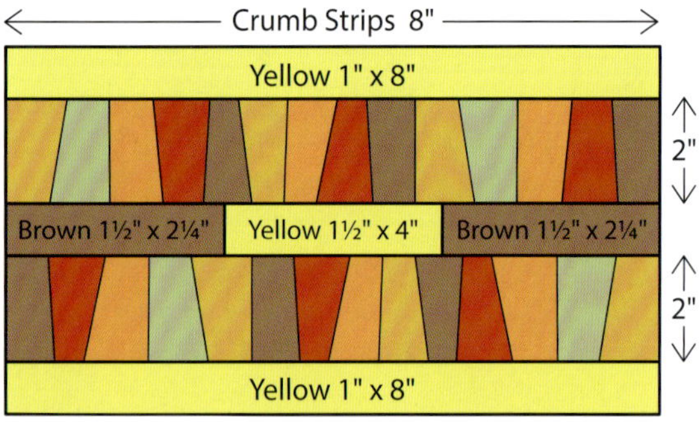

3. Stitch the stripes RST with the previous one. Press seams after every addition. From top to bottom, horizontally, stitch as follows:
- (1) 1" x 8" (2.5 x 20.3cm) yellow
- (1) 2" x 8" (5.1 x 20.3cm) crumb
- (1) 1½" x 8" (3.8 x 20.3cm) brown/yellow/brown strip
- (1) 2" x 8" (5.1 x 20.3cm) crumb
- (1) 1" x 8" (2.5 x 20.3cm) yellow

4. Trim the mug rug front evenly from center out to 5" x 7" (12.8 x 17.8cm).

5. Make a quilt sandwich as follows: Lay (1) 5" x 7" (12.7 x 17.8cm) rust print fabric RS down. Lay (1) 5" x 7" (12.7 x 17.8cm) batting on top of the fabric. Lay the mug rug front on top of the batting RS up.

6. Stitch around the quilt sandwich as close to the edge as possible to keep all layers together. Quilt as desired.

7. Sew the bias tape to the front of the mug rug. Fold the bias tape over the edge and hand sew to the back.

Multicolor Vertical Stripe Mug Rug

1. Trim (2) crumb strips to 2" x 6" (5.1 x 15.2cm).

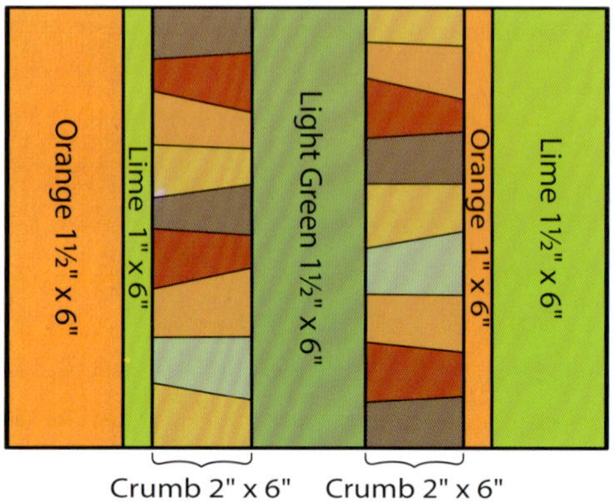

2. Stitch the stripes RST with the previous one. Press seams after every addition. From left to right, vertically, stitch as follows:
- (1) 1½" x 6" (3.8 x 15.2cm) orange
- (1) 1" x 6" (2.5 x 15.2cm) lime green
- (1) 2" x 6" (5.1 x 15.2cm) crumb
- (1) 1½" x 6" (3.8 x 15.2cm) light green
- (1) 2" x 6" (5.1 x 15.2cm) crumb
- (1) 1" x 6" (2.5 x 15.2cm) orange
- (1) 1½" x 6" (3.8 x 15.2cm) lime green

3. Trim the mug rug front evenly from center out to 5" x 7" (12.8 x 17.8cm).

4. Make a quilt sandwich as follows: Lay (1) 5" x 7" (12.7 x 17.8cm) lime green fabric RS down. Lay (1) 5" x 7" (12.7 x 17.8cm) batting on top of the fabric. Lay the mug rug front on top of the batting RS up.

5. Stitch around the quilt sandwich as close to the edge as possible to keep all layers together. Quilt as desired.

6. Sew the bias tape to the front of the mug rug. Fold the bias tape over the edge and hand sew to the back.

Selvage-Edge Bias Mug Rugs

Finished Size: 6" (15.2cm) diameter

For some reason, I've always been intrigued by the selvage edge of fabrics. It seems to be a secret code about that particular fabric, the collection, the designer if applicable, and colors used in the printing. To me, they are just cool, so I have saved them for many years. When I went to make round bias-stitched mug rugs, I thought that incorporating the selvage edge strips would be fun and colorful. I hope you do too!

Material Requirements

- (1) 24" x 44" (61 x 111.8cm) colorful fabric
- Fat Quarter or (1) 9" x 44" (22.9 x 111.8cm) red fabric
- Fat Quarter or (1) 9" x 44" (22.9 x 111.8cm) green fabric
- Fat Quarter or (1) 9" x 44" (22.9 x 111.8cm) blue fabric
- Fat Quarter or (1) 9" x 44" (22.9 x 111.8cm) yellow fabric
- Fat Quarter or (1) 9" x 44" (22.9 x 111.8cm) orange fabric
- Fat Quarter or (1) 9" x 44" (22.9 x 111.8cm) purple fabric
- (18–24) selvage edge strips
- (6) 6" (15.2cm) diameter needled cotton batting
- White thread
- Basic tools (page 7)

Cutting Requirements

Colorful Fabric

- (6) 2" x 42" (5.1 x 106.70cm)
- (6) 6" (15.2cm) diameter for backing

Red Fabric

- (2) 2" x 9" (5.1 x 22.9cm)
- (1) 6" x 6" (15.2 x 15.2cm) for bias tape, cut on bias

Green Fabric

- (2) 2" x 9" (5.1 x 22.9cm)
- (1) 6" x 6" (15.2 x 15.2cm) for bias tape, cut on bias

Blue Fabric

- (2) 2" x 9" (5.1 x 22.9cm)
- (1) 6" x 6" (15.2 x 15.2cm) for bias tape, cut on bias

Yellow Fabric

- (2) 2" x 9" (5.1 x 22.9cm)
- (1) 6" x 6" (15.2 x 15.2cm) for bias tape, cut on bias

Orange Fabric

- (2) 2" x 9" (5.1 x 22.9cm)
- (1) 6" x 6" (15.2 x 15.2cm) for bias tape, cut on bias

Purple Fabric

- (2) 2" x 9" (5.1 x 22.9cm)
- (1) 6" x 6" (15.2 x 15.2cm) for bias tape, cut on bias

Selvage Strips

- (18–24) ½" (1.3cm) wide x various lengths

Instructions

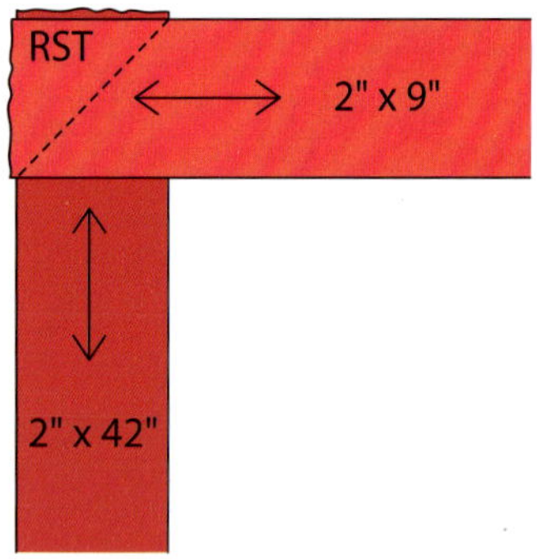

1. Sew (1) 2" x 9" (5.1 x 22.9cm) red strip RST to (1) 2" x 42" (5.1 x 106.7cm) colorful strip at a right angle. Add the other 2" x 9" (5.1 x 22.9cm) red strip to the other end.

2. Create a 60" (152.4cm) length of ½" (1.3cm) double-fold bias tape, according to the instructions on page 9.

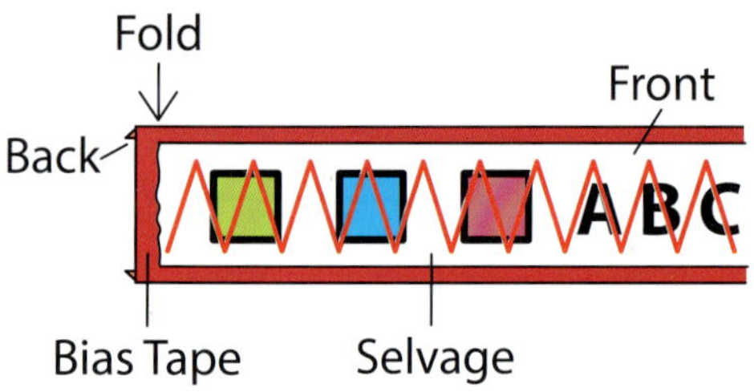

3. Zigzag stitch (3–4) selvage-edge strips to the center of the bias tape intermittently, depending on their length, approximately 6" (15.2cm) apart.

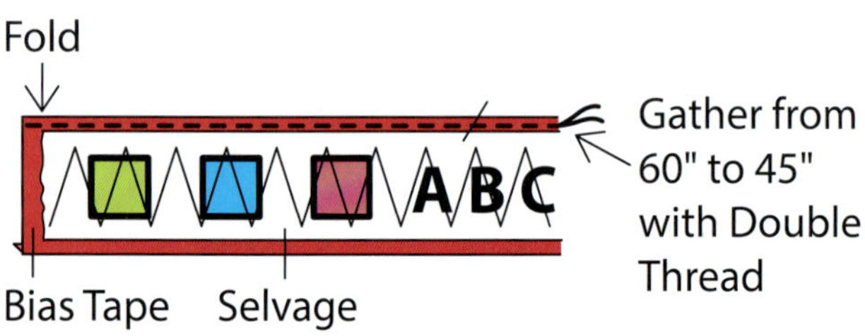

4. Evenly gather the embellished 60" (152.4cm) bias tape to 45" (114.3cm) with doubled thread. These gathers will make the next step much easier.

5. Working from one end, coil the bias strip flat by starting with a tight circle at the center. Continue around with the bias, keeping the strips flush with the next.

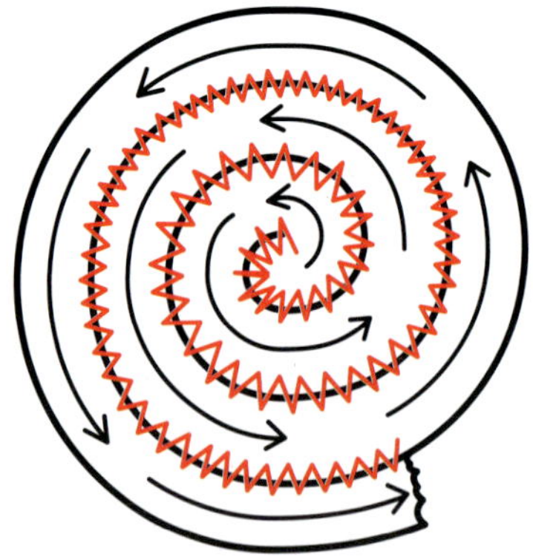

6. Secure the rows with large zigzag stitches, starting at the center and working out. Follow the ditch between the coiled bias tape as the mug rug is rotated. When finished, tuck the end under and stitch in place.

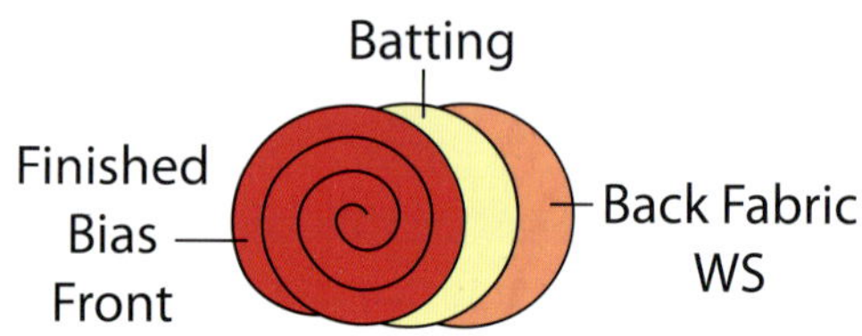

7. Make a quilt sandwich as follows: Lay (1) 6" (15.2cm) colorful print fabric RS down. Lay (1) 6" (15.2cm) diameter batting on top of the fabric. Lay the mug rug front on top of the batting RS up, showing the selvage. Stitch around the quilt sandwich as close to the edge as possible to keep all layers together.

8. Zigzag stitch the front of the mug rug over the previous stitching, going through three layers of fabric.

9. Make bias tape from (1) 6" x 6" (15.2 x 15.2cm) red strip. Stitch the bias tape around the outside edge.

10. Repeat steps 1–9 for (5) more mug rugs. In step 9, use the green, blue, yellow, orange, or purple fabrics for the bias tape.

Crazy Quilt Tasseled Coasters

Finished Size: 6" (15.2cm) diameter

For those of you that love color like me, you'll enjoy these coasters. First, you'll get the chance to make a crazy quilt block; then, you'll cut it into six circular coasters. Sewing the tassels onto the circle is as much fun as choosing the tassel colors to use. Crazy quilting is a great way to use up fabric scraps—you might recognize some of the project fabrics from this book. I also added other scraps that I found in my studio.

Material Requirements

- (1) 11" x 11" (28 x 28cm) red print fabric
- (1) 11" x 11" (28 x 28cm) orange print fabric
- (1) 12" x 18" (30.5 x 45.7cm) sturdy leather-like fusible fabric
- (1) 12" x 18" (30.5 x 45.7cm) cotton needled batting
- Fabric scraps in assorted colors and sizes
- (96) 1" (2.5cm) tassels in assorted colors
- Red thread
- White thread
- CQ pattern (page 111)
- Basic tools (page 7)

Cutting Requirements

Leather-Like Fusible Fabric

- (6) Pattern CQ-A

Instructions

1. Gather different fabric scraps and be sure they are pressed. (I like to press with pressing spray for crisp flat pieces of fabric to work with.) You will trim the fabrics as you sew the block.

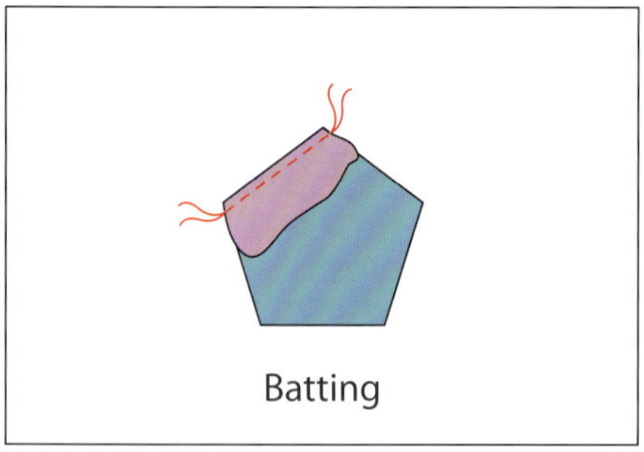

2. Lay (1) scrap RS up in the center of the batting. Lay a scrap RST with the central scrap, so one edge lines up along one edge. Stitch along this edge. Flip the fabric back and press flat on the batting.

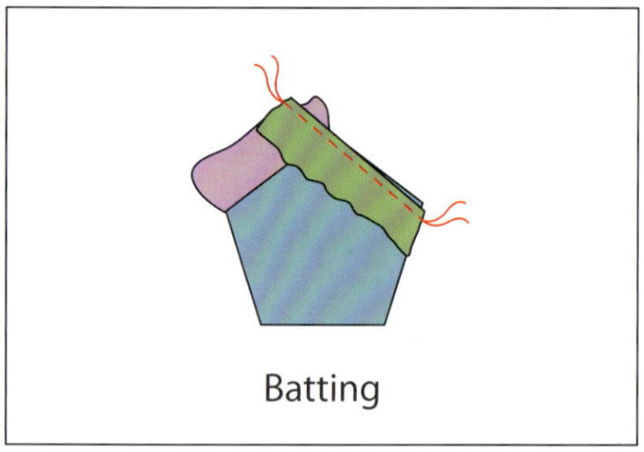

3. Lay another scrap RST along another edge. Stitch, flip, and press. Repeat until the entire piece of batting is covered.

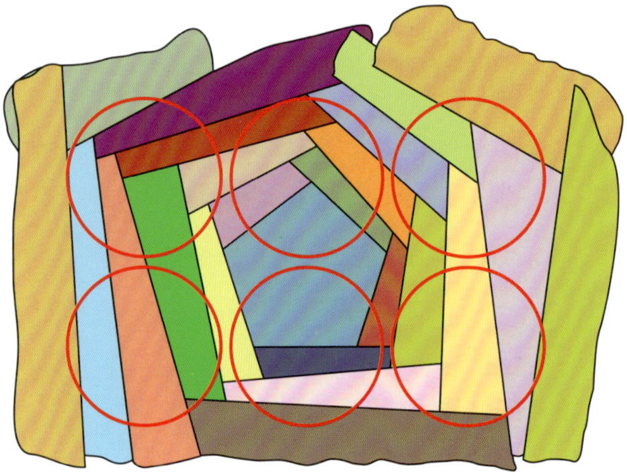

4. Trace Pattern CQ-A (6) times onto the crazy quilt block with a water-erasable pen for (6) crazy quilt circles. Cut out the circles.

5. Press (1) crazy quilt circle to the fusible side of the leather-like fabric, following the manufacturer's instructions.

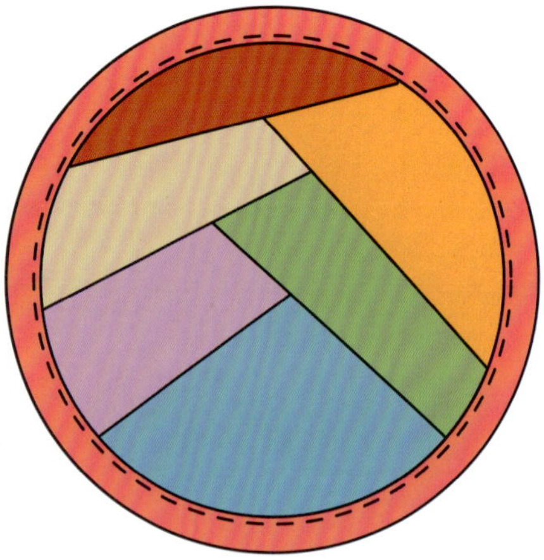

6. Make 2 yards of bias tape from the red print fabric and orange print fabric, as explained on page 9. Cut each color into (3) 24" (61cm) strips. There will be (3) orange-bound coasters and (3) red-bound coasters.

7. Flip the bias tape over the edge and hand stitch to the back.

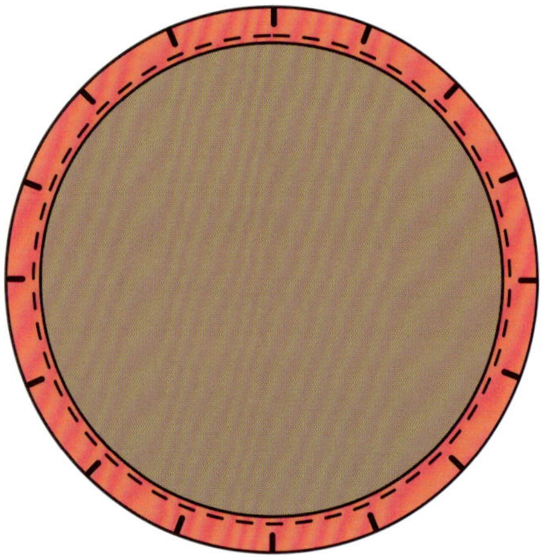

8. With a water-erasable marker, mark the back of the bias tape where the tassels will be attached.

9. Hand stitch (16) tassels around the coaster and knot the thread after each.

10. Repeat steps 5–9 for the remaining (5) crazy quilt circles.

MODERN PATCHWORK
Projects

Bold colors, asymmetry, interesting new construction, and improvisation are the basis of modern patchwork. This includes graphic, abstract, and minimalist leaning designs. Historical blocks can be reincarnated with modern fabrics and new proportions. In the newest modern designs, you may find neutral fabrics and jewel tone fabrics emerging.

In the **Modern "Squircles" Mug Rug** set, we focus on a rounded square used in interesting ways with color blocking and a vibrant fabric.

The **Log Cabin Puzzle Coasters** started as a set of historical blocks that morphed into a large asymmetrical Log Cabin design that is then divided for a puzzle-type coaster set.

Modern "Squircles" Mug Rugs

Finished Size: 5" x 8" (12.7 x 20.3cm)

"Squircles"? What are squircles? In the quilting world, they are a meld of a circle and a square. The corners are not sharp like squares but rounded from the edges. Squircles are often singularly hand cut, each one different from the last. In this project, we will use a template for ease and consistency.

Material Requirements

- Fat Quarter of multicolor fabric
- Fat Quarter of orange solid fabric
- Fat Quarter of blue solid fabric
- Fat Quarter of green solid fabric
- Fat Quarter of red solid fabric
- Fat Quarter of yellow solid fabric
- Fat Quarter of pink solid fabric
- (6) 5" x 8" (12.7 x 20.3cm) needled cotton batting
- (1) 18" x 36" (45.7 x 91.4cm) iron-on adhesive (I/O)
- Solid color-coordinating threads
- MS pattern (page 112)
- Basic tools (page 7)

Cutting Requirements

Multicolor Fabric

- (23) Pattern MS-A with I/O
- (12) 1" x 18" (2.5 x 45.7cm)

Orange Fabric

- (2) 5" x 8" (12.7 x 20.3cm)
- (2) 1" x 8" (2.5 x 20.3cm) with I/O

Blue Fabric

- (2) 5" x 8" (12.7 x 20.3cm)
- (2) 1½" x 6" (3.8 x 15.2cm) with I/O

Green Fabric

- (2) 5" x 8" (12.7 x 20.3cm)
- (2) 1" x 5" (2.5 x 15.2cm) with I/O

Red Fabric

- (2) 5" x 8" (12.7 x 20.3cm)
- (2) 1" x 8" (2.5 x 20.3cm) with I/O

Yellow Fabric

- (2) 5" x 8" (12.7 x 20.3cm)
- (2) 1" x 8" (2.5 x 20.3cm) with I/O

Pink Fabric

- (2) 5" x 8" (12.7 x 20.3cm)
- (3) 1" x 6" (2.5 x 15.2cm) with I/O

Note

For decorative quilting, I used a HandiQuilter Amara stationary quilting machine. A traditional sewing machine can also be used with a quilting foot after lowering the feed dogs.

Blue Mug Rug

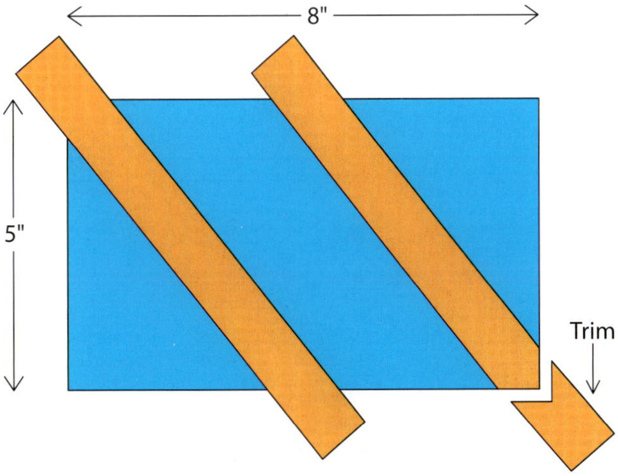

1. Press (2) 1" x 8" (2.5 x 20.3cm) orange strips diagonally WS down to (1) 5" x 8" (12.7 x 20.3cm) blue fabric RS.

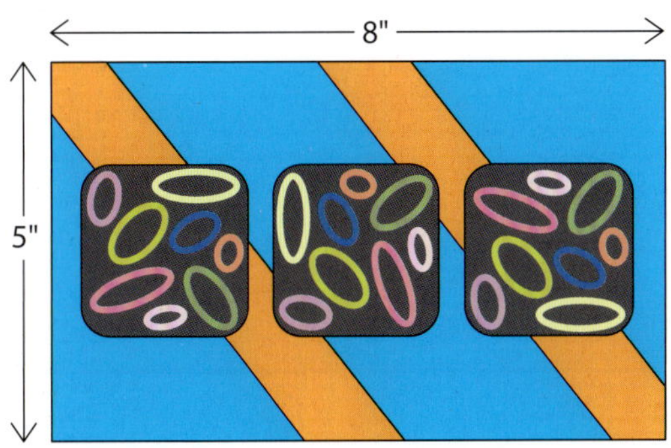

2. Press (3) Pattern MS-A squircles WS down to the mug rug front. Ensure they are placed evenly on top of the orange stripes.

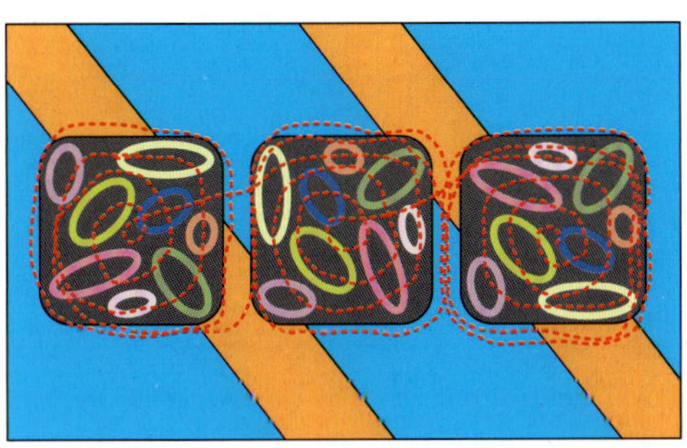

3. Place the mug rug front WS down on (1) 5" x 8" (12.7 x 20.3cm) batting. With a quilting machine or with a sewing machine and quilting foot, quilt random circles around the squircles.

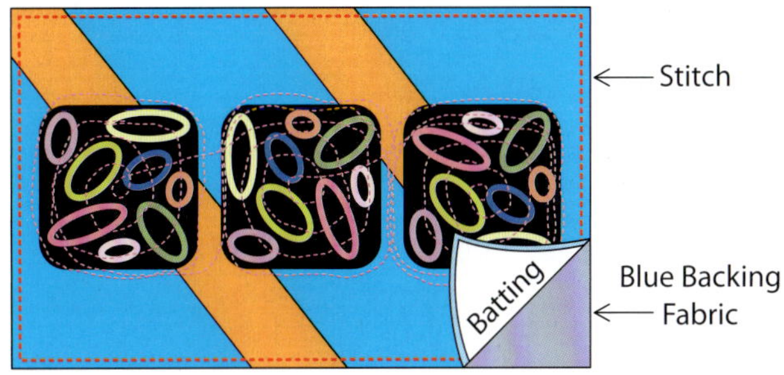

4. Place the quilted mug rug front and batting WST with (1) 5" x 8" (12.7 x 20.3cm) blue fabric. Stitch around the quilt sandwich as close to the edge as possible to keep all layers together.

5. Stitch (2) 1" x 18" (2.5 x 45.7cm) multicolor strips together. Although this strip is not cut on the bias, make a ¼" (6.4cm) double-fold bias tape. Sew the bias tape to the front of the mug rug, flip over edge, and hand stitch it to the back, as explained on page 10.

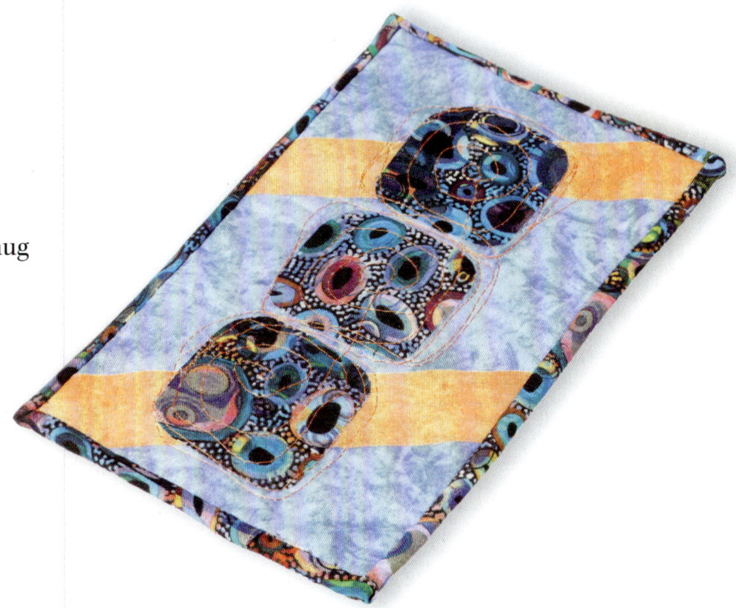

Orange Mug Rug

1. Press (2) 1" x 5" (2.5 x 12.7cm) green strips as shown WS down to (1) 5" x 8" (12.7 x 20.3cm) orange fabric RS. Press (3) squircles in place WS down as shown.

2. Repeat steps 3–5 of the Blue Mug Rug, using orange as the backing fabric.

Green Mug Rug

1. Press (3) 1" x 6" (2.5 x 15.2cm) pink strips as shown WS down to (1) 5" x 8" (12.7 x 20.3cm) green fabric RS. Press (4) squircles in place WS down as shown.

2. Repeat steps 3–5 of the Blue Mug Rug, using green as the backing fabric.

Red Mug Rug

1. Press (2) 1" x 8" (2.5 x 20.3cm) yellow strips as shown WS down to (1) 5" x 8" (12.7 x 20.3cm) red fabric RS. Press (3) squircles in place WS down as shown.

2. Repeat steps 3–5 of the Blue Mug Rug, using red as the backing fabric.

Yellow Mug Rug

1. Press (2) 1" x 8" (2.5 x 20.3cm) red strips as shown WS down to (1) 5" x 8" (12.7 x 20.3cm) yellow fabric RS. Press (5) squircles in place WS down as shown.

2. Repeat steps 3–5 of the Blue Mug Rug, using yellow as the backing fabric.

Pink Mug Rug

1. Press (2) 1½" x 6" (3.8 x 15.2cm) blue strips as shown WS down to (1) 5" x 8" (12.7 x 20.3cm) pink fabric RS. Press (5) squircles in place WS down as shown.

2. Repeat steps 3–5 of the Blue Mug Rug, using pink as the backing fabric.

Log Cabin Puzzle Coasters

Finished Size: 6" x 7" (15.2 x 17.8cm)

Just like most fellow quilters, I love incorporating the Log Cabin design into my projects. To make this set of coasters, we will create a table mat with a unique Log Cabin spin. When complete, we'll cut the table mat into six equal blocks that will individually be finished with bias tape. This coaster set can be displayed in a basket or laid out on the coffee table in the full design to hold flowers, books, and candles.

Material Requirements

- Fat Quarter or (1) ¼" x 44" (0.6 x 111.8cm) ivory floral fabric
- Fat Quarter or (1) ¼" x 44" (0.6 x 111.8cm) rust solid fabric
- Fat Quarter or (1) ¼" x 44" (0.6 x 111.8cm) sage green solid fabric
- Fat Quarter or (1) ¼" x 44" (0.6 x 111.8cm) dark brown print fabric
- (1) 18" x 44" (45.7 x 111.8cm) brown solid fabric
- (1) 18" x 44" (45.7 x 111.8cm) brown plaid fabric
- (1) 16" x 20" (40.6 x 50.8cm) needled cotton batting
- Off-white thread
- Brown thread
- Basic tools (page 7)

Cutting Requirements

Ivory Floral Fabric

- (1) 1½" x 1½" (3.8 x 3.8cm)
- (2) 7½" x 1½" (19.1 x 3.8cm)
- (3) 8½" x 1½" (21.6 x 3.8cm)
- (1) 9½" x 1½" (24.1 x 3.8cm)
- (1) 12½" x 1½" (31.8 x 3.8cm)
- (1) 6½" x 1½" (16.5 x 3.8cm)
- (1) 4½" x 1½" (11.4 x 3.8cm)
- (1) 11½" x 1½" (29.2 x 3.8cm)
- (1) 17½" x 1½" (44.5 x 3.8cm)

Rust Solid Fabric

- (1) 3½" x 1½" (8.9 x 3.8cm)
- (1) 4½" x 1½" (11.4 x 3.8cm)
- (3) 5½" x 1½" (14 x 3.8cm)
- (1) 7½" x 1½" (19.1 x 3.8cm)

Sage Green Solid Fabric

- (1) 3½" x 1½" (8.9 x 3.8cm)
- (3) 5½" x 1½" (14 x 3.8cm)
- (1) 6½" x 1½" (16.5 x 3.8cm)
- (1) 7½" x 1½" (19.1 x 3.8cm)
- (1) 10½" x 1½" (26.7 x 3.8cm)
- (1) 11½" x 1½" (29.2 x 3.8cm)

Dark Brown Print Fabric

- (1) 2½" x 1½" (6.4 x 3.8cm)
- (2) 3½" x 1½" (8.9 x 3.8cm)
- (1) 5½" x 1½" (14 x 3.8cm)
- (1) 6½" x 1½" (16.5 x 3.8cm)
- (1) 10½" x 1½" (26.7 x 3.8cm)
- (2) 14½" x 1½" (36.8 x 3.8cm)
- (1) 17½" x 1½" (44.5 x 3.8cm)

Brown Solid Fabric

- (6) 2" x 36" (5.1 x 91.4cm) for bias tape, cut with grain

Brown Plaid Fabric

- (1) 14" x 18" (35.6 x 45.7cm) for backing

Instructions

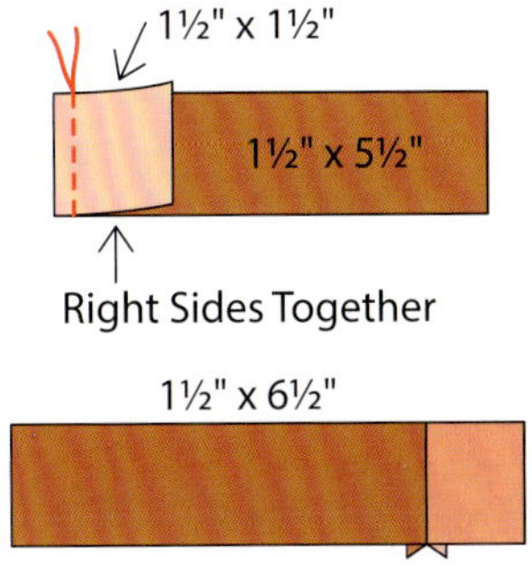

1. Stitch (1) 1½" x 1½" (3.8 x 3.8cm) floral fabric with RST to (1) 5½" x 1½" (14 x 3.8cm) rust fabric (Pieces 1 and 2). Open and press seam to darker fabric. Press between each fabric addition.

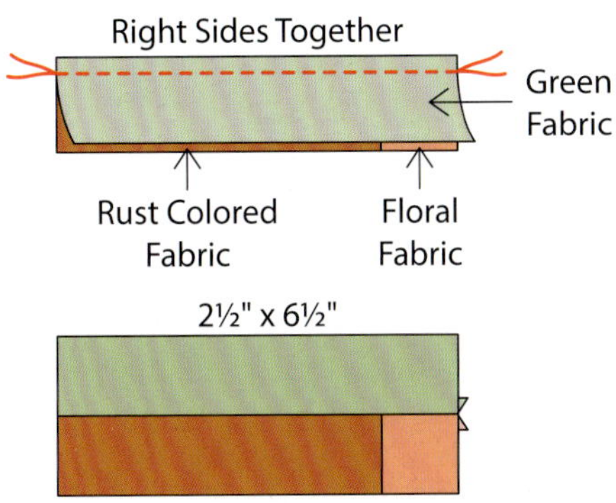

2. Stitch (1) 6½" x 1½" (16.5 x 3.8cm) green fabric (Piece 3) with RST to the top of Pieces 1 and 2 as shown.

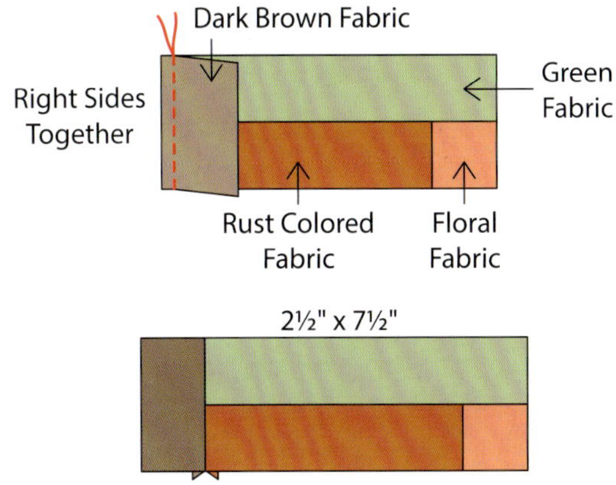

3. Stitch (1) 2½" x 1½" (6.4 x 3.8cm) dark brown fabric (Piece 4) with RST to Pieces 1–3 as shown.

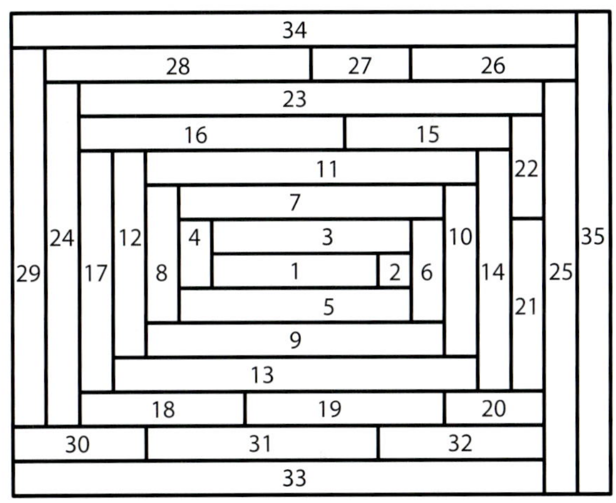

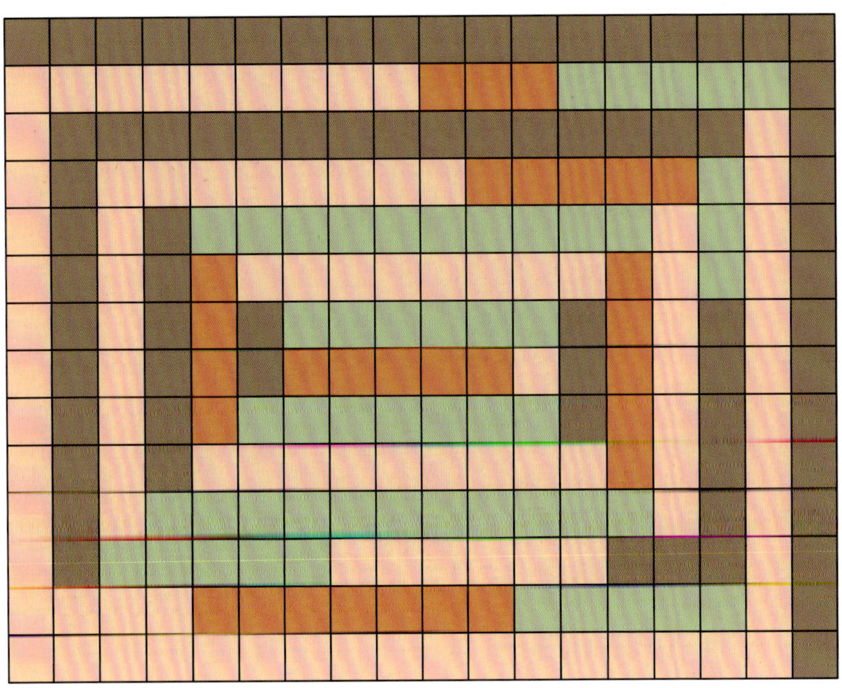

4. Continue joining strips around in a circle, following the diagrams. You should end up with a 14" x 18" (35.6 x 45.7cm) quilt block front.

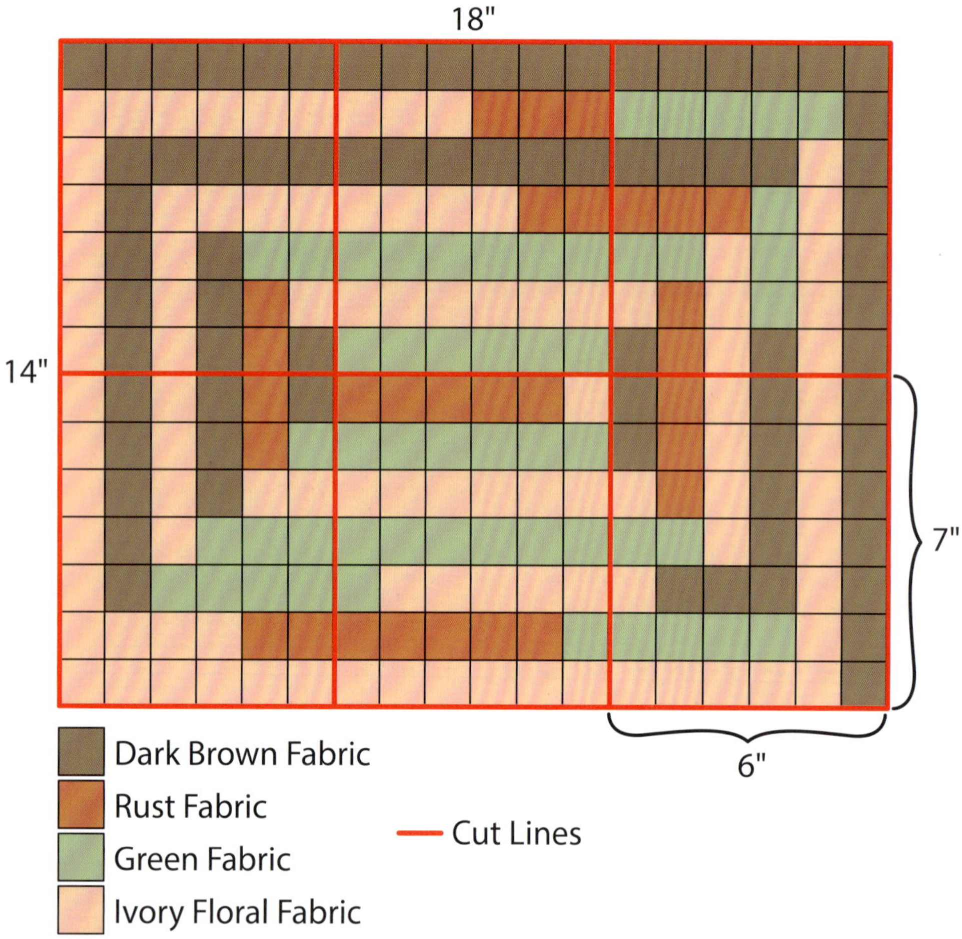

5. Make a quilt sandwich as follows: Lay (1) 14" x 18" (35.6 x 45.7cm) brown plaid fabric RS down. Lay the batting on top of the backing. Lay the quilt front on top of the batting RS up. Stitch around the outside edges to secure.

6. Quilt the entire quilt sandwich with ivory thread as desired. I stitched diagonal lines across the block.

7. Cut the quilt sandwich into (6) 6" x 7" (15.2 x 17.8cm) pieces as shown.

8. Make (1) ½" (1.3cm) double-fold bias tape from (1) 2" x 36" (5.1 x 91.4cm) brown fabric. Repeat for (5) more.

9. Stitch the bias tape to the front of (1) cut piece, as explained on page 10. Fold over the edge and hand sew to the back.

KAWANDI
Projects

Kawandi is a quilting technique that was developed in the Siddi community of Western India and is used to recycle old saris into a new fabric. The construction is characterized as working from the "outside in." The backing fabric edge is hemmed to the inside. Folded pieces of scrap fabric are stitched to the backing fabric in a circular fashion, moving the outside edges to the center. A long running stitch holds it all together in a continuous presentation of stitches.

Corner triangles are called *phula* (flowers). *Tikli* is the addition of fabric scraps to cover sparse areas of the completed project.

The **Traditional Kawandi Mug Rugs with a Twist** incorporates the basic kawandi technique with batting for added cushion and a cork circle for a textural twist.

The **Kawandi Coasters** are created from one large kawandi mat that is cut into smaller pieces and trimmed with bias tape.

Traditional Kawandi Mug Rugs with a Twist

Finished Size: 6" x 9" (15.2 x 22.9cm)

It's been said that including a few grains of rice in the center of a kawandi quilt behind a fabric piece can bring a blessing to the person receiving it. There are filler pieces of fabric added on top of the stitched quilt that are called *tikli* and the corner triangles are called *phula*. Embroidery floss, perle cotton, or standard thread can be used to stitch a kawandi quilt. I used striped fabric for the binding and polka-dot fabric for the back.

Material Requirements

- (1) 9" x 9" (22.9 x 22.9cm) black/white striped fabric for bias tape
- (1) 9" x 6" (22.9 x 15.2cm) black polka-dot fabric
- (1) 9" x 9" (22.9 x 22.9cm) yellow/white striped fabric for bias tape
- (1) 9" x 6" (22.9 x 15.2cm) yellow polka-dot fabric
- (1) 9" x 9" (22.9 x 22.9cm) red/white striped fabric for bias tape
- (1) 9" x 6" (22.9 x 15.2cm) red polka-dot fabric
- (1) 9" x 9" (22.9 x 22.9cm) green/white striped fabric for bias tape
- (1) 9" x 6" (22.9 x 15.2cm) green polka-dot fabric
- (1) 9" x 9" (22.9 x 22.9cm) blue/white striped fabric for bias tape
- (1) 9" x 6" (22.9 x 15.2cm) blue polka-dot fabric
- (1) 9" x 9" (22.9 x 22.9cm) orange/white striped fabric for bias tape
- (1) 9" x 6" (22.9 x 15.2cm) orange polka-dot fabric
- (1) 9" x 13" (22.9 x 33cm) cork fabric
- (6) 9" x 6" (22.9 x 15.2cm) needled cotton batting
- (8–10) print scraps from each color: black, yellow, red, green, blue, and orange
- Thread in colors: yellow, red, green, blue, and orange
- KMR pattern (page 112)
- Basic tools (page 7)

Cutting Requirements

Black Print Scrap Fabric

- (4) Pattern KMR-A

Yellow Print Scrap Fabric

- (4) Pattern KMR-A

Red Print Scrap Fabric

- (4) Pattern KMR-A

Green Print Scrap Fabric

- (4) Pattern KMR-A

Blue Print Scrap Fabric

- (4) Pattern KMR-A

Orange Print Scrap Fabric

- (4) Pattern KMR-A

Fabric Scraps (All Colors)

- Cut random-sized rectangle shapes that are at least 2" x 3" (5.1 x 7.6cm)

Cork Fabric

- (6) 4" (10.2cm) circles

Black Kawandi Mug Rug

1. Gather the black fabric scraps and have pins ready to use. Lay (1) 9" x 6" (22.9 x 15.2cm) batting piece on the work surface.

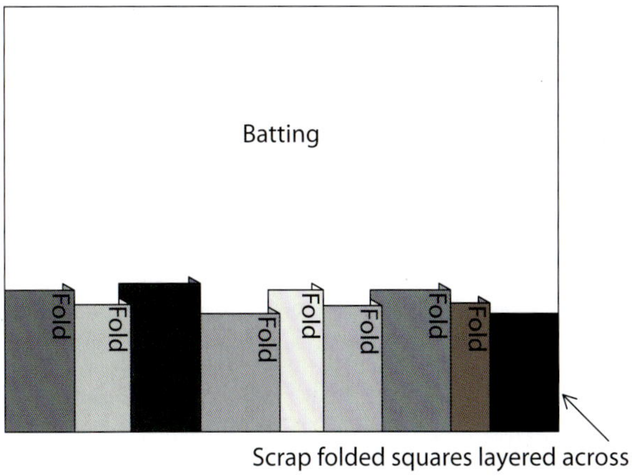

2. Pin (1) scrap to the bottom-right corner of the batting with both the right edge and bottom folded under ¼" (6.4mm). Repeat with a second scrap. Finger press or press with an iron. The folded edge will slightly overlap the first scrap to conceal the raw edge. Repeat until the bottom row is complete as shown.

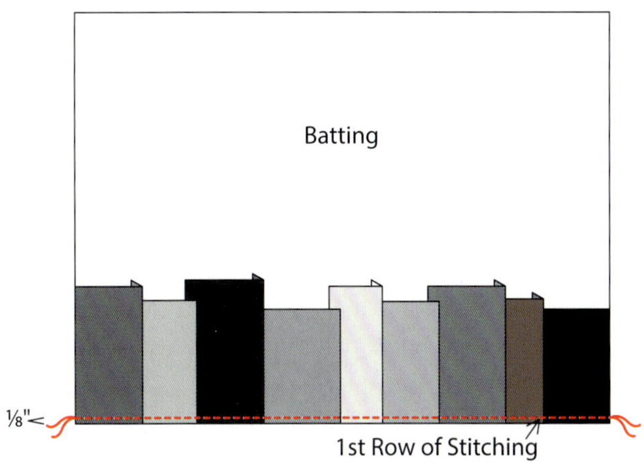

3. With a needle and single thread, hide the knot between the first scrap and the batting. Stitch small running stitches along the bottom of the mug rug ⅛" (3.2mm) from the outside edge. Stitch through the fabric and batting. Stop at the corner where the fabrics ended.

4. Add scraps around the remaining edges of the mug rug as in step 2. Make sure that all right-side edges of the scraps are folded or tucked under.

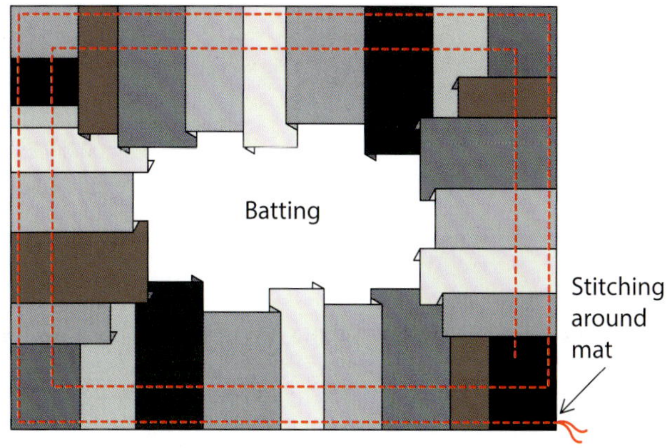

5. Stitch ⅛" (3.2mm) around the entire perimeter. The stitch lines will complete a continuous square. The stitching turns with the direction you are stitching.

6. Keep adding scraps, folding as needed to cover messy edges, and complete a second and third row. Add more scraps as needed to cover the mug rug. Stitch the entire mug rug as new scraps are adding and rows complete.

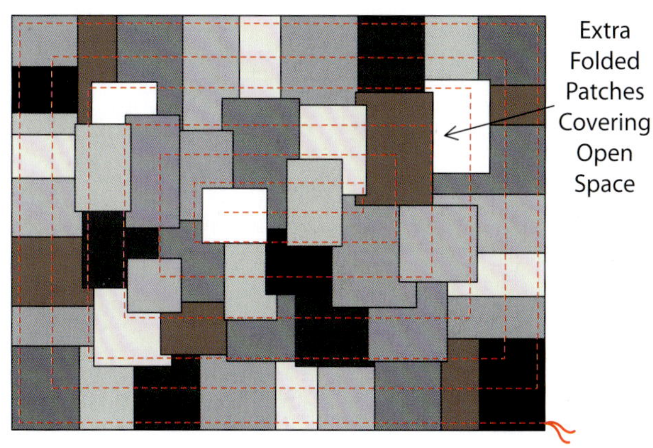

7. Stitch tiny scraps of fabric (*tikli*) in various places to hide stubborn holes and add interesting texture as shown.

8. Make a quilt sandwich as follows: Lay (1) 9" x 6" (22.9 x 15.2cm) black polka-dot fabric RS down. Lay the front/batting piece on top of the fabric, batting side down. Stitch close to the edge to keep all layers together for edging.

9. Use (1) 9" x 9" (22.9 x 22.9cm) black/white striped fabric to make ½" (1.3cm) double-fold bias tape.

10. Stitch the bias tape to the front of the mug rug, as explained on page 10. Fold the bias tape over the edge and hand sew to the back.

11. Sew (1) cork circle to the mug rug front, 1" (2.5cm) from the side and 1¼" (3.2cm) from both the top and bottom.

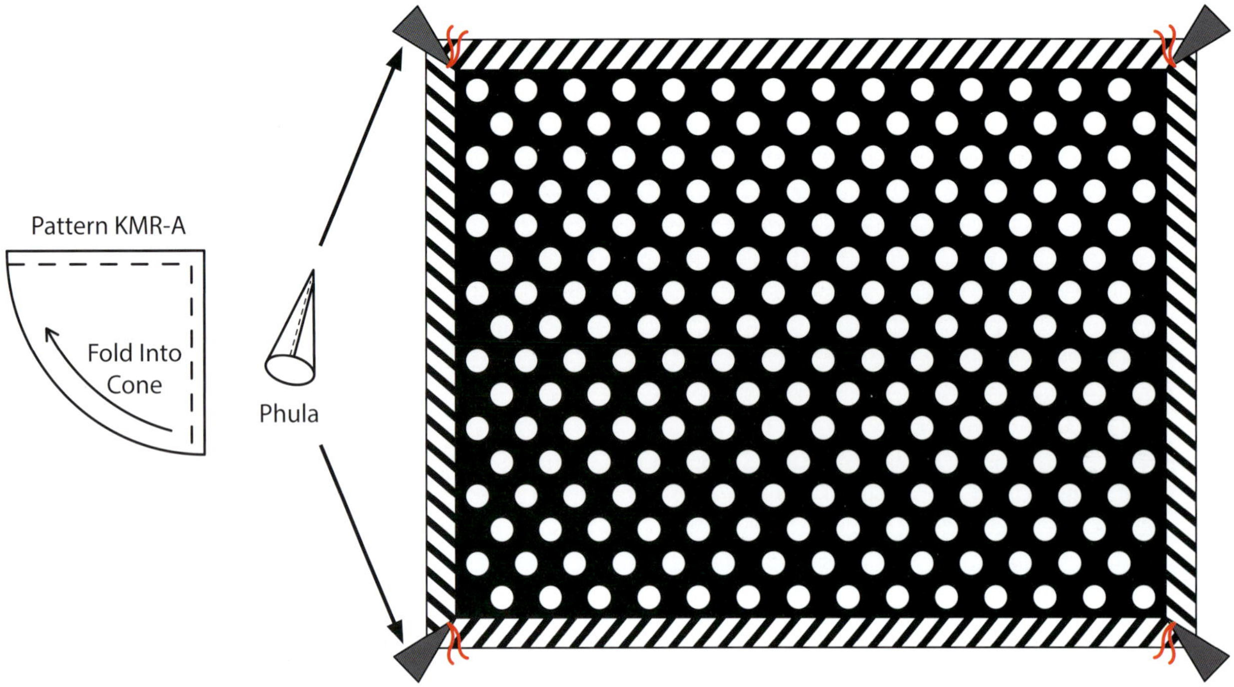

12. Fold and hand stitch the Pattern KMR-A pieces (*phula*) into cone shapes and sew them to the back of the mug rug as shown.

13. Repeat steps 1–12 to make the other (5) kawandi mug rugs, matching colors as appropriate.

Tip

When using cork fabric, do not launder in a machine. Wipe clean with a damp cloth.

Kawandi Coasters

Finished Size: 3½" (8.9cm) diameter

I love this technique for restful quilting when watching a movie with family. Since this technique can be worked with a variety of fabric scraps, I look at used clothing and household fabrics in a very new light! Traditionally, kawandi is hand stitched as the patches are added. For this set of coasters, I machine stitched the pieces for a more durable piece when cut apart.

Material Requirements

- (30) 2" x 3" (5.1 x 7.6cm) green fabric scraps
- (1) 13" x 13" (33 x 33cm) green striped fabric for bias tape
- (1) 9" x 12" (22.9 x 30.5cm) green polka-dot fabric for backing
- (1) 9" x 12" (22.9 x 30.5cm) cotton needled batting
- White thread
- GQ pattern (page 111)
- Basic tools (page 7)

Cutting Requirements

- Cut random sized square shapes from fabric scraps that are no larger than 2" x 3" (5.1 x 7.6cm). Do not cut the striped or polka-dot fabric. This will be used for the bias trim around each coaster and the backing.

Instructions

1. Lay (1) 9" x 12" (22.9 x 30.5cm) green polka-dot fabric piece RS down on the work surface. Lay (1) 9" x 12" (22.9 x 30.5cm) batting piece on the backing. Gather the fabric scraps and have pins ready to use.

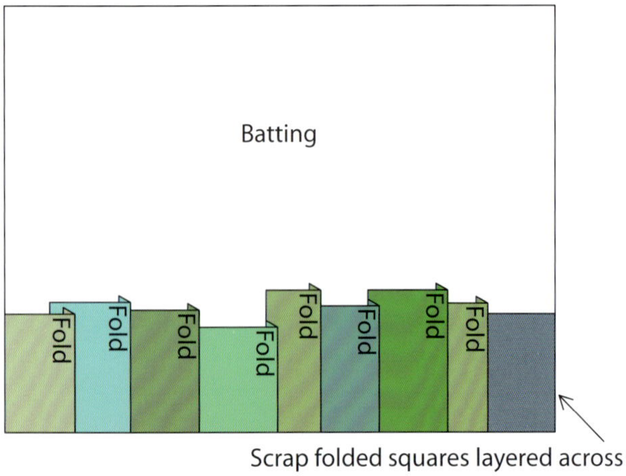

2. Pin (1) scrap to the bottom-right corner of the batting with both the right edge and bottom folded under ¼" (6.4mm). Repeat with a second scrap. Finger press or press with an iron. The folded edge will slightly overlap the first scrap to conceal the raw edge. Repeat until the bottom row is complete as shown.

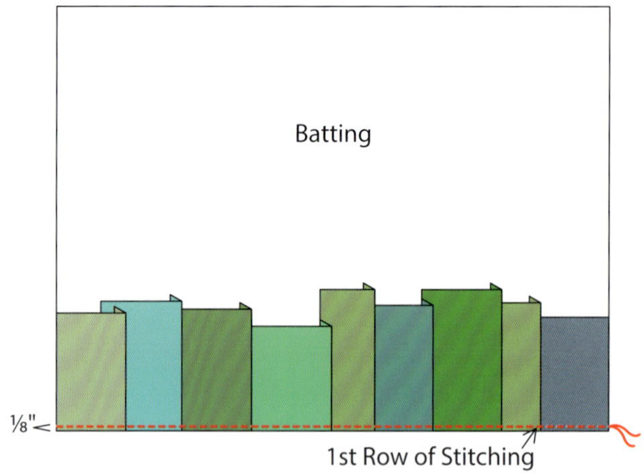

3. Machine stitch along the bottom ⅛" (3.2mm) from the outside edge. Stitch through the quilt sandwich. Stop at the corner where the fabrics ended.

4. Add scraps around the remaining edges as in step 2. Make sure that all right-side edges of the scraps are folded or tucked under.

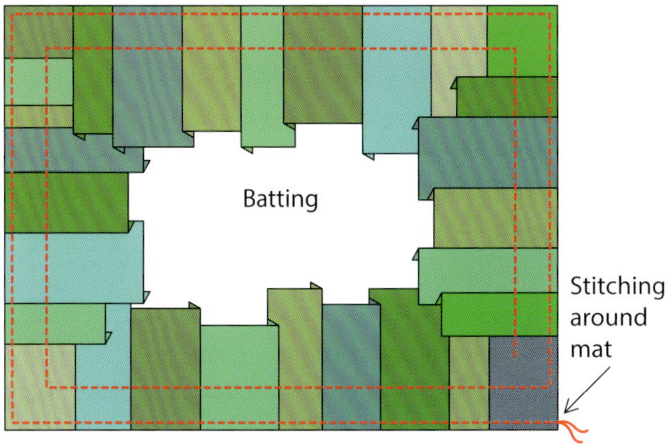

5. Stitch ⅛" (3.2mm) around the entire perimeter. The stitch lines will complete a continuous square. The stitching turns with the direction you are stitching.

6. Keep adding scraps, folding as needed to cover messy edges, and complete a second and third row. Add more scraps as needed to cover quilted piece. Stitch the entire piece as new scraps are added and rows are completed.

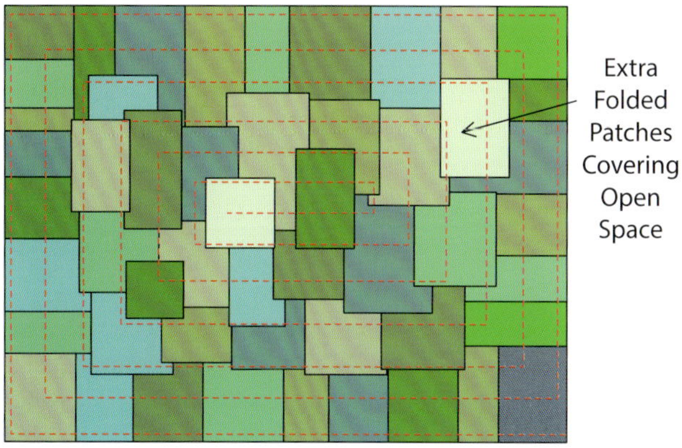

7. Stitch tiny scraps of fabric (*tikli*) in various places to hide stubborn holes and add interesting texture as shown.

8. Using Pattern GQ-A, cut (6) circles from the finished quilt.

9. Make 2 yards (182.9cm) of ½" (1.3cm) double-fold green-striped bias tape.

10. Stitch the bias tape to the front of the coaster, as explained on page 10. Fold the bias tape over the edge and hand sew to the back.

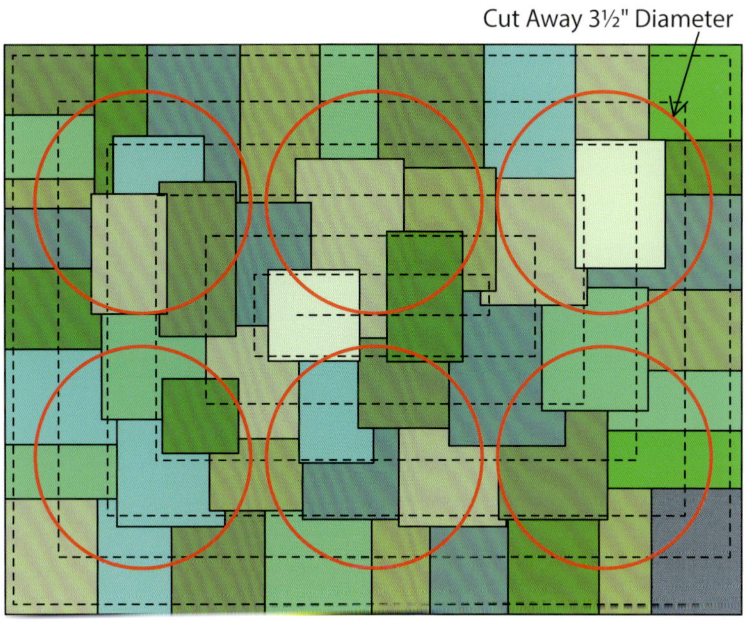

RECYCLED DENIM
Projects

Did you know that denim has an enormous effect on our environment? It can take 1,500 to 2,000 gallons (5,700 to 7,600L) of water to produce a single pair of jeans. If you throw them away, they may sit in the landfill for 200 years. They contain toxic dyes that can leach into the surrounding environment. Decomposing denim releases methane, a harmful greenhouse gas. Domestic textile waste consists of 17 million tons discarded annually.

Let's make a difference; let's recycle.

The **Recycled Jean Pocket Mug Rugs** are created from just that, jean pockets! Pockets are fun and can be used in so many clever ways. I used fabric patches and a simple running stitch, inspired by sashiko, to embellish these.

In the **Reverse Appliqué Denim Mug Rugs**, we will use the remainder of a pair of jeans to create "groovy" mug rugs reflecting the '70s. These mug rugs are designed with a minimalist vintage look using hand-drawn reverse appliqué and imperfect stitching. They can be made more refined if desired.

Reverse Appliqué Denim Mug Rugs

Finished Size: 6" x 6" (15.2 x 15.2cm)

Whether we outgrow our jeans or stain them, a pair of jeans that should be discarded always seems to be around the house. Don't throw them away; use the pockets for the Recycled Jean Pocket Mug Rugs (page 40) and use the legs for these mug rugs. I prefer dark denim but use what you have or what you find in a resale shop. These mug rugs reflect 1970s fashion and were designed with hand-drawn appliqué shapes to lend to the vintage look.

Material Requirements

- Fat Quarter of yellow print fabric
- Fat Quarter of orange print fabric
- Fat Quarter of pink floral fabric
- Fat Quarter of yellow/green mottled print fabric
- Fat Quarter of multicolored fabric
- Fat Quarter of red mottled print fabric
- Fat Quarter of blue print fabric
- (6) 6" x 6" (15.2 x 15.2cm) cotton needled batting
- (1) pair of denim jeans
- Embroidery floss or perle cotton in colors: peach, yellow, light green, pink, red, white, hot pink, magenta, and light blue
- Utility knife
- RAD patterns (pages 112–117)
- Basic tools (page 7)

Cutting Requirements

Yellow Print Fabric

- (2) 2" x 15" (5.1 x 38.1cm)
- (1) 6" x 6" (15.2 x 15.2cm)

Orange Print Fabric

- (1) 4" x 4" (10.2 x 10.2cm)

Pink Floral Fabric

- (2) 2" x 15" (5.1 x 38.1cm)
- (1) 8" x 8" (20.3 x 20.3cm)

Yellow/Green Print Fabric

- (2) 2" x 15" (5.1 x 38.1cm)
- (1) 8" x 8" (20.3 x 20.3cm)

Multicolored Fabric

- (2) 2" x 15" (5.1 x 38.1cm)
- (1) 8" x 8" (20.3 x 20.3cm)

Red Print Fabric

- (2) 2" x 15" (5.1 x 38.1cm)
- (1) 8" x 8" (20.3 x 20.3cm)

Blue Print Fabric

- (2) 2" x 15" (5.1 x 38.1cm)
- (1) 8" x 8" (20.3 x 20.3cm)

Denim Jeans (For All Mug Rugs)

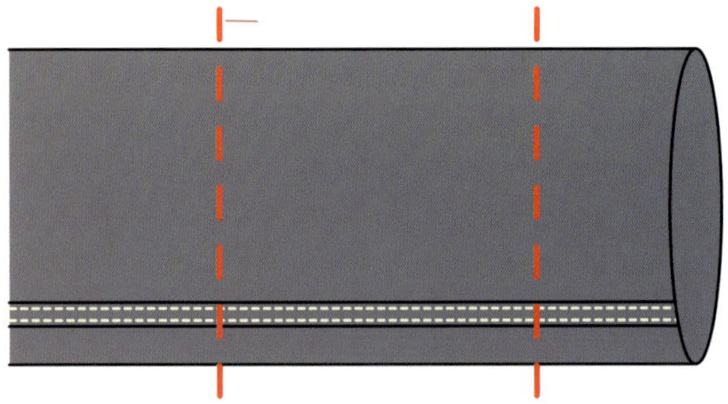

1. Lay out the jean leg flat, aligning the side seam RS up on the workspace. Cut (6) 6" (15.2cm) sections from the leg with the side seam included. This should result in (6) tubes of denim fabric.

2. Cut the tubes into (12) 6" x 6" (15.2 x 15.2cm) squares, (6) fronts with the seam and (6) backings without the seam.

Sunshine Mug Rug

1. Using a utility knife, cut Pattern RAD-A in the bottom-right side of (1) jean square front, orienting the seam on the left.

2. Place (1) 4" x 4" (10.2 x 10.2cm) orange fabric WS down on top of (1) 6" x 6" (15.2 x 15.2cm) yellow fabric in the bottom-right corner. Place the cut jean front WS down on top of the yellow/orange layered fabric. Trim the orange so it only shows through the body of the sun. Stitch the orange fabric in place on the yellow fabric.

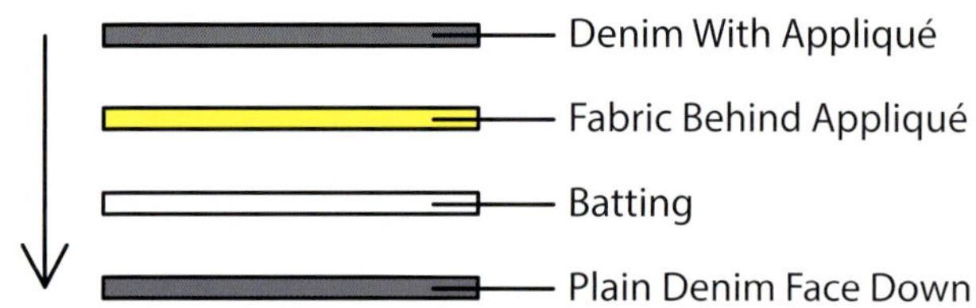

3. Make a quilt sandwich as follows: Lay (1) jean back RS down. Lay (1) batting on top. Lay (1) yellow/orange layered fabric on top RS up. Lay the jean front on top RS up. Make sure the fabrics show through the holes as desired.

4. Pin in place. Stitch around the quilt sandwich as close to the edge as possible to keep all layers together.

5. Blanket stitch (see page 11) along the left side of the seam with a single strand of yellow perle cotton or double strand of yellow embroidery thread. This stitching should only be on the front fabric.

6. Blanket stitch around all the holes with a single strand of yellow perle cotton or double strand of yellow embroidery thread. This stitching should only be on the front fabric.

7. Stitch light green lazy daisy leaves (see page 11) as shown. Stitch yellow French knots in groups of (3) among the loops.

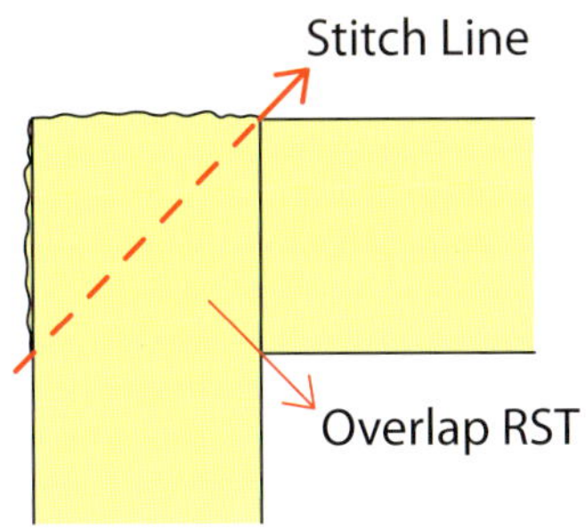

8. Make bias tape from (2) 2" x 15" (5.1 x 38.1cm) yellow print strips. The (2) 2" x 15" (5.1 x 38.1cm) yellow print strips should be sewn RST on one short end to create a 2" x 30" (5.1 x 76.2cm) strip. Stitch the bias tape around the outside edge, as explained on page 10.

9. Flip the bias tape over the edge and hand stitch to the back.

Love Mug Rug

1. Using a utility knife, cut Pattern RAD-B in the right side of (1) jean square front, orienting the seam on the left.

2. Repeat steps 3–9 of the Sun Mug Rug. Use pink floral fabric behind the jean front and for the bias tape. Use green perle cotton or embroidery thread for the blanket stitches. Use hot pink thread for the lazy daisies. Use magenta thread for the French knots.

Moon Mug Rug

1. Using a utility knife, cut Pattern RAD-C in the right side of (1) jean square front, orienting the seam on the left.

2. Repeat steps 3–9 of the Sun Mug Rug. Use yellow/green print fabric behind the jean front and for the bias tape. Use yellow perle cotton or embroidery thread for the blanket stitches. Use green thread for the lazy daisies. Use pink thread for the French knots.

Rainbow Mug Rug

1. Using a utility knife, cut Pattern RAD-D in the bottom-right corner of (1) jean square front, orienting the seam on the left.

2. Repeat steps 3–9 of the Sun Mug Rug. Use multicolor fabric behind the jean front and for the bias tape. Use light blue perle cotton or embroidery thread for the blanket stitches. Use green and peach thread for the lazy daisies. Use pink thread for the French knots.

Peace Sign Mug Rug

1. Using a utility knife, cut Pattern RAD-E in the right side of (1) jean square front, orienting the seam on the left.

2. Repeat steps 3–9 of the Sun Mug Rug. Use red print fabric behind the jean front and for the bias tape. Use red perle cotton or embroidery thread for the blanket stitches. Use green and white thread for the lazy daisies. Use yellow thread for the French knots.

Flower Mug Rug

1. Using a utility knife, cut Pattern RAD-F in the right side of (1) jean square front, orienting the seam on the left.

2. Repeat steps 3–9 of the Sun Mug Rug. Use blue print fabric behind the jean front and for the bias tape. Use white perle cotton or embroidery thread for the blanket stitches. Use green and peach thread for the lazy daisies. Use yellow thread for the French knots.

Recycled Jean Pocket Mug Rugs

Finished Size: 4" x 4" (10.2 x 10.2cm)

Blue jean pockets can be used in so many clever ways. They can be small bags, decorated magnets, and other accessories and decorations.

Material Requirements

- Fat Quarter of green plaid fabric
- Fat Quarter of red paisley print fabric
- Fat Quarter of yellow print fabric
- (1) 1" x 4½" (2.5 x 11.4cm) gray stripe print fabric
- Fat Quarter of brown plaid print fabric
- Fat Quarter of blue stripe print fabric
- Fat Quarter of red floral print fabric
- (1) 6" x 6" (15.2 x 15.2cm) red houndstooth fabric
- (6) 4" x 4" (10.2 x 10.2cm) denim jean pockets
- (6) 4½" x 4½" (11.4 x 11.4cm) needled cotton batting
- (1) 12" x 18" (30.5 x 45.7cm) iron-on adhesive (I/O)
- Off-white pearl cotton thread (and other colors if desired)
- Thread in colors: off-white, white, red, and orange
- (24) ¼" (6.4mm) snap-together silver grommets
- Awl or sharp tool to punch holes
- Water-soluble marker
- Stitch patterns (pages 118–119)
- Basic tools (page 7)

Cutting Requirements

Green Plaid

- (1) 2½" x 3½" (6.4 x 8.9cm) with I/O
- (2) 2" x 20" (5.1 x 50.8cm)

Red Paisley Print

- (2) 1½" x 4" (3.8 x 10.2cm) with I/O
- (2) 2" x 20" (5.1 x 50.8cm)

Yellow Print

- (1) 3" x 3¾" (7.6 x 9.5cm) with I/O
- (2) 2" x 20" (5.1 x 50.8cm)

Gray Stripe Print

- (1) 1" x 4½" (2.5 x 11.4cm) with I/O

Brown Plaid Print

- (1) 2" x 2½" (5.1 x 6.4cm) with I/O
- (2) 2" x 20" (5.1 x 50.8cm)

Blue Stripe Print

- (2) 1" x 4" (2.5 x 10.2cm) with I/O
- (2) 2" x 20" (5.1 x 50.8cm)

Red Floral Print

- (2) 1½" x 1½" (3.8 x 3.8cm) with I/O
- (2) 2" x 20" (5.1 x 50.8cm)

Red Houndstooth

- (2) 1½" x 1½" (3.8 x 3.8cm) with I/O

Note

When cutting the pockets from your jeans, include the base denim of the jeans that will serve as the backing fabric in your quilt sandwich. This means the mug rug backing will be wrong side out. If you only have the pocket front, cut a piece of denim from elsewhere on the jeans to a size and shape that matches the front. You can face this backing piece right side out if desired.

Green Plaid Mug Rug

1. Press (1) 2½" x 3½" (6.4 x 8.9cm) green plaid rectangle to (1) pocket.

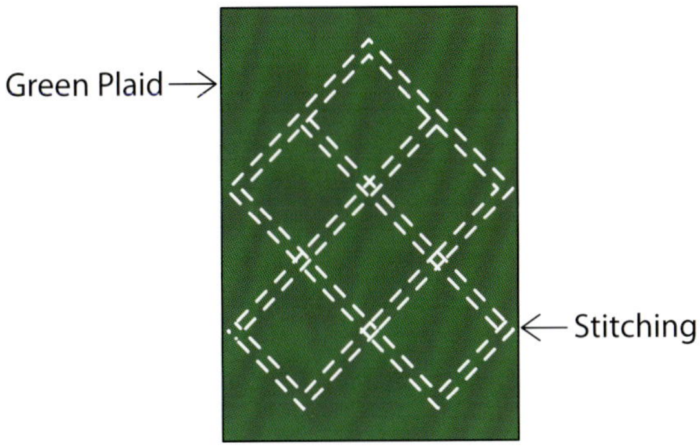

2. With a water-soluble marker, draw the stitch pattern to the fabric appliqué.

3. Using the off-white pearl cotton thread and needle, make a running stitch of the design. Only stitch through the front layer of the pocket.

4. Insert (1) batting piece between the front and back of the pocket.

5. Stitch (2) 2" x 20" (5.1 x 50.8cm) green plaid strips together. Make a ½" (1.3cm) double-fold bias tape.

6. Sew the bias tape to the front of the mug rug, flip over edge, and hand stitch it to the back, as explained on page 10. This will close the top of the pocket.

7. Use the awl or sharp tool to punch one hole in each of the four corners. Punch in the denim only. Attach the snap-together grommets by putting through the hole on the front and then snap the back in place.

> **Note**
>
> If these mug rugs will be used on a surface that is easily scratched, the grommets can be omitted or covered on the back with felt.

Red Paisley Mug Rug

1. Press (2) 1½" x 4" (3.8 x 10.2cm) paisley fabric pieces to the front of (1) pocket.

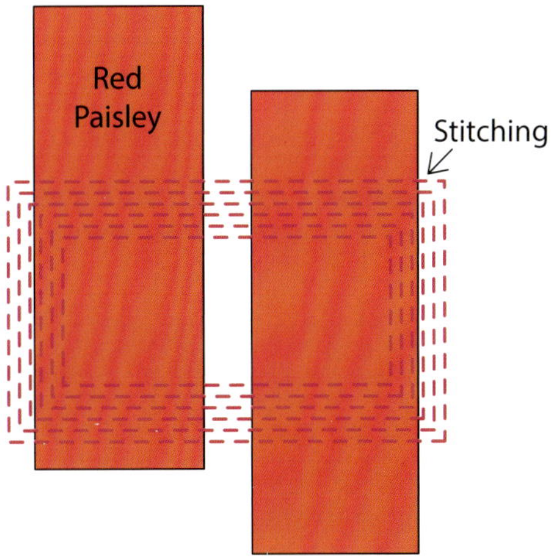

2. Repeat steps 2–7 of the Green Plaid Mug Rug. Use red or off-white pearl cotton thread for the running stitch. Use the paisley fabric as the bias tape.

Yellow Print Mug Rug

1. Press (1) 3" x 3¾" (7.6 x 9.5cm) yellow print rectangle to the front of (1) pocket. Press (1) 1" x 4½" (2.5 x 11.4cm) gray striped fabric across it as shown.

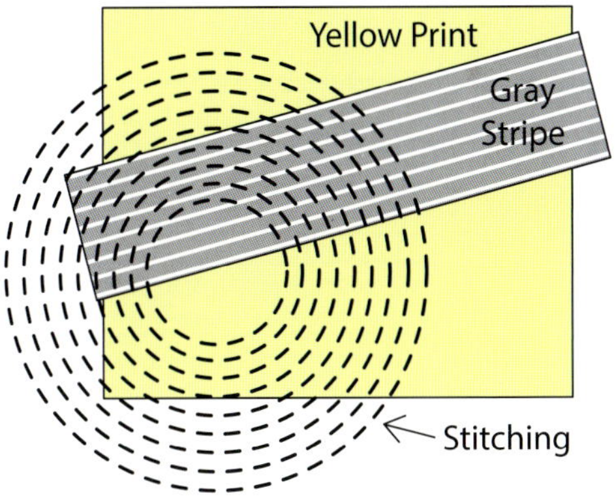

2. Repeat steps 2–7 of the Green Plaid Mug Rug. Use the yellow print fabric as the bias tape.

Brown Plaid Mug Rug

1. Press (1) 2" x 2½" (5.1 x 6.4cm) brown plaid rectangle to the front of (1) pocket.

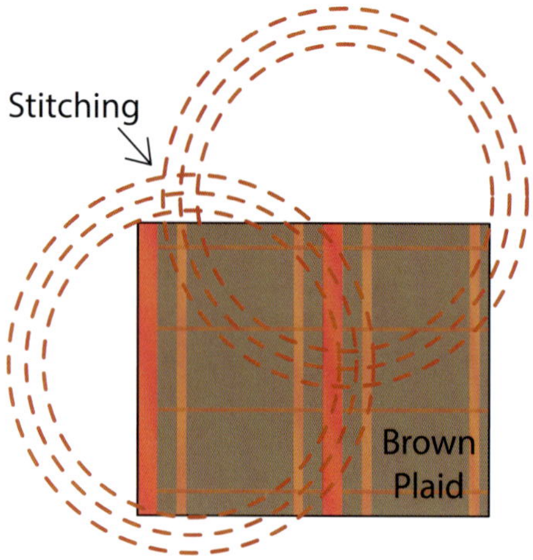

2. Repeat steps 2–7 of the Green Plaid Mug Rug. Use orange or off-white pearl cotton thread for the running stitch. Use the brown plaid fabric as the bias tape.

Blue Stripe Mug Rug

1. Press (2) 1" x 4" (2.5 x 10.2cm) blue stripe strips to the front of (1) pocket.

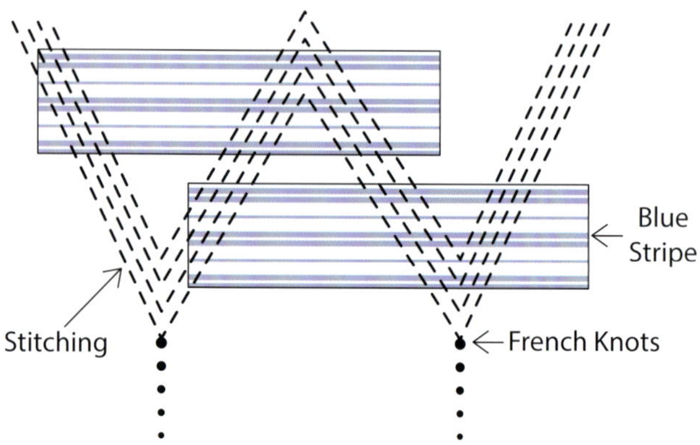

2. Repeat steps 2–7 of the Green Plaid Mug Rug. Use the blue stripe fabric as the bias tape.

Red Floral Mug Rug

1. Press (2) 1½" x 1½" (3.8 x 3.8cm) red floral fabric squares and (2) 1½" x 1½" (3.8 x 3.8cm) red houndstooth squares to the front of (1) pocket.

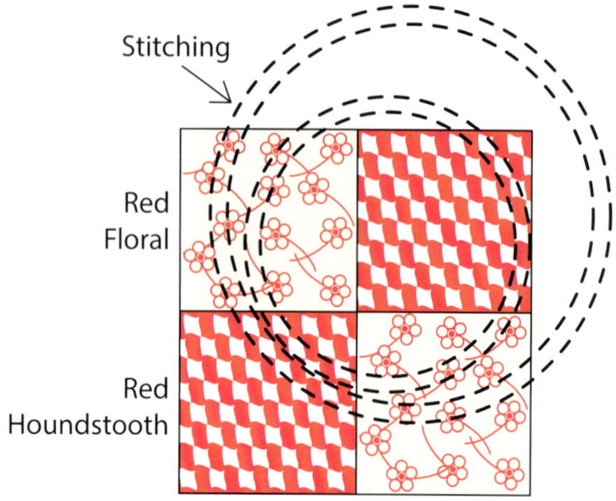

2. Repeat steps 2–7 of the Green Plaid Mug Rug. Use the red floral fabric as the bias tape.

MEMORY
Projects

When a loved one is lost, preserving special memories through meaningful fabrics makes for a thoughtful gift.

Daddy's Wonky Mug Rugs incorporates my father's plaid and canvas clothing. I looked for a unique way to use these special fabrics, and wonky circles seemed the best fit for these textures. Wonky circles are hand-drawn or irregular circles. When drawing the wonky circle, avoid trying to find perfection; they should be slightly off kilter.

Grandma's Quilted Mug Rugs are created from an old, torn quilt that my grandma made. When it is hard to throw away, use parts of the quilt in memory mug rugs. These are edged with fabric yo-yos and colorful buttons that are reflected in the quilt. Yo-yos are created with scraps of fabric that are cut into circles and gathered around the outside edge. When the thread is pulled tight, a yo-yo is created.

Daddy's Wonky Mug Rugs

Finished Size: 5½" x 5½" (14 x 14cm)

When my father passed away, my brother, sister, mother, and I wanted something of his to hold on to. For our immediate family, I made teddy bears and my sister made pillows. While working on this book, I thought about using pieces of his shirts to make mug rugs. This would have been a great reminder every time we reached for a drink or entertained friends and family.

Wonky circles are circular shapes that are not perfectly round. When layering wonky circles, the individual circles are usually not modeled after the last wonky circle. They are cut independently.

Material Requirements

- Blue plaid shirt
- Red plaid shirt
- Light khaki pants or (1) 18" x 36" (45.7 x 91.4cm) khaki lightweight canvas
- (3) 1¼" x 6" (3.2 x 15.2cm) red shirt placket, optional
- Iron-on adhesive (I/O)
- Thread (light khaki, red, and blue)
- Light khaki crochet cotton thread
- (13) buttons
- Basic tools (page 7)

Cutting Requirements

Red Plaid

- (1) 3" (7.6cm) wonky circle with I/O
- (5) 4" (10.2cm) wonky circles with I/O
- (1) 5" (12.7cm) wonky circle with I/O
- (3) 1½" x 8" (3.8 x 20.3cm)
- (3) 1½" x 6" (3.8 x 15.2cm)
- (1) 2½" x 6" (6.4 x 15.2cm) with I/O
- (3) 1" x 8" (2.5 x 20.3cm) button placket, remove buttons

Blue Plaid

- (3) 3" (7.6cm) wonky circles with I/O
- (1) 4" (10.2cm) wonky circle with I/O
- (2) 5" (12.7cm) wonky circles with I/O
- (2) 2½" x 2½" (6.4 x 6.4cm) with I/O
- (1) 3" x 8" (7.6 x 20.3cm) with I/O
- (3) 1½" x 6" (3.8 x 15.2cm)
- (1) 4" x 6" (10.2 x 15.2cm) with I/O

Light Khaki

- (1) 2" (5.1cm) wonky circle with I/O
- (2) 3" (7.6cm) wonky circles with I/O
- (2) 5" (12.7cm) wonky circles with I/O
- (11) 5½" x 5½" (14 x 14cm)

Batting

- (6) 5½" x 5½" (14 x 14cm)

Mug Rug 1

1. Press (1) 5" (12.7cm) blue wonky circle on top of (1) 5½" x 5½" (14 x 14cm) khaki square.

2. Press (1) 4" (10.2cm) red wonky circle on top of the blue wonky circle.

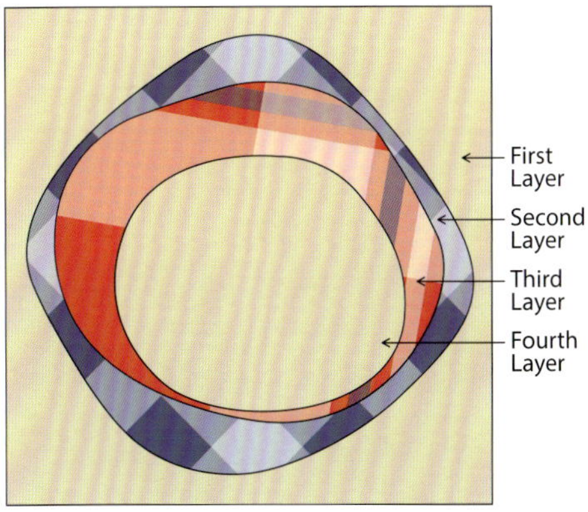

3. Press (1) 3" (7.6cm) khaki wonky circle on the red wonky circle.

4. Zigzag stitch around all wonky circles with matching thread.

5. Stitch (3) buttons on the khaki square.

6. Make a quilt sandwich as follows: Lay (1) 5½" x 5½" (14 x 14cm) khaki square RS down. Lay (1) 5½" x 5½" (14 x 14cm) batting on top of the fabric. Lay the mug rug front on top of the batting RS up.

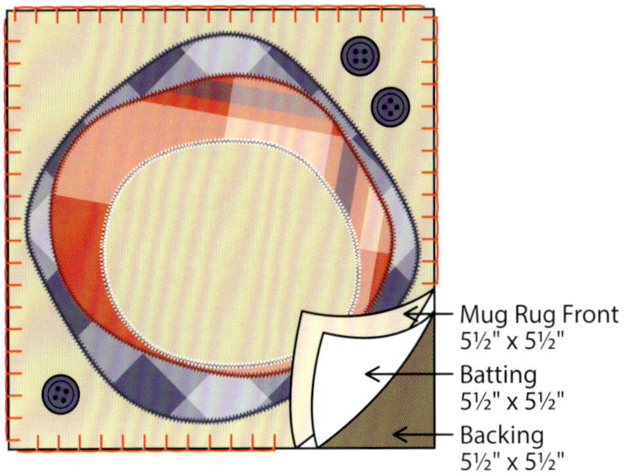

7. Blanket stitch with crochet cotton thread around the entire mug rug.

Mug Rug 2

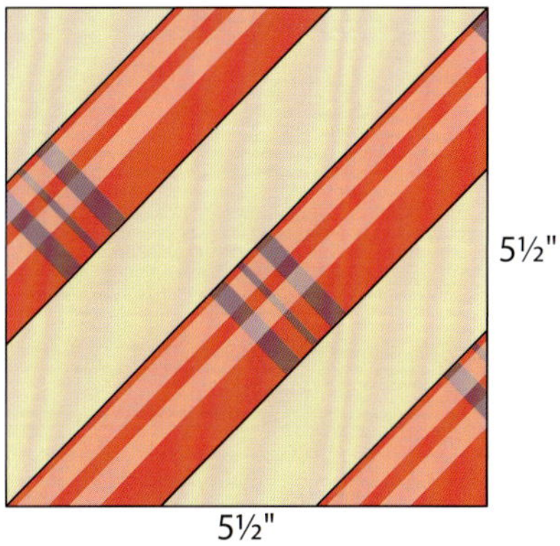

1. Fold both long edges of (3) 1½" x 8" (3.8 x 20.3cm) red strips under ¼" (6.4mm). Pin and stitch these strips diagonally onto (1) 5½" x 5½" (14 x 14cm) khaki square. Trim excess fabric.

2. Press (1) 5" (12.7cm) blue wonky circle on top of the mug rug front.

3. Press (1) 4" (10.2cm) red wonky circle to the blue wonky circle.

4. Press (1) 3" (7.6cm) khaki wonky circle to the red wonky circle.

5. Zigzag stitch around all wonky circles with matching thread.

6. Pin (1) 1" x 8" (2.5 x 20.3cm) red plaid button placket to the mug rug front at an angle. Trim excess fabric. Quilt in place with straight lines.

7. Stitch (2) buttons on the button placket.

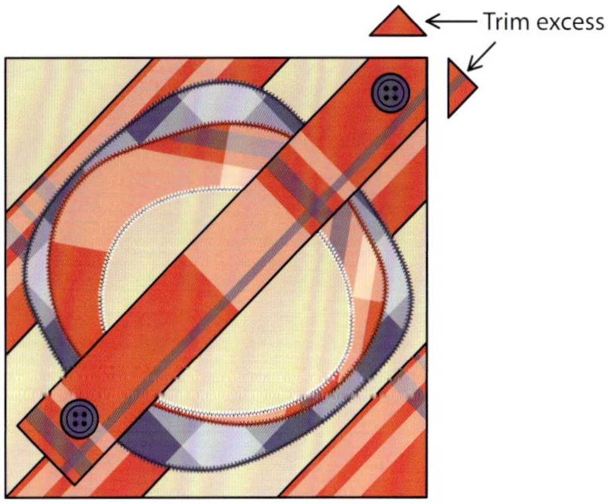

8. Repeat steps 6 and 7 of Mug Rug 1.

Mug Rug 3

1. Press (2) 2½" x 2½" (6.4 x 6.4cm) blue squares to the corners of (1) 5½" x 5½" (14 x 14cm) khaki square, opposite each other.

2. Press (1) 5" (12.7cm) red wonky circle on top of the mug rug front.

3. Press (1) 4" (10.2cm) blue wonky circle on the red wonky circle.

4. Press (1) 3" (7.6cm) red wonky circle on the blue wonky circle.

5. Zigzag stitch around all wonky circles with matching thread.

6. Stitch (3) buttons on the khaki square.

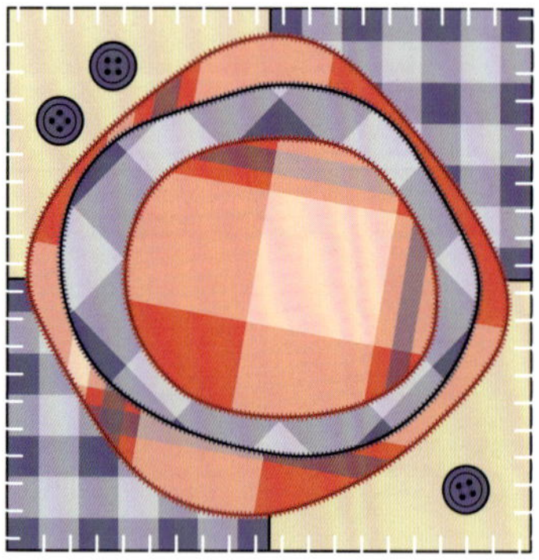

7. Repeat steps 6 and 7 of Mug Rug 1.

Mug Rug 4

1. Press (1) 3" x 8" (7.6 x 20.3cm) blue plaid strip diagonally across (1) 5½" x 5½" (14 x 14cm) khaki square. Trim excess fabric.

2. Press (1) 4" (10.2cm) red wonky circle on top of the mug rug front.

3. Press (1) 3" (7.6cm) blue wonky circle on the red wonky circle.

4. Trim (1) 1" x 8" (2.5 x 20.3cm) red plaid button placket as desired. Pin to the mug rug front at an angle.

5. Press (1) 2" (5.1cm) khaki wonky circle on the placket.

6. Zigzag stitch around all wonky circles and strips with matching thread.

7. Stitch (1) button on the blue plaid strip.

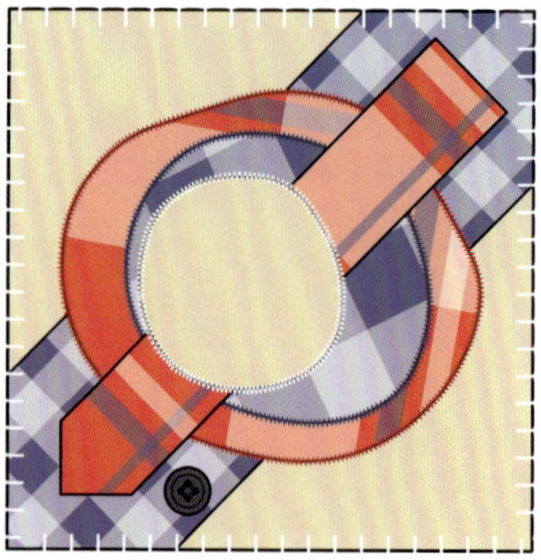

8. Repeat steps 6 and 7 of Mug Rug 1.

Mug Rug 5

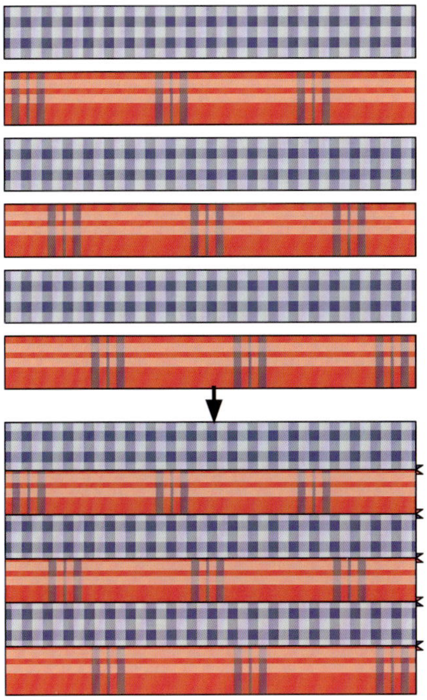

1. Stitch (3) 1½" x 6" (3.8 x 15.2cm) blue plaid strips and (3) 1½" x 6" (3.8 x 15.2cm) red plaid strips side by side, alternating the colors. Trim to 5½" x 5½" (14 x 14cm).

2. Press (1) 5" (12.7cm) khaki wonky circle on top of the mug rug front.

3. Press (1) 4" (10.2cm) red wonky circle on the khaki wonky circle.

4. Press (1) 3" (7.6cm) blue wonky circle on the red wonky circle.

5. Zigzag stitch around all wonky circles with matching thread.

6. Stitch (2) buttons to the blue-and-red strip layer.

7. Repeat steps 6 and 7 of Mug Rug 1.

Mug Rug 6

1. Press (1) 4" x 6" (10.2 x 15.2cm) blue plaid piece on top of (1) 5½" x 5½" (14 x 14cm) khaki square, aligning to one edge.

2. Press (1) 2½" x 6" (6.4 x 15.2cm) red plaid on top of the same khaki square, aligning to the open edge. The khaki square should be completely covered.

3. Press (1) 5" (12.7cm) khaki wonky circle on top of the mug rug front.

4. Press (1) 4" (10.2cm) red wonky circle to the khaki wonky circle.

5. Pin (1) 1" x 8" (2.5 x 20.3cm) red plaid button placket at an angle on the mug rug front. Trim excess fabric.

6. Press (1) 3" (7.6cm) blue wonky circle on the mug rug front.

7. Zigzag stitch around all wonky circles and strips with matching thread.

8. Stitch (2) buttons to the blue-and-red pieced layer.

9. Repeat steps 6 and 7 of Mug Rug 1.

Grandma's Quilted Mug Rugs

Finished Size: 7" (17.8cm) diameter

Using an heirloom quilt from grandma to make mug rugs sounds incredibly harsh. I suggest only using your grandma's quilt if it is damaged beyond repair or if it is at the request of the entire family. For the nostalgic look, a quilt found in a resale shop works great. Again, I'd use a damaged or torn quilt; it seems sacrilegious to cut a quilt apart.

Whether it is grandma's or not, vintage-looking circular mug rugs will add comfort and warmth when used under a steaming mug of coffee, tea, or hot chocolate. They are also perfect under a vase of sweet, gathered flowers.

Material Requirements

- (6–8) Fat Quarters in various colors
- Old quilt
- (96) ¼" (6.4mm) two-hole buttons
- Yellow thread
- Basic tools (page 7)
- GQ pattern (page 111)

Cutting Requirements

Fat Quarters

- (96) Pattern GQ-A

Instructions

1. Trace Pattern GQ-A (6) times onto the quilt with a water-erasable pen for (6) circles. Cut out the circles.

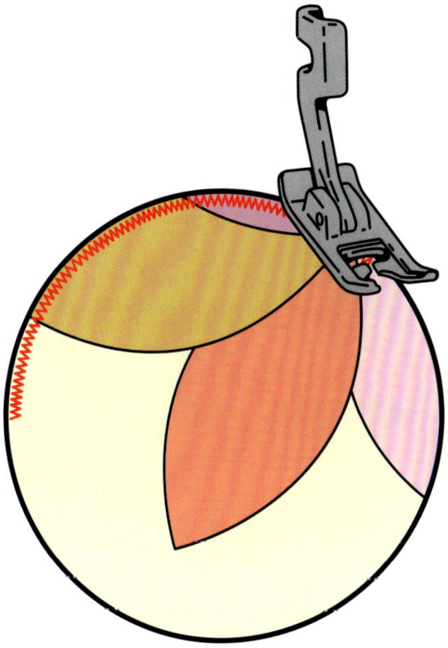

2. To keep the layers of the quilt circles intact, zigzag stitch around the perimeter near the edge of all (6) circles.

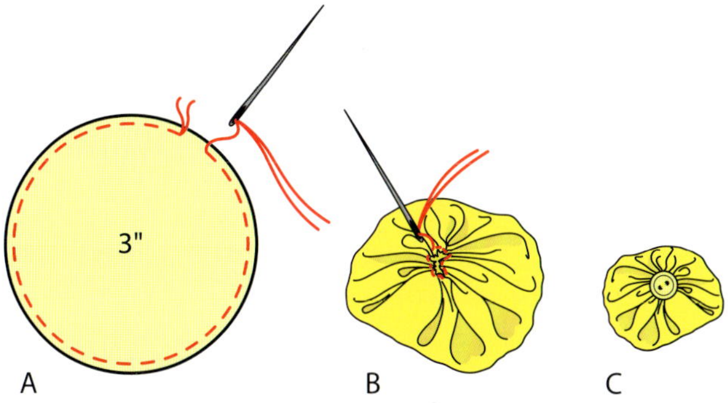

3. Stitch around perimeter of (1) Pattern GQ-A circle. Use small straight stitches close to the edge. At the end, pull into a tight circle. Knot the thread in the center. Move gathers as needed to make a uniform fabric yo-yo. Stitch a button in the center of the yo-yo.

4. Repeat step 3 with the remaining (95) Pattern GQ-A circles.

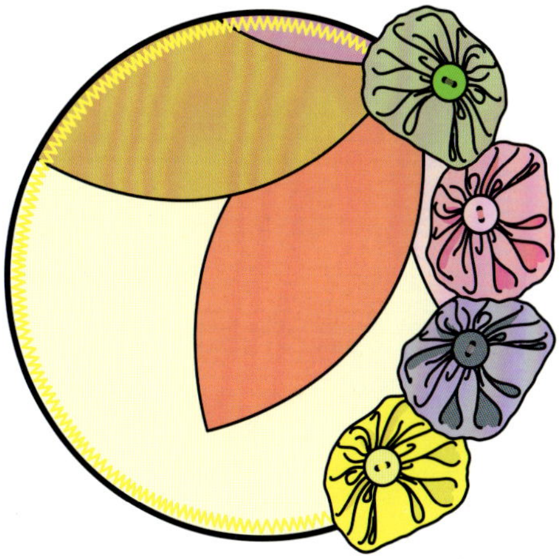

5. Plan the placement of (16) random yo-yos around the perimeter of the quilt circle, then hand stitch them. Place the yo-yo button up on the front of the quilt circle.

6. Repeat step 5 for the remaining (5) quilt circles.

PHOTO TRANSFER
Projects

For the projects in this book, I used photo transfer paper. There are many ways to transfer photos to fabric, but I find this the easiest and cleanest way to achieve the results I am looking for. These items will last longer if handwashed when necessary.

The **Italy Photo Transfer Mug Rugs** are a reminder of a recent trip to Rome. How would I preserve and enjoy my photos of St. Peter's Basilica? Of course, a photo album is usually preferred, but my sister and mother enjoy these gifts as reminders of the trip we took together.

The **Artwork Transfer Mug Rugs** are dear to me. I have eight grandchildren and a never-ending supply of drawings from them. This is a wonderful way to enjoy these pieces of artwork daily!

Artwork Transfer Mug Rugs

Finished Size: 6" x 8" (15.2 x 20.3cm)

When my grandchildren visit, they often color pictures for me. I gathered them up one day and thought that it would be fun to create a memory using something from them. I found this fabric that to me looks like crayon drawings, and away I went, creating the fun mug rugs featured in this set. The different color cotton fabrics can be solids, batiks, or small prints.

Material Requirements

- Fat Quarter or (1) ¼" x 44" (0.6 x 111.8cm) white cotton fabric
- Fat Quarter or (1) ¼" x 44" (0.6 x 111.8cm) colorful cotton fabric
- Fat Quarter or (1) ¼" x 44" (0.6 x 111.8cm) yellow cotton fabric
- Fat Quarter or (1) ¼" x 44" (0.6 x 111.8cm) blue cotton fabric
- Fat Quarter or (1) ¼" x 44" (0.6 x 111.8cm) green cotton fabric
- Fat Quarter or (1) ¼" x 44" (0.6 x 111.8cm) rust cotton fabric
- Fat Quarter or (1) ¼" x 44" (0.6 x 111.8cm) red cotton fabric
- Fat Quarter or (1) ¼" x 44" (0.6 x 111.8cm) hot pink cotton fabric
- (1) 18" x 44" (45.7 x 111.8cm) melon cotton fabric
- (1) 14" (35.6cm) hot pink medium-size rickrack
- (1) 14" (35.6cm) purple medium-size rickrack
- (1) 12" (30.5cm) green medium-size rickrack
- (1) 14" (35.6cm) lime green medium-size rickrack
- (1) 12" (30.5cm) blue medium-size rickrack
- (1) 12" (30.5cm) red medium-size rickrack
- (6) 6" x 8" (15.2 x 20.3) needled cotton batting
- (6) 3½" x 4½" (8.9 x 11.4cm) crayon drawings with ½" (1.3cm) allowance
- Transfer paper (I used Transfer Magic)
- Solid color-coordinating threads
- Basic tools (page 7)

Cutting Requirements

White Fabric

- (6) 6" x 6" (15.2 x 15.2cm)

Colorful Fabric

- (6) 5½" x 8" (14 x 20.3cm)

Yellow Fabric

- (2) 1½" x 8" (3.8 x 20.3cm)
- (1) 5½" x 8" (14 x 20.3cm)

Blue Fabric

- (2) 1½" x 8" (3.8 x 20.3cm)
- (1) 5½" x 8" (14 x 20.3cm)

Green Fabric

- (1) 1½" x 6" (14 x 15.2cm)
- (1) 1½" x 8" (3.8 x 20.3cm)
- (1) 5½" x 8" (14 x 20.3cm)

Rust Fabric

- (2) 1½" x 6" (14 x 15.2cm)
- (1) 5½" x 8" (14 x 20.3cm)

Red Fabric

- (2) 1½" x 8" (3.8 x 20.3cm)
- (1) 5½" x 8" (14 x 20.3cm)

Hot Pink Fabric

- (2) 1½" x 6" (14 x 15.2cm)
- (1) 5½" x 8" (14 x 20.3cm)

Melon Fabric

- (6) 2" x 30" (5.1 x 76.2cm) for bias tape, cut straight

Blue Rickrack

- (2) 6" (15.2cm)

Red Rickrack

- (2) 6" (15.2cm)

Hot Pink Rickrack

- (1) 6" (15.2cm)
- (1) 8" (15.2cm)

Purple Rickrack

- (1) 6" (15.2cm)
- (2) 8" (15.2cm)

Green Rickrack

- (2) 6" (15.2cm)

Lime Green Rickrack

- (1) 6" (15.2cm)
- (1) 8" (15.2cm)

Heart Mug Rug (Vertical)

1. Follow the manufacturer's instructions to transfer the drawings to the 6" x 6" (15.2 x 15.2cm) white fabric. Trim to ½" (1.3cm) around the image, approximately 3½" x 4½" (8.9 x 11.4cm).

2. Pin (1) transfer to (1) 5½" x 8" (14 x 20.3cm) colorful fabric as desired. The mug rugs can all be symmetrical and centered, can favor one side, or can position near the top or bottom. Use horizontal photos on horizontal colorful fabric and vertical photos on vertical colorful fabric.

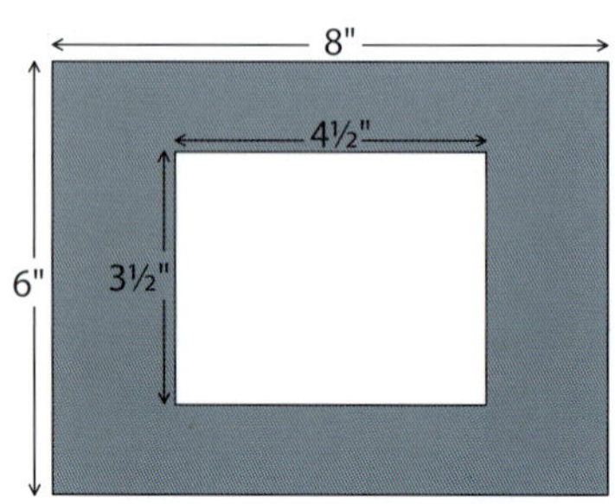

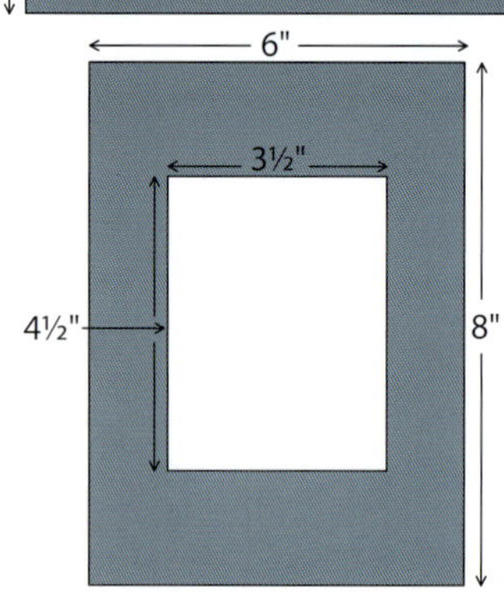

3. Sew the WS of the transfer fabric to the RS of the colorful fabric with white thread and a ¼" (6.4mm) seam. Make sure the photo orientation matches the fabric shape.

4. Fold both long edges of (1) 1½" x 8" (3.8 x 20.3cm) yellow strip under ¼" (6.4mm). Pin and stitch the strip onto (1) mug rug front, covering (1) long seam of the transfer to the colorful fabric.

5. Repeat step 4 with another yellow strip on the other long seam.

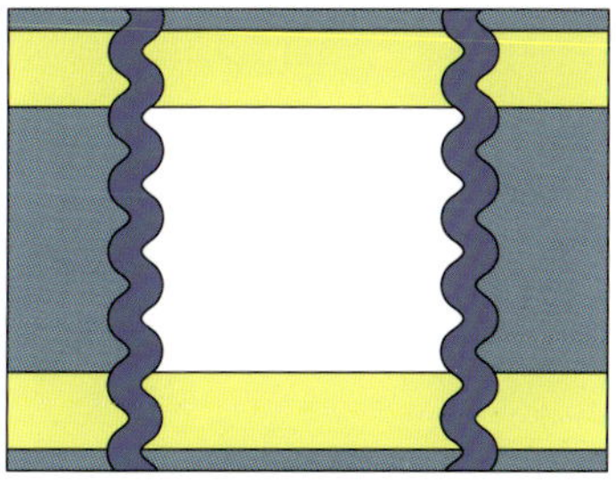

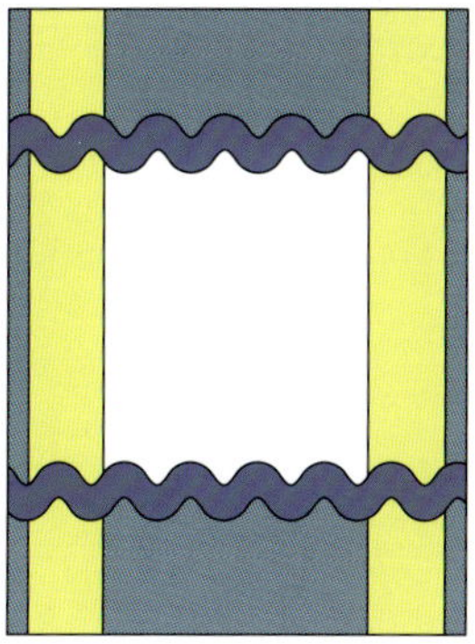

6. Pin and sew (1) blue rickrack across (1) short seam of the transfer to the colorful fabric. Repeat with another blue rickrack on the other short seam.

7. Make a quilt sandwich as follows: Lay (1) 5½" x 8" (14 x 20.3cm) yellow fabric RS down. Lay the batting piece on top of the fabric. Lay the mug rug front on top of the batting RS up. Stitch close to the edge to keep all layers together.

8. Make ½" (1.3cm) double-fold bias tape from (1) 2" x 30" (5.1 x 76.2cm) melon strip, as explained in step 6 on page 9. Fold the bias tape over the edge and hand sew to the back, as explained on page 10.

Ladybug Mug Rug (Vertical)

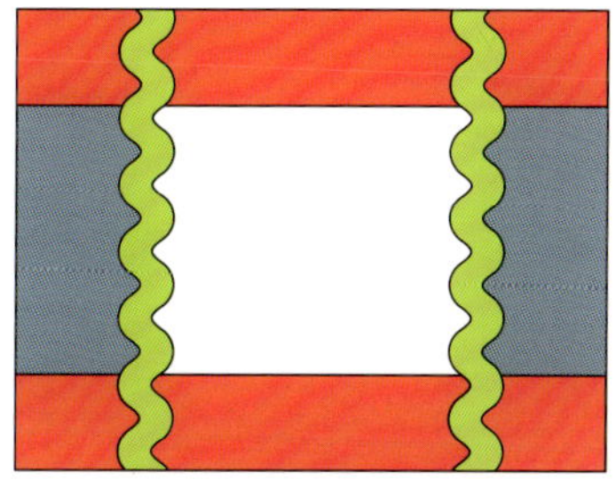

1. Repeat steps 2–8 of the Heart Mug Rug. Use red fabric for the (2) vertical strips and backing fabric. Use green rickrack for the (2) horizontal strips.

Bunny Mug Rug (Vertical)

1. Repeat steps 2 and 3 of the Heart Mug Rug.

2. Fold both long edges of (1) 1½" x 6" (14 x 15.2cm) hot pink strip under ¼" (6.4mm). Pin and stitch the strip onto (1) mug rug front, covering (1) short seam of the transfer to the colorful fabric.

3. Repeat step 2 with another hot pink strip, placing ½" (1.3cm) above the other strip.

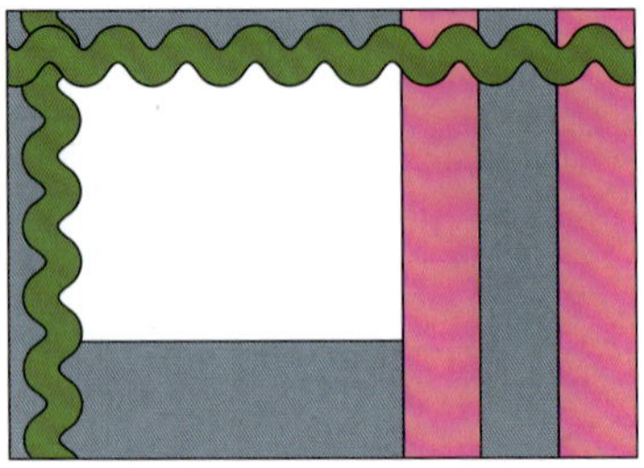

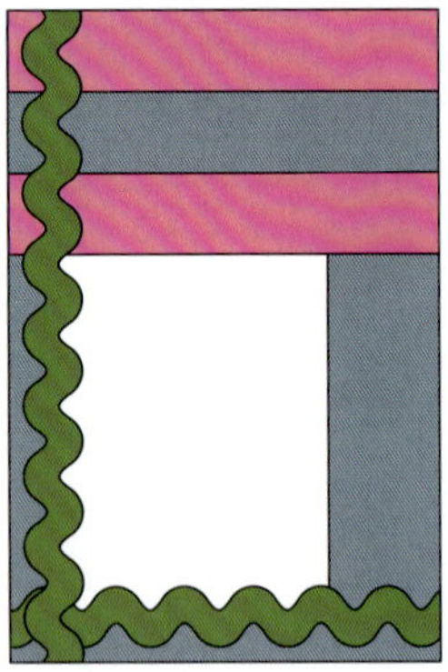

4. Pin and sew (1) lime green rickrack across the other short seam of the transfer to the colorful fabric. Repeat with another lime green rickrack on (1) long seam.

5. Repeat steps 7 and 8 of the Heart Mug Rug. Use hot pink fabric for the backing fabric.

Dragonfly Mug Rug (Horizontal)

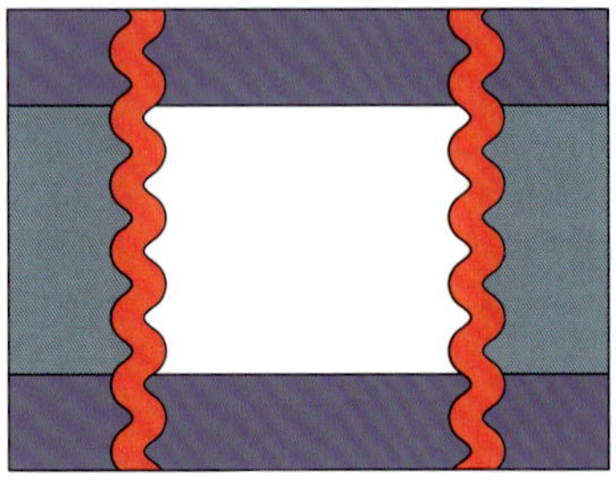

1. Repeat steps 2–8 of the Heart Mug Rug. Use blue fabric for the (2) horizontal strips and backing fabric. Use red rickrack for the (2) vertical strips.

Owl Mug Rug (Horizontal)

1. Repeat steps 2 and 3 of the Heart Mug Rug.

2. Fold both long edges of (1) 1½" x 8" (3.8 x 20.3cm) green strip under ¼" (6.4mm). Pin and stitch the strip onto (1) mug rug front, covering (1) long seam of the transfer to the colorful fabric.

3. Repeat step 2 with (1) 1½" x 6" (14 x 15.2cm) green strip on (1) short seam.

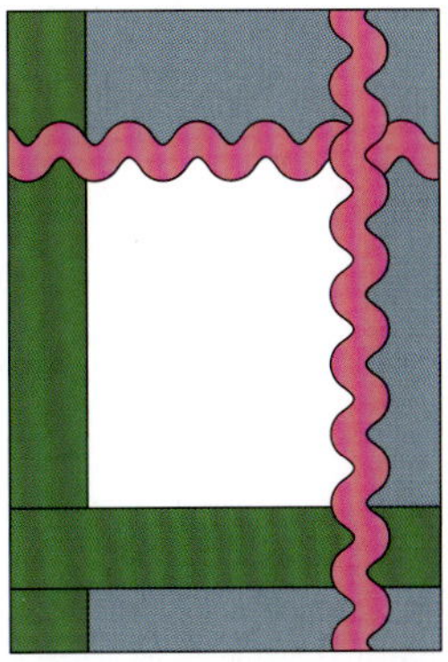

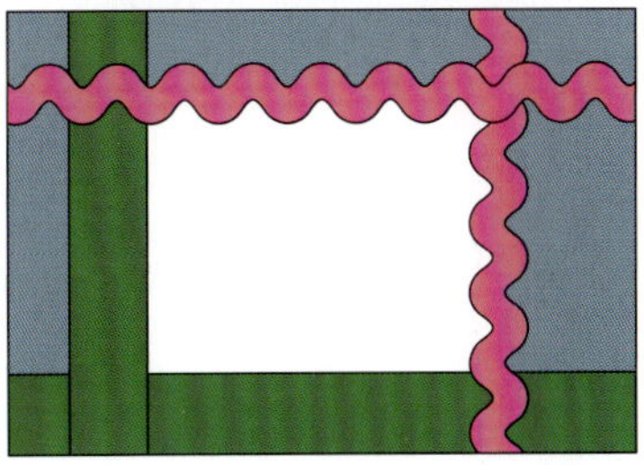

4. Pin and sew (1) hot pink rickrack across the other short seam of the transfer to the colorful fabric. Repeat with another hot pink rickrack on the other long seam.

5. Repeat steps 7 and 8 of the Heart Mug Rug. Use green fabric for the backing fabric.

Bear Mug Rug (Horizontal)

1. Repeat steps 2 and 3 of the Heart Mug Rug.

2. Fold both long edges of (1) 1½" x 6" (14 x 15.2cm) rust strip under ¼" (6.4mm). Pin and stitch the strip onto (1) mug rug front, covering (1) short seam of the transfer to the colorful fabric.

3. Repeat step 2 with another rust strip, placing ½" (1.3cm) to the right of the other strip.

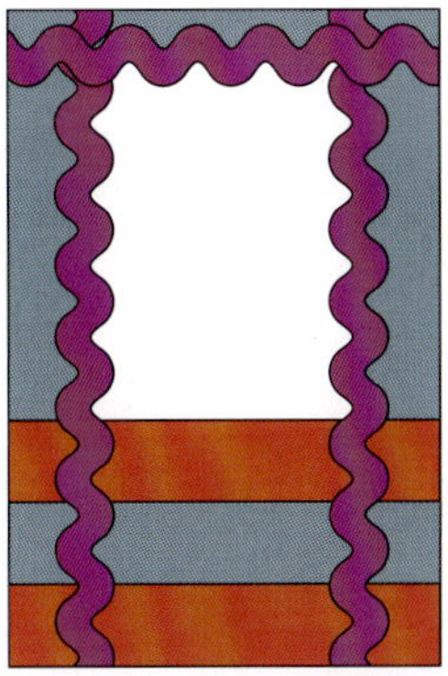

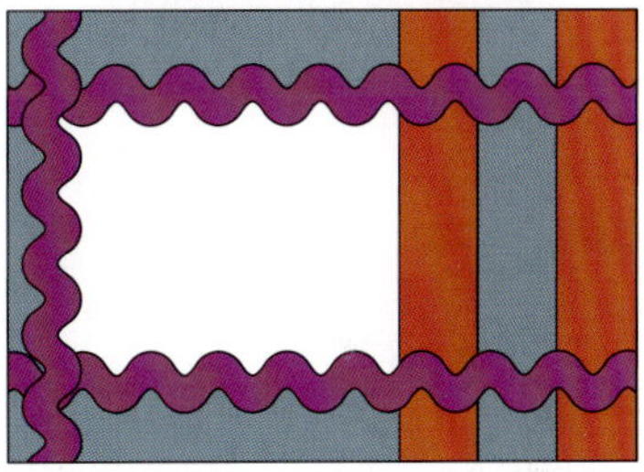

4. Pin and sew (1) purple rickrack across the other short seam of the transfer to the colorful fabric. Repeat with (2) purple rickrack pieces on (2) long seams.

5. Repeat steps 7 and 8 of the Heart Mug Rug. Use rust fabric for the backing fabric.

Woven Photo Transfer Mug Rugs

Finished Size: 7" x 8" (17.8 x 20.3cm)

I recently saw some woven photos used in mixed media and wondered if the same could be done with transferred photos on fabric projects. I am delighted by the results. I used family vacation photos from our yearly trip to Minnesota, and the hardest part of this project was choosing the photos I wanted to use.

Material Requirements

- (1) 12" x 44" (30.5 x 111.8cm) white fabric
- (1) 36" x 44" (91.4 x 111.8cm) brown print fabric
- Fat Quarter or (1) 9" x 44" (22.9 x 111.8cm) aqua solid fabric
- (6) 7" x 8" (17.8 x 20.3cm) cotton needled batting
- Fusible interfacing (I used HeatnBond Lite)
- (12) 4" x 5" (10.2 x 12.7cm) photos (2 of each photo)
- Transfer paper (I used Transfer Magic)
- Brown thread
- Pins and foamboard or masking tape, optional
- Basic tools (page 7)

Cutting Requirements

Brown Print Fabric

- (6) 7" x 8" (17.8 x 20.3cm)
- (24) 2" x 8" (5.1 x 20.3cm)
- (6) 2" x 36" (5.1 x 91.4cm) for bias tape
- (4) 1½" x 1½" (3.8 x 3.8cm)

Aqua Solid Fabric

- (2) 3" x 3" (7.6 x 7.6cm)
- (4) 2"x 8" (5.1 x 20.3cm)
- (4) 1½" x 3½" (3.8 x 8.9cm)

Cotton Needled Batting

- (6) 7" x 8" (17.8 x 20.3cm)

Fusible Interfacing

- (6) 4½" x 5½" (11.4 x 14cm)

Woven Photo (For All Mug Rugs)

1. Follow the manufacturer's instructions to print the (12) photos onto transfer paper.

2. Transfer the transfer-paper photos to the white fabric, leaving at least 1" (2.5cm) between the photos. Set aside the release papers that you remove from the photos.

3. Cut (1) photo to ¼" (6.4mm) larger around, creating a 4½" x 5½" (11.4 x 14cm) piece. Repeat with the duplicate photo.

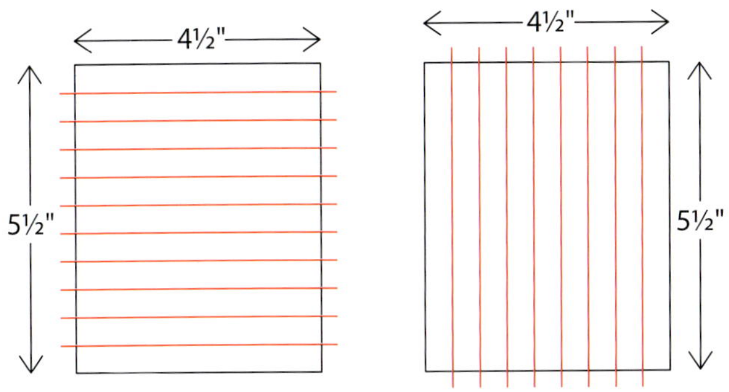

4. Cut (1) photo in ½" (1.3cm) strips vertically and the (1) duplicate photo in ½" (1.3cm) strips horizontally.

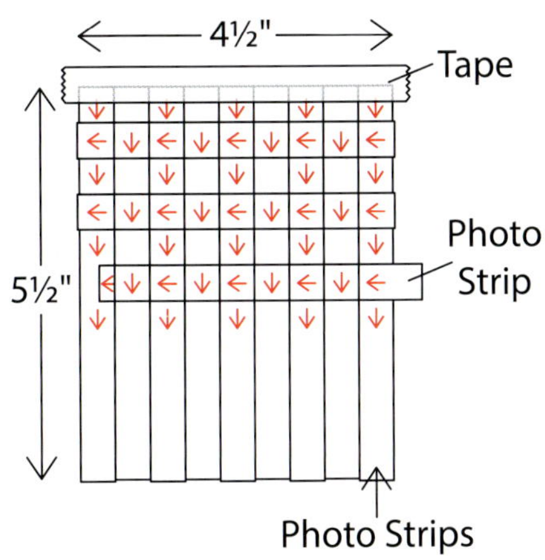

5. Weave the (2) photos together, matching the image. This can be done by taping or pinning strips to a foam board, either the horizontal or vertical strips, and then weaving the other direction strips into them.

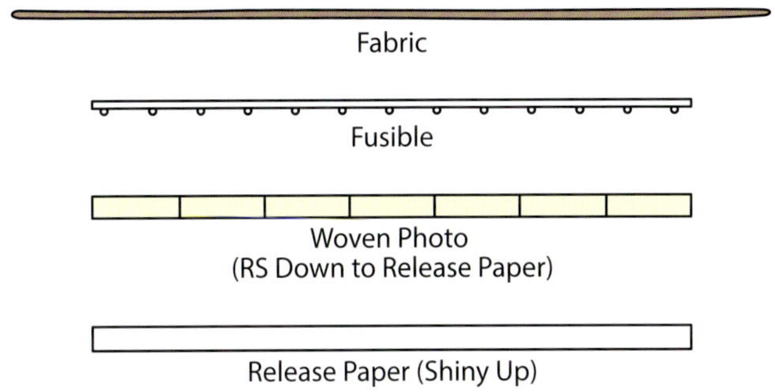

6. Lay the woven photo RS down on the slippery side of the release paper, which was set aside. Place (1) fusible interfacing piece bumpy side down on top of the woven photo. Place a pressing cloth over the fusible and follow the manufacturer's instructions to adhere.

7. Trim the photo to 4½" x 5½" (11.4 x 14cm) if needed.

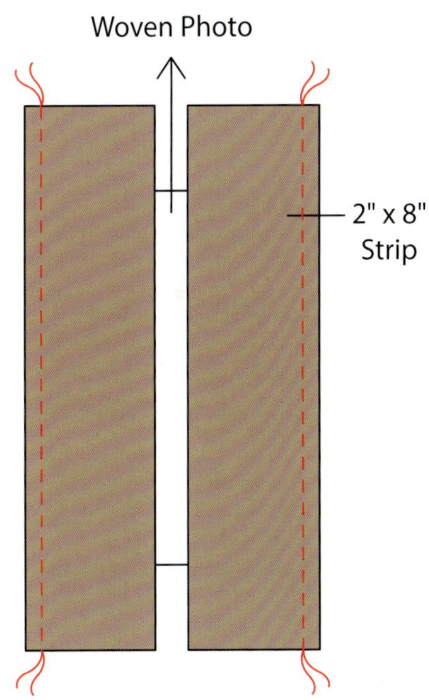

8. Stitch (1) 2" x 8" (5.1 x 20.3cm) brown strip RST to the right edge of the photo. Stitch a second 2" x 8" (5.1 x 20.3cm) brown strip to the left edge. Press open.

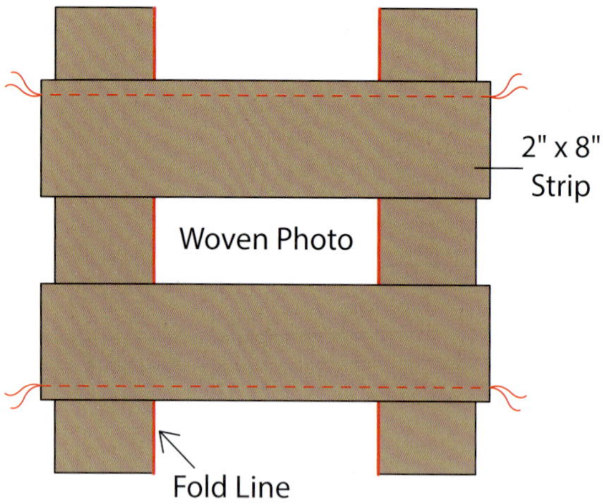

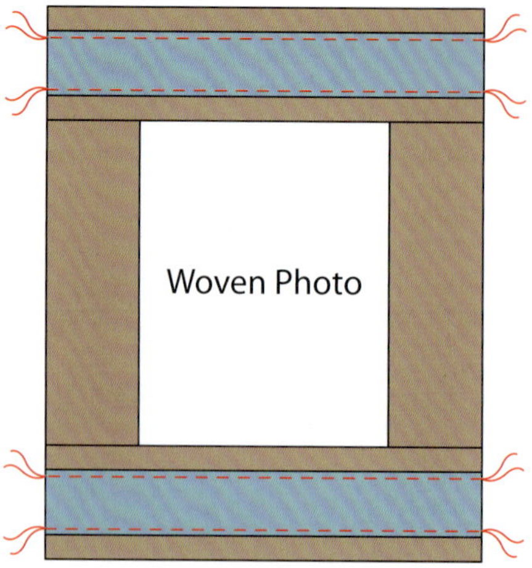

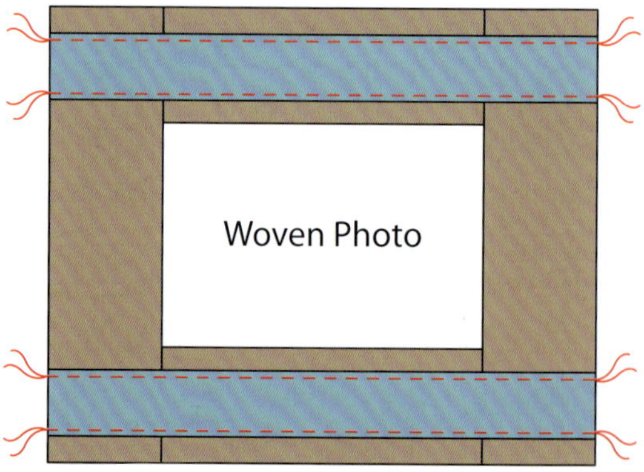

9. Stitch (1) 2" x 8" (5.1 x 20.3cm) brown strip RST to the top of the photo. Stitch a second 2" x 8" (5.1 x 20.3cm) brown strip to the bottom. These strips should be sewn across the first (2) strips. Press open.

10. Repeat steps 1–9 for the remaining (5) photos.

Stripes Mug Rug

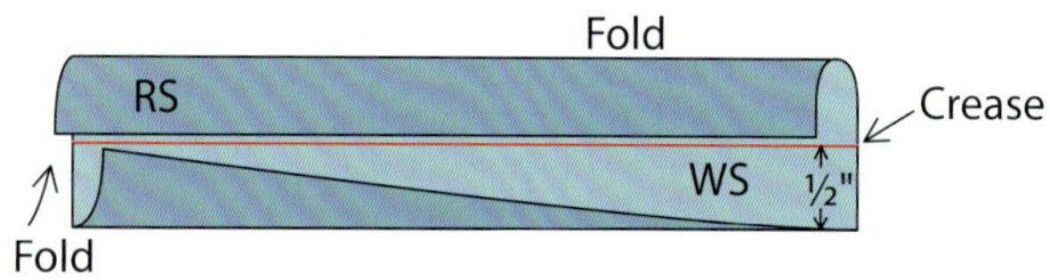

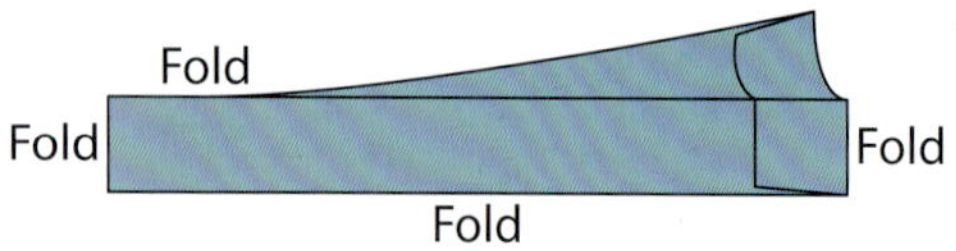

1. Iron (2) 2" x 8" (5.1 x 20.3cm) aqua strips in half lengthwise. Open up and fold each outer edge to the center fold. Press the fold firmly. Fold the ends inside for clean square ends.

2. Stitch the aqua stripes to the top and bottom of (1) fabric frame using brown thread along both long edges.

3. Repeat with a second fabric frame. If you have a horizontal mug rug and a vertical mug rug, trim them with the aqua strips on top and bottom.

4. Make a quilt sandwich as follows: Lay (1) 7" x 8" (17.8 x 20.3cm) brown piece RS down. Lay (1) 7" x 8" (17.8 x 20.3cm) batting on top of the fabric. Lay the mug rug front on top of the batting RS up. Stitch around the outside edges close to the edge.

5. Use (1) 2" x 36" (5.1 x 91.4cm) brown fabric to make ½" (1.3cm) double-fold bias tape. Stitch the bias tape to the front of the mug rug, as explained on page 10. Fold the bias tape over the edge and hand sew to the back.

Corners Mug Rug

1. Cut (1) 3" x 3" (7.6 x 7.6cm) aqua square in half diagonally from corner to corner. Fold the longest side of the square under for a ¼" (6.4mm) hem.

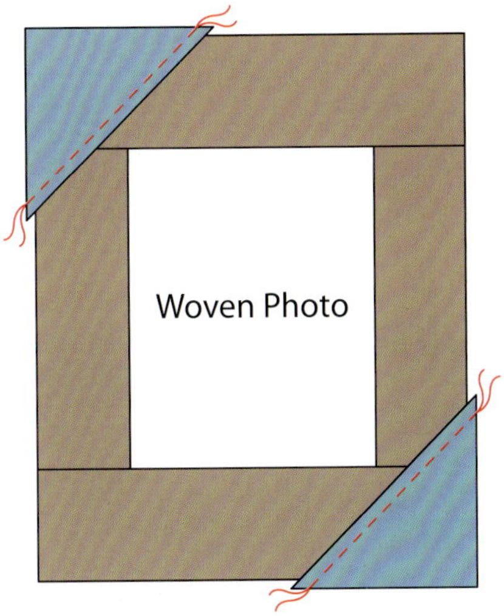

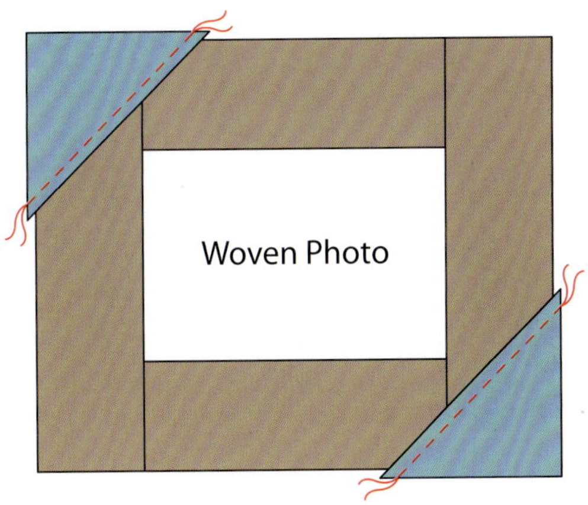

2. Pin the aqua corners to the top-left and bottom-right corners, whether vertical or horizontal. Stitch the hemmed edge to the mug rug using brown thread.

3. Repeat steps 1 and 2 with a second fabric frame.

4. Repeat steps 4 and 5 of the Stripes Mug Rug.

Squares Mug Rug

1. Fold (2) edges of (1) 1½" x 3½" (3.8 x 8.9cm) aqua square into the center. Press the outer folds. Fold the ends inside the folded strip for a finished square look.

2. Fold (1) 1½" x 1½" (3.8 x 3.8cm) brown square the same as the aqua strip. Fold around the center of the aqua strip like a buckle. Stitch the aqua/brown strip to the left side of (1) fabric frame, whether vertical or horizontal.

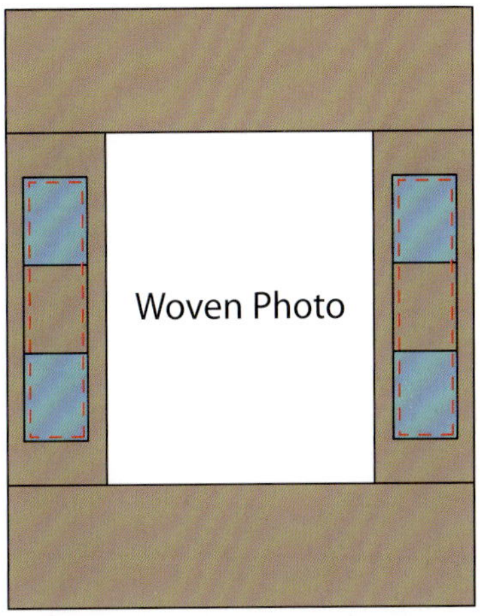

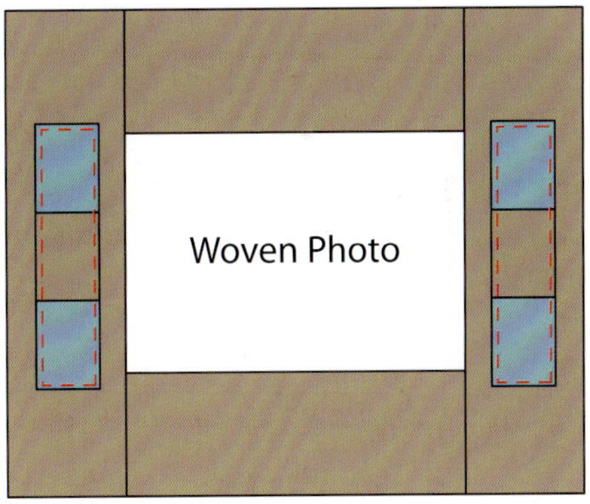

3. Repeat steps 1 and 2, placing on the other side of the fabric frame.

4. Repeat steps 1–3 with a second fabric frame.

5. Repeat steps 4 and 5 of the Stripes Mug Rug.

WOVEN
Projects

Weaving is the art of interlacing two pieces of fabric or yarn at right angles. The horizontal yarn is the weft and the vertical yarn is the warp.

In the **Woven Burlap Mug Rugs**, we will be weaving yarn into a grid fabric: open-weave burlap. There is also a strip of hemmed fabric that is sewn across the burlap between the groups of yarns for added color, texture, and interest.

The **Woven Cork Fabric Mug Rugs** weaves strips of cork fabric. This has a polycotton fabric attached to the back of the cotton fibers. I used a perforated cork fabric with ¼" x ¼" (6.4 x 6.4mm) holes to weave through. Another creative note about these mug rugs is that we will be using the back of the cork fabric as its own distinct color and texture throughout.

The **Woven Photo Transfer Mug Rugs** will incorporate transfer photos on white fabric. We will cut that fabric into strips and then weave the photos back together for a unique texture in the mug rug.

Woven Burlap Mug Rugs

Finished Size: 6" x 8" (15.2 x 20.3cm), including fringe

Simple to do, these woven burlap mug rugs add a soft texture to your gathering space. Weaving is done with a large tapestry needle and fluffy yarn through burlap ribbon. The fabric strips were added to break things up a bit and add another texture. If you are adventurous, add wooden or stone beads onto the fringes when the mug rugs are complete. Because of the texture, these are recommended for mugs only.

Material Requirements

- (1) 6" x 48" (15.2 x 122cm) blue burlap ribbon
- (1) 6" x 48" (15.2 x 122cm) salmon burlap ribbon
- (1) 9" x 44" (22.9 x 111.8cm) coordinating fabric
- (1) 9" x 36" (22.9 x 91.4cm) needled cotton batting
- (1) skein #6/super bulky yarn in a variegated colorway: blue, green, and brown
- Tapestry needle
- Blue thread
- Salmon thread
- Basic tools (page 7)

Cutting Requirements

Blue Burlap Ribbon

- (6) 6" x 8" (15.2 x 20.3cm)

Salmon Burlap Ribbon

- (6) 6" x 8" (15.2 x 20.3cm)

Coordinating Fabric

- (12) 2" x 8" (5.1 x 20.3cm)

Yarn

- (180) 10" (25.4cm)

Tip

Pull and stretch the burlap ribbon or fabric to square it up.

Tip

The 6" (15.2cm) wide burlap ribbon is easy to find, but six strips can be made from ⅓ yard (30.5cm) of burlap fabric as well.

Instructions

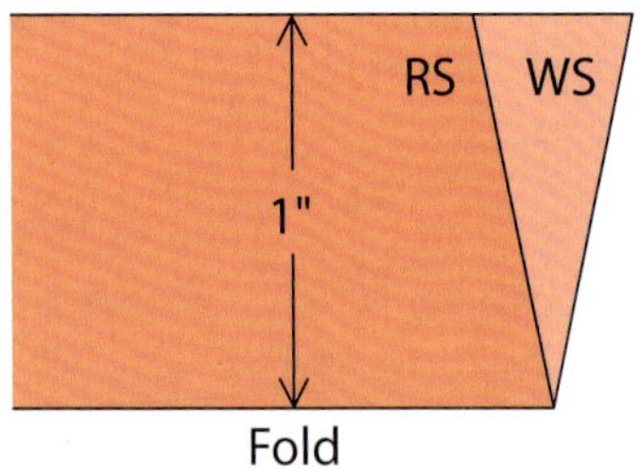

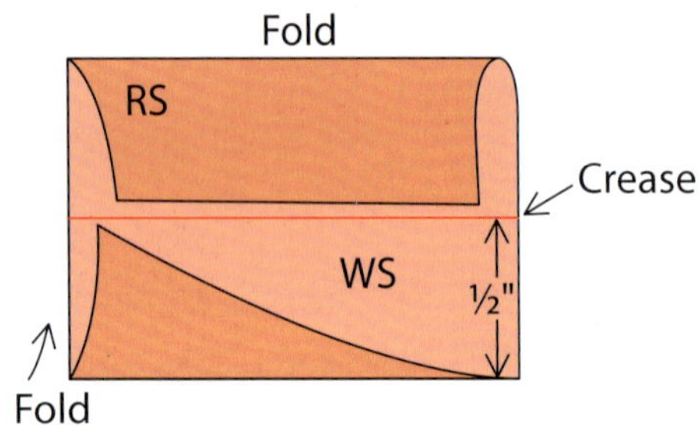

1. Iron (1) 2" x 8" (5.1 x 20.3cm) fabric strip in half lengthwise for a 1" x 8" (2.5 x 20.3cm) strip. Open up and fold (1) long edge to the center fold line. Press. Repeat for the other long edge. Press again, being sure the folds are sharp and the center fold line is gone.

2. Repeat step 1 for a second fabric strip.

3. Stitch around the perimeter of (1) burlap ribbon with matching thread.

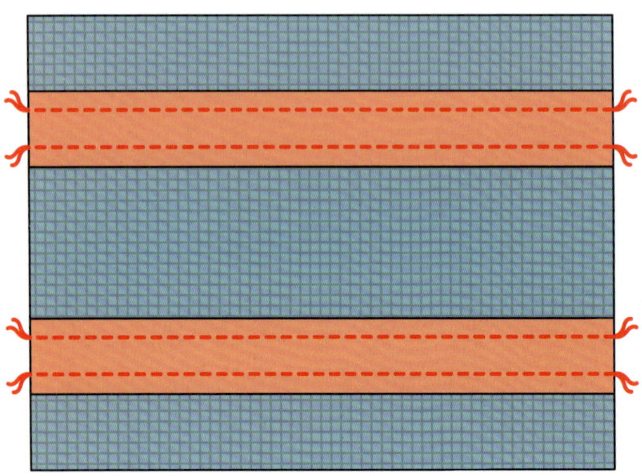

4. Pin (1) folded fabric strip WS down to the burlap, 1" (2.5cm) away from (1) long edge of the burlap. Repeat with the second fabric strip on the other long edge. Stitch these strips in place with ¼" (6.4mm) seams.

5. Repeat steps 1–4 for the remaining (5) mug rugs. There is a total of (3) blue mug rugs and (3) salmon mug rugs. Trim all mug rugs to 8" (20.3cm) long.

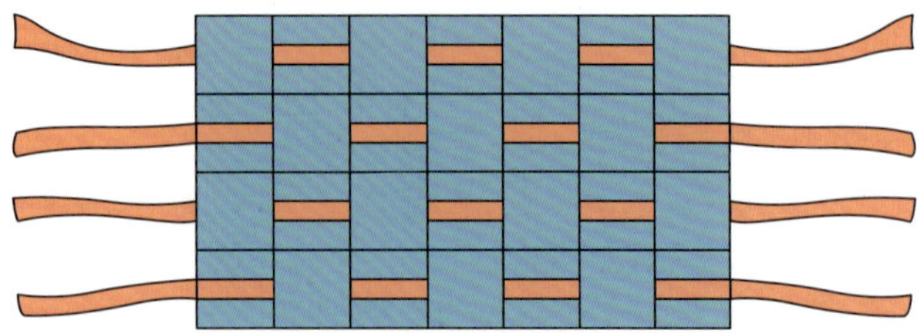

Enlarged Grid

6. Thread a length of yarn onto the tapestry needle. Weave the yarn in and out of the burlap holes from right to left. Above and below the fabric strips, start next to the fabric strip and work out to burlap edges. This will alleviate stress on the outside edges of the burlap ribbon.

7. Repeat step 6 for the other (5) mug rugs.

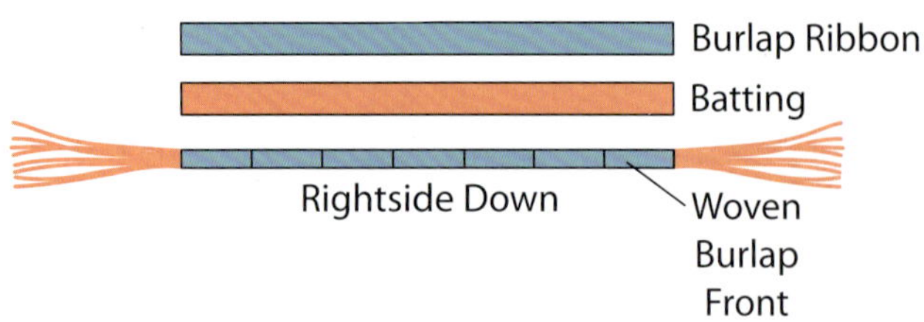

8. Make a quilt sandwich as follows: Lay (1) burlap RS down. Lay (1) batting on top. Lay (1) matching burlap/fabric front on top RS up. Stitch close to the edge with matching thread to keep all layers together.

9. Trim the yarn fringe to 1½" (3.8cm) long on all mug rugs.

Woven Cork Fabric Mug Rugs

Finished Size: 5" x 8" (12.7 x 20.3cm)

Cork fabric isn't just for bulletin boards and handbags. In this project, we are using Belagio Enterprises cork fabric. It is lightweight, durable, and has so many great characteristics: the edges seal when cut, it can be woven easily because it can be cut to the size needed for weft and warp, and it can be sewn to hold the final shape. However, any ¼" x ¼" (6.4 x 6.4mm) square open-weave fabric will work for this design. When making these cork mug rugs, we will be using the cork fabric front and back for contrast.

Material Requirements

- (2) 15" x 18" (38.1 x 45.7cm) or 18" x 25" (45.7 x 63.5cm) basketweave cork fabric
- (2) 15" x 18" (38.1 x 45.7cm) or 12" x 25" (30.5 x 63.5cm) crocodile print cork fabric
- (2) 15" x 18" (38.1 x 45.7cm) or 12" x 25" (30.5 x 63.5cm) circles print cork fabric
- (2) 15" x 18" (38.1 x 45.7cm) or 12" x 25" (30.5 x 63.5cm) fox print cork fabric
- (6) 5" x 8" (12.7 x 20.3cm) needled cotton batting
- Brown thread
- Basic tools (page 7)

Cutting Requirements

Basketweave Cork Fabric

- (6) 5" x 8" (12.7 x 20.3cm)

Crocodile Print Cork Fabric

- (4) 5" x 8" (12.7 x 20.3cm)
- (4) 1" x 18" (2.5 x 45.7cm)
- (4) 3" x 3" (7.6 x 7.6cm)
- (24) ¼" x 5" (6.4 x 12.7cm)

Circles Print Cork Fabric

- (4) 5" x 8" (12.7 x 20.3cm)
- (4) 1" x 18" (2.5 x 45.7cm)
- (4) 3" x 3" (7.6 x 7.6cm)
- (24) ¼" x 5" (6.4 x 12.7cm)

Fox Print Cork Fabric

- (4) 5" x 8" (12.7 x 20.3cm)
- (4) 1" x 18" (2.5 x 45.7cm)
- (4) 3" x 3" (7.6 x 7.6cm)
- (24) ¼" x 5" (6.4 x 12.7cm)

Crocodile Print Mug Rug

1. Lay (1) 5" x 8" (12.7 x 20.3cm) basketweave cork piece WS down at a horizontal angle.

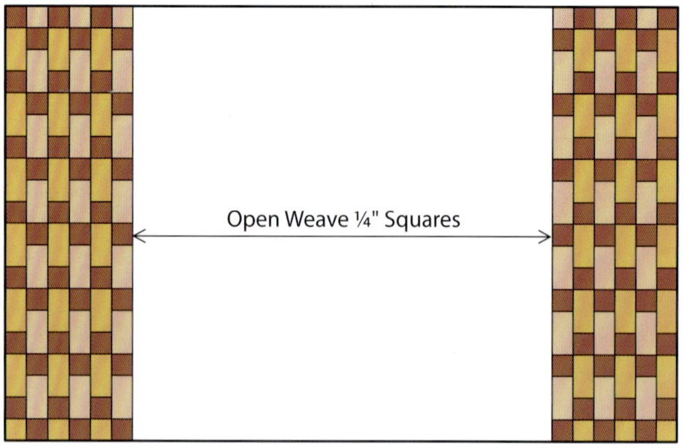

2. Weave (12) ¼" x 5" (6.4 x 12.7cm) crocodile print strips into the first (6) and last (6) columns of the basketweave cork. The first strip will be RS up and the second strip WS up; continue to alternate the orientation of the strips.

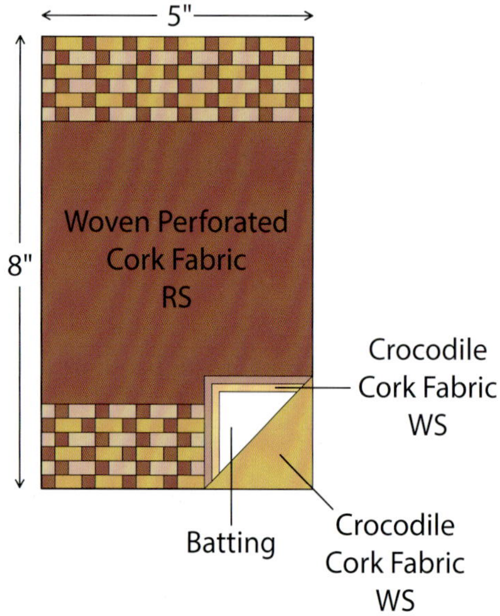

3. Make a quilt sandwich as follows: Lay (1) 5" x 8" (12.7 x 20.3cm) crocodile print RS down. Lay (1) 5" x 8" (12.7 x 20.3cm) batting on top of the fabric. Lay (1) 5" x 8" (12.7 x 20.3cm) crocodile print RS up. Lay the mug rug front on top of the batting RS up. You should be able to see the crocodile print through the open-weave cork.

4. Stitch around the quilt sandwich as close to the edge as possible to keep all layers together.

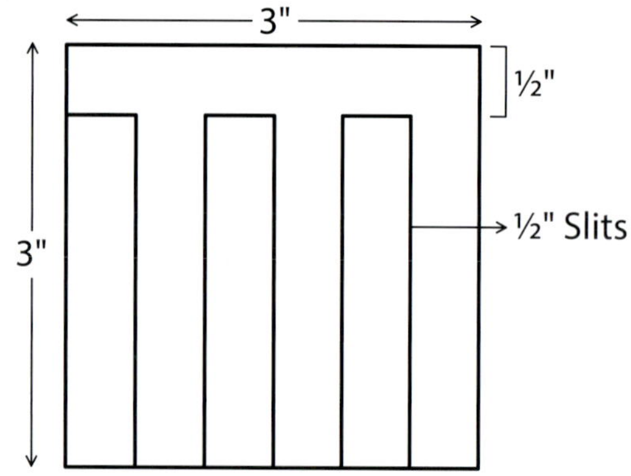

5. Cut slits in the (2) 3" x 3" (7.6 x 7.6cm) crocodile cork squares, ½" (1.3cm) apart from one end to the top, leaving 1" (2.5cm) at the top as shown.

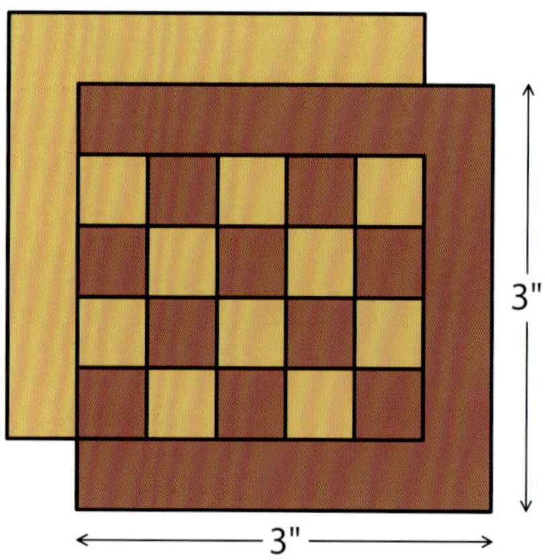

6. Flip (1) square upside down, showing the WS of the cork. Weave the ends of the (2) squares as shown.

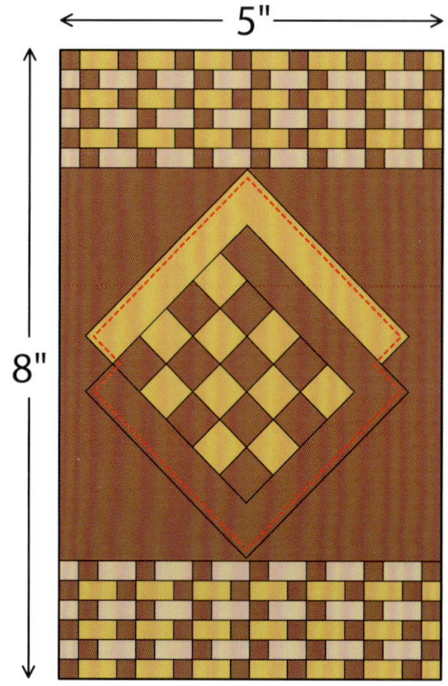

7. Sew the (2) woven squares to the front center of the mug rug as shown.

8. Stitch (2) 1" x 18" (2.5 x 45.7cm) crocodile print strips together to create a 36" (91.4cm) length of ½" (1.3cm) double-fold bias tape.

9. Encase the edge of the mug rug with the bias tape. Sew by machine all around like a bias tape, but stitch the back and front at the same time. The seam should be ⅜" (1cm) from the outside edge.

10. Repeat steps 1–9 to make a second crocodile print mug rug. In step 3, lay both 5" x 8" (12.7 x 20.3cm) crocodile print pieces RS down, so the WS is seen through the open-weave cork.

Circles Print Mug Rug

1. Follow steps 1–10 to make (2) circles print mug rugs, (1) with the top print RS up and (1) with the print RS down.

Fox Print Mug Rug

1. Follow steps 1–10 to make (2) fox print mug rugs, (1) with the top print RS up and (1) with the print RS down.

ROPE SEWING
Projects

Rope sewing is a technique of joining rope, paracord, or cotton clothesline with a wide zigzag stitch. Rope sewing is used to make baskets, coasters, table mats, and rugs. In rope sewing, a sewing machine is usually used, but these items can be stitched by hand sewing as well.

The **Blue Rope Mug Rugs** are quick and easy to put together. They make for great gifts. Using just one skein of clothesline rope and ½ yard (45.7cm) of fabric, these are also great for children sewing groups to teach this basic technique.

The **Mug Rugs with Rope-Sewn Coaster Pad** shows you how to make a rope-sewn square using paracord. The narrow, softer cord makes it easier to turn corners. While the mug rug has you rope sewing directly onto a fabric base, you could just as easily make a coaster without a base following the rope-sewing section of the instructions.

Blue Rope Mug Rugs

Finished Size: 8" (20.3cm) diameter

Rope sewing is a quick technique meant to simply join the rows of rope or cord together. I enjoyed using colored cord and fabric-covered cord for a difference in texture and appearance. Next time I make this group of mug rugs, I might go a step further and make a basket with the same technique to hold the mug rugs.

Material Requirements

- (1) 18" x 44" (45.7 x 111.8cm) multicolor fabric
- (1) 12" x 17" (30.5 x 43.2cm) leather-like fusible interfacing
- (1) ¼" (6.4mm) x 30 yards (27.4m) blue cotton rope
- Blue thread
- BR pattern (page 120)
- Basic tools (page 7)

Cutting Requirements

Multicolor Fabric

- (6) 5" x 5" (12.7 x 12.7cm)
- (12) 1" x 36" (2.5 x 91.4cm)

Leather-Like Fusible Interfacing

- (12) Pattern BR-A

Blue Cotton Rope

- (6) 4½ yard (4.1m)

Instructions

1. Lay (1) Pattern BR-A interfacing disc WST with (1) 5" x 5" (12.7 x 12.7cm) multicolor square. Place a pressing cloth on top and follow the manufacturer's instructions to adhere.

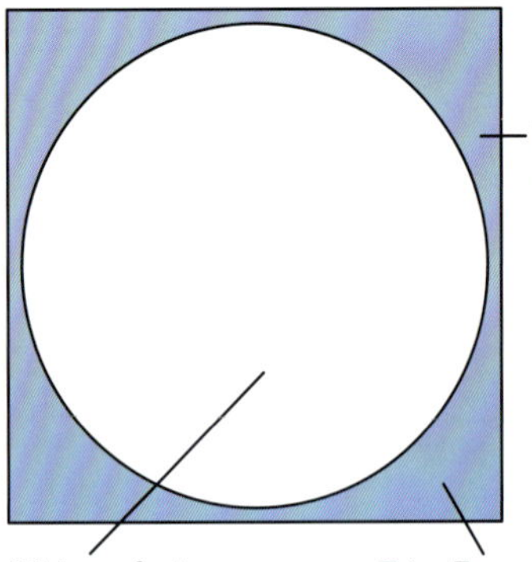

2. Lay (1) Pattern BR-A interfacing disc WS down on top of the disc from step 1 for a double thickness. Press using a pressing cloth as before. Trim the multicolor fabric to the disc.

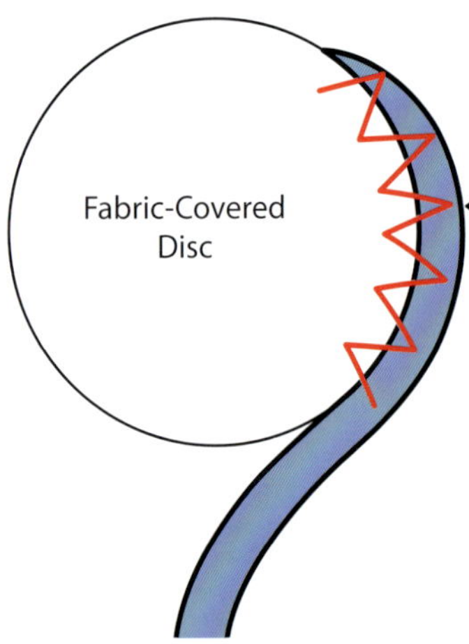

3. Place one end of (1) 4½ yard (4.1m) rope length next to the fabric-covered disc with the RS facing up. On the sewing machine, sew the rope to the disc with a wide zigzag; it must catch both the disc and the rope when sewing.

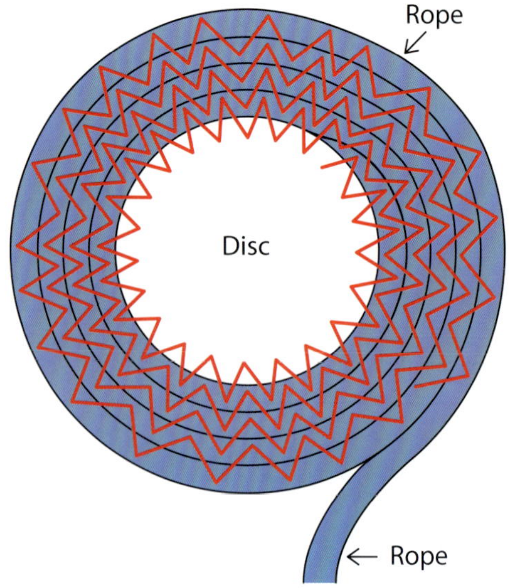

4. Repeat this technique until you have (4) complete rows around the disc.

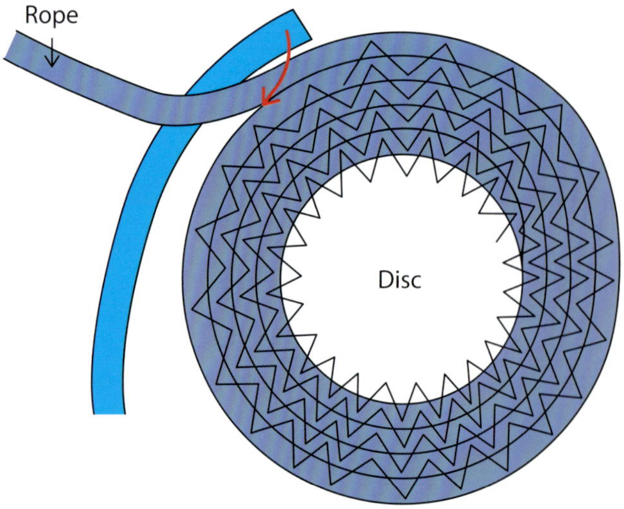

5. Starting with one end of (1) 1" x 36" (2.5 x 91.4cm) multicolor strip, wrap it tightly around the rope from where you stopped stitching, using the entire length of the fabric.

Tip

The fabric strips should be diagonally wrapped around the rope to stretch out the coverage.

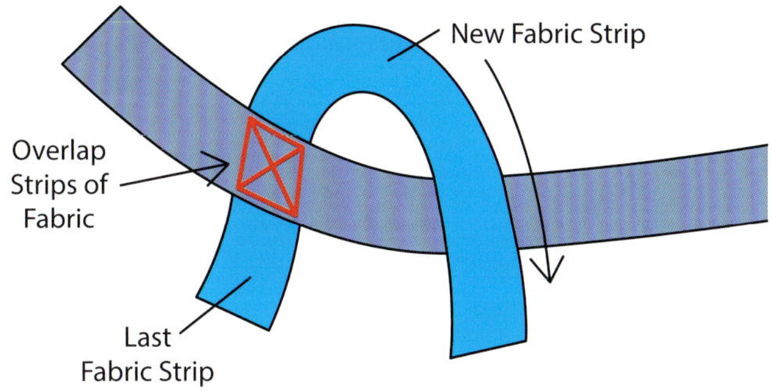

6. Add another strip to complete the fabric wrap. You should end with (2–3) rows of fabric-covered rope.

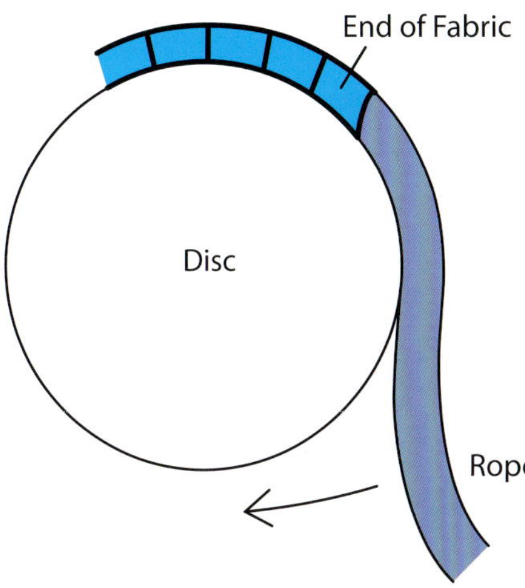

7. Stitch the fabric-covered rope to the disc like in step 3, continuing until the end of the rope. The last (2) rows of the mug rug will not be fabric covered. Stitch over the end of the rope several times back and forth to end.

8. Repeat steps 1–7 for the remaining (5) mug rugs.

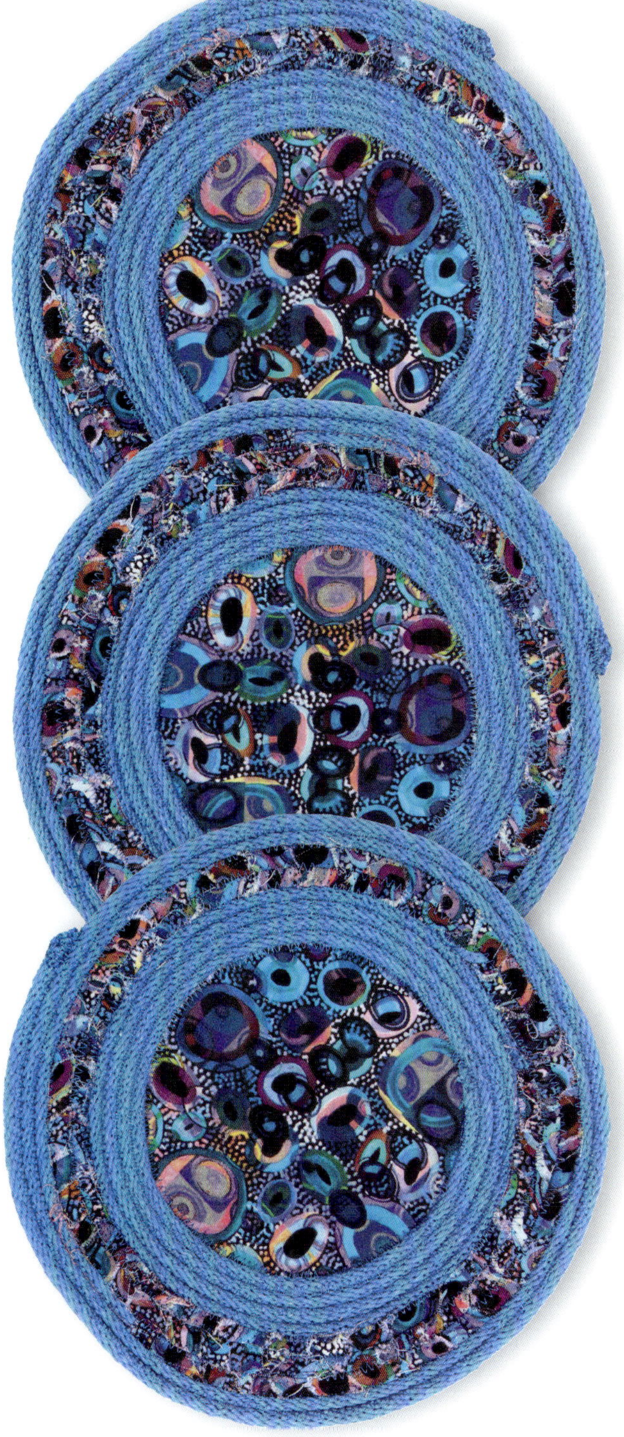

Mug Rugs with Rope-Sewn Coaster Pad

Finished Size: 8½" x 5¼" (21.6 x 13.3cm)

This decorative mug rug is the perfect opportunity to practice a touch of quilting and little rope sewing with paracord. When you're done, you'll have a reinforced pad for your heated beverages and a little spot for a treat or two. Use coordinating thread or try a metallic or variegated option to dress up a solid-color cord.

Material Requirements

- ¼ yard (22.9cm) cotton print fabric
- (1) 10" (22.9cm) cotton batting
- (1) ⅛" (3.2mm) x 5½ feet (1.7m) paracord
- Coordinating or metallic thread
- 90/14 or jeans sewing machine needle
- 1" x 1" (2.5 x 2.5cm) iron-on stabilizer, optional
- Basic tools (page 7)

Cutting Requirements

Print Fabric

- (2) 10" x 7" (22.9 x 17.8 cm)
- (1) 1½" x 36" (3.8 x 91.4cm) for bias tape

Batting

- (1) 10" x 7" (22.9 x 17.8 cm)

Instructions

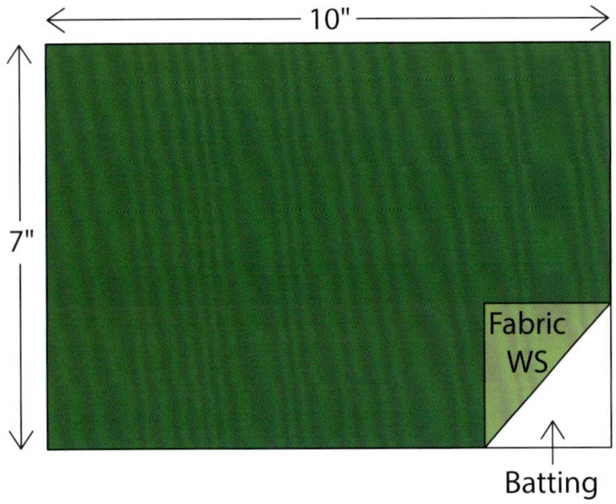

1. Lay (1) fabric rectangle WS down on top of (1) batting rectangle.

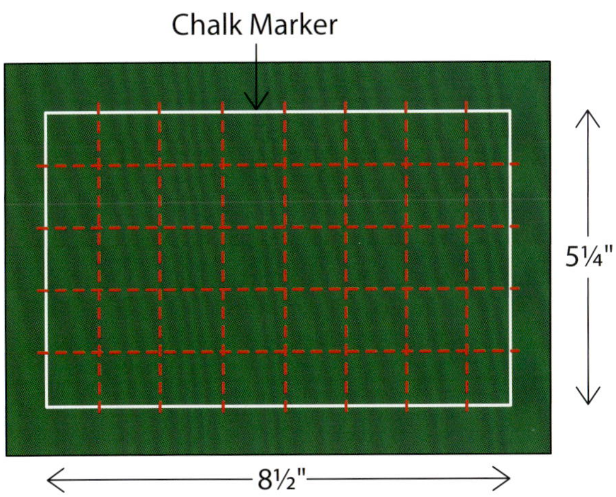

2. Using a chalk marker or wash-away marking pen, draw an 8½" x 5¼" (21.6 x 13.3cm) rectangle on the fabric layer. Quilt as desired, making sure to stitch slightly beyond the drawn lines. The examples were quilted with a 1⅛" (2.9cm) grid (turquoise piece) and a meandering line (brown piece).

3. Make a quilt sandwich as follows: Lay (1) fabric rectangle RS down. Lay the front/batting piece on top of the fabric, batting side down. Stitch close to the edge to keep all layers together for edging.

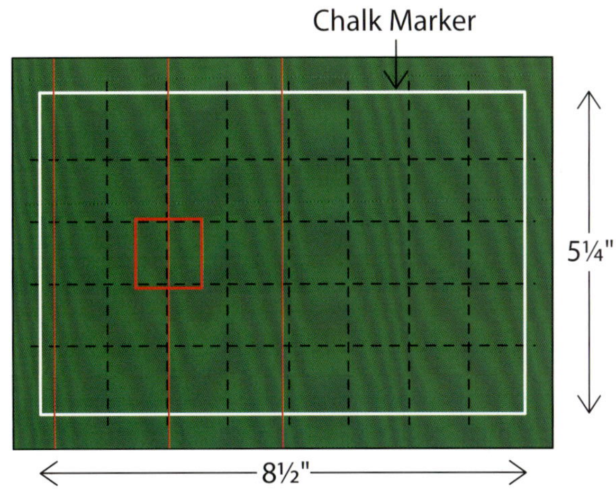

4. Mark a ¼" (6.4mm) seam allowance from the short side of the drawn rectangle from step 2. Mark the center point of the long side, then mark the midpoint between the seam allowance and the center. Finally, mark the center point of the short side. Draw a 1" x 1" (2.5 x 2.5cm) square for starting your rope sewing.

Note

If you prefer, you can use a small piece of iron-on stabilizer and position it on your rectangle to serve as your starting square.

5. Zigzag across the end of your paracord with a 2.0 width and length to prevent raveling.

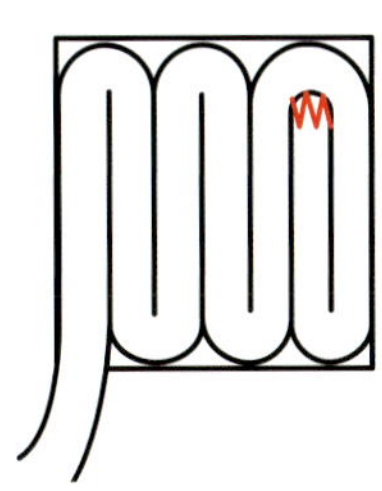

6. Place the end of the paracord slightly in from the corner of the starting square. Pin in place, run the cord down to the bottom of the square, then back up to the top. With a slightly larger zigzag (3.0), stitch across the ditch between the cord, starting at the bottom.

7. Continue to run the cord up and down to fill in the square as shown, zigzag stitching as you go.

8. When you get to the bottom-right corner, coil the rope around the square, zigzagging across the ditch to join each row to the previous one and pivoting at the corners. The finished square will have (9) rows around the center square.

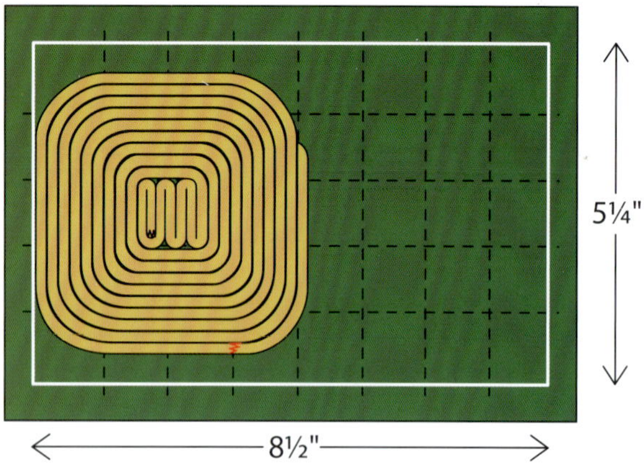

9. When you get to a stopping point, clip your paracord and zigzag the end as you did the beginning. Tuck the end under the last cord row and finish zigzagging your square.

10. Using a quilt ruler, check and redraw (if needed) the 8½" x 5¼" (21.6 x 13.3cm) rectangle from step 2. Make sure there is adequate space around the rope-sewn coaster pad to attach a ¼" (6.4mm) binding strip. Cut the mug rug along the drawn lines.

11. Use (1) 1½" x 36" (3.8 x 91.4cm) print fabric to make ½" (1.2cm) double-fold bias tape.

12. Stitch the bias tape to the front of the mug rug, as explained on page 10. Fold the bias tape over the edge and hand sew to the back.

FELT
Projects

Sewing with felt is a fun and relaxing way to create coasters, mug rugs, wall hangings, table mats, and many more projects. I love working with felt, fabric, and beads in my design work, though I had to stay away from beading with coasters. I didn't want to sabotage the use of the coasters!

The **Felt Fruit Mug Rugs** are a creative way to blend fabrics and felts together. An easy blanket stitch is used to complete the details of the fruit.

The **Felt Handbag Coasters** are designed with women in mind, so they can be great for secret gifts, used at book clubs, craft clubs, or given as gifts. What woman doesn't appreciate a new handbag? I also enjoyed using some of my sewing machine's decorative stitches to finish the details.

Felt Fruit Mug Rugs

Finished Size: 5½" x 5½" (14 x 14cm)

One of my passions is "painting" with felt, fabric, and thread. I love the way these materials work together to create beautiful, dimensional projects. For this set, I focused on the fabric choices working with the basic fruit outlines to create fun and simplicity in the mug rugs. I used a quilt charm pack of fabrics for the background of the fruits. This is why the fabrics are pinked on the edges. If you use fabric instead of precuts and like the pinked look, you will need to pink your own background fabric.

Material Requirements

- (1) 6" x 6" (15.2 x 15.2cm) dark red print fabric
- (1) 6" x 6" (15.2 x 15.2cm) orange print fabric
- (1) 6" x 6" (15.2 x 15.2cm) peach print fabric
- (4) 6" x 6" (15.2 x 15.2cm) dark green print fabric
- (1) 6" x 6" (15.2 x 15.2cm) green print fabric
- (3) 6" x 6" (15.2 x 15.2cm) light green print fabric
- (1) 6" x 6" (15.2 x 15.2cm) very light green print fabric
- (1) 6" x 6" (15.2 x 15.2cm) purple print fabric
- (1) 6" x 6" (15.2 x 15.2cm) black solid fabric
- (2) 6" x 6" (15.2 x 15.2cm) charcoal print fabric
- (2) 6" x 6" (15.2 x 15.2cm) dark brown print fabric
- (1) 6" x 6" (15.2 x 15.2cm) brown print fabric
- (1) 6" x 6" (15.2 x 15.2cm) ivory print fabric
- (6) 4½" x 4½" (11.4 x 11.4cm) needled cotton batting
- (1) wine felt square
- (1) dark red felt square
- (1) rust felt square
- (1) orange felt square
- (2) peach felt squares
- (2) dark green felt squares
- (1) green felt square
- (2) light olive green felt squares
- (1) lime green felt square
- (2) purple felt squares
- (2) dark brown felt squares
- (1) brown felt square
- (3) ivory felt squares
- Iron-on adhesive (I/O)
- Black thread
- FF patterns (pages 120–121)
- Basic tools (page 7)

Cutting Requirements

Dark Red Print Fabric
- (1) 1" x 5" (2.5 x 12.7cm) with I/O
- (1) Pattern FF-J with I/O

Orange Print Fabric
- (1) 1" x 5" (2.5 x 12.7cm) with I/O
- (9) Pattern FF-R with I/O

Peach Print Fabric
- (1) 1" x 5" (2.5 x 12.7cm) with I/O
- (1) Pattern FF-E with I/O

Dark Green Print Fabric
- (1) 5" x 5" (12.7 x 12.7cm), pinked
- (1) Pattern FF-L with I/O
- (2) Pattern FF-U with I/O

Green Print Fabric
- (2) Pattern FF-G with I/O

Light Green Print Fabric
- (2) 5" x 5" (12.7 x 12.7cm), pinked
- (1) 1" x 5" (2.5 x 12.7cm) with I/O
- (1) Pattern FF-V with I/O

Very Light Green Print Fabric
- (1) Pattern FF-K with I/O

Purple Print Fabric
- (1) 1" x 5" (2.5 x 12.7cm) with I/O
- (11) ¾" (1.9cm) diameter with I/O

Black Solid Fabric
- (12) Pattern FF-S with I/O

Charcoal Print Fabric
- (2) 5" x 5" (12.7 x 12.7cm), pinked

Dark Brown Print Fabric
- (2) Pattern FF-F with I/O

Brown Print Fabric
- (1) Pattern FF-F with I/O

Ivory Print Fabric
- (1) 5" x 5" (12.7 x 12.7cm), pinked
- (1) 1" x 5" (2.5 x 12.7cm) with I/O
- (1) Pattern FF-E with I/O

Dark Red Felt
- (1) Pattern FF-I with I/O

Wine Felt
- (1) 5½" x 5½" (14 x 14cm)
- (1) Pattern FF-A with I/O

Rust Felt
- (1) 5½" x 5½" (14 x 14cm)
- (1) Pattern FF-A with I/O

Orange Felt
- (1) 5½" x 5½" (14 x 14cm)
- (1) Pattern FF-P with I/O

Peach Felt
- (1) Pattern FF-B with I/O
- (9) Pattern FF-Q with I/O

Dark Green Felt
- (2) 5½" x 5½" (14 x 14cm)
- (1) Pattern FF-H with I/O
- (1) Pattern FF-T with I/O

Green Felt
- (2) Pattern FF-C with I/O

Light Olive Green Felt
- (1) Pattern FF-G with I/O
- (1) Pattern FF-N with I/O
- (1) Pattern FF-T with I/O

Lime Green Felt
- (1) Pattern FF-W with I/O

Purple Felt
- (1) 5½" x 5½" (14 x 14cm)
- (1) Pattern FF-M with I/O

Dark Brown Felt
- (2) Pattern FF-D with I/O
- (1) Pattern FF-D reversed with I/O

Brown Felt
- (1) Pattern FF-O with I/O

Ivory Felt
- (1) Pattern FF-B with I/O
- (1) Pattern FF-X with I/O

Note

When blanket stitching the mug rugs, use one strand of thread. Only stitch through the top layer, not the felt backing.

Peach Mug Rug

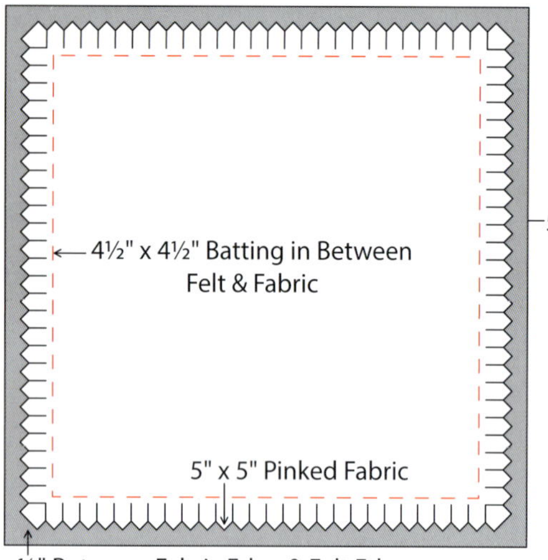

1. Place (1) batting in the center of (1) 5½" x 5½" (14 x 14cm) rust felt. Pin (1) 5" x 5" (12.7 x 12.7cm) charcoal fabric RS up on top of the batting in the center of the rust felt.

2. Blanket stitch between the points of the pinked fabric.

3. Press (1) 1" x 5" (2.5 x 12.7cm) peach fabric at 1" (2.5cm) from the left edge, vertically. Blanket stitch around this strip.

4. Press (1) Pattern A rust felt to the mug rug. Press (1) Pattern B peach felt inside. Press (1) Pattern E peach fabric inside. Blanket stitch around each layer before attaching the next one.

5. Press (1) Pattern F dark brown fabric in the center of the peach vertically. Blanket stitch around.

6. Press (1) Pattern D dark brown felt in place. Blanket stitch around. Press (2) Pattern C green felt in place. Press (2) Pattern G green fabric in place. Blanket stitch around both leaf fabric and felt at once.

Watermelon Mug Rug

1. Place (1) batting in the center of (1) 5½" x 5½" (14 x 14cm) dark green felt. Pin (1) 5" x 5" (12.7 x 12.7cm) light green fabric RS up on top of the batting in the center of the dark green felt.

2. Blanket stitch between the points of the pinked fabric.

3. Press (1) 1" x 5" (2.5 x 12.7cm) dark red fabric at 1" (2.5cm) from the left edge, vertically. Blanket stitch around this strip.

4. Press (1) Pattern J dark red fabric to the mug rug. Press (1) Pattern I dark red felt, (1) Pattern K very light green fabric, (1) Pattern L dark green fabric, and (1) Pattern H dark green felt in place. Blanket stitch around the entire watermelon slice and layers.

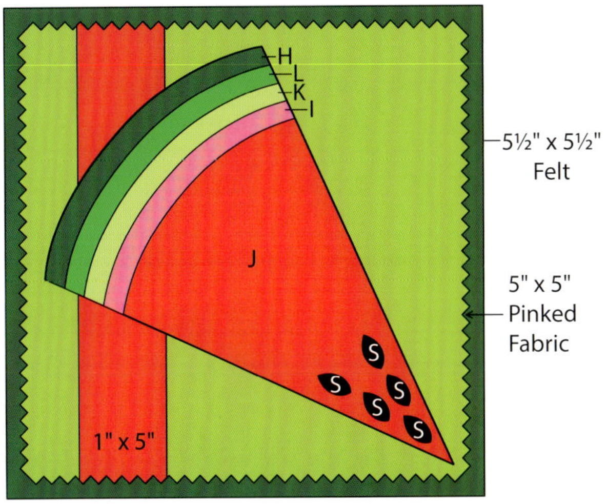

5. Press (5) Pattern S black fabric in place for watermelon seeds.

Grapes Mug Rug

1. Place (1) batting in the center of (1) 5½" x 5½" (14 x 14cm) purple felt. Pin (1) 5" x 5" (12.7 x 12.7cm) light green fabric RS up on top of the batting in the center of the purple felt.

2. Blanket stitch between the points of the pinked fabric.

3. Press (1) 1" x 5" (2.5 x 12.7cm) purple fabric at 1" (2.5cm) from the left edge, vertically. Blanket stitch around this strip.

4. Press (1) Pattern M purple felt to the mug rug. Press (1) Pattern N light olive green felt and (1) Pattern G light olive green felt in place. Press (1) Pattern O brown felt in place.

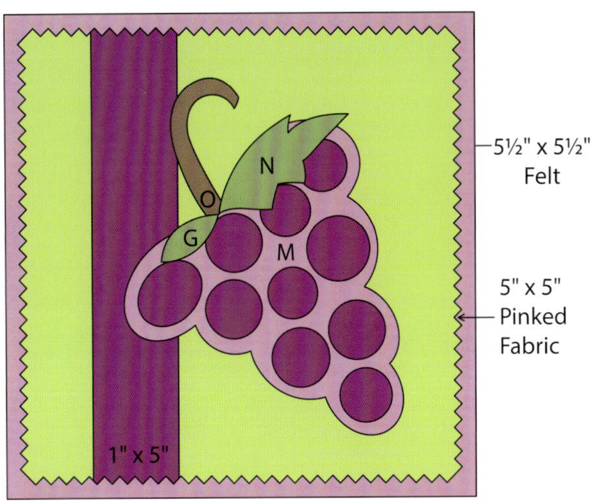

5. Press (11) purple fabric circles to the grapes shape for individual grapes. Blanket stitch around the grapes, leaves, and stem.

Orange Mug Rug

1. Place (1) batting in the center of (1) 5½" x 5½" (14 x 14cm) orange felt. Pin (1) 5" x 5" (12.7 x 12.7cm) dark green fabric RS up on top of the batting in the center of the orange felt.

2. Blanket stitch between the points of the pinked fabric.

3. Press (1) 1" x 5" (2.5 x 12.7cm) orange fabric at 1" (2.5cm) from the left edge, vertically. Blanket stitch around this strip.

4. Press (1) Pattern P orange felt to the mug rug. Press (9) Pattern Q peach felt in place. Press (9) Pattern R orange fabric in place. Blanket stitch the orange and slices.

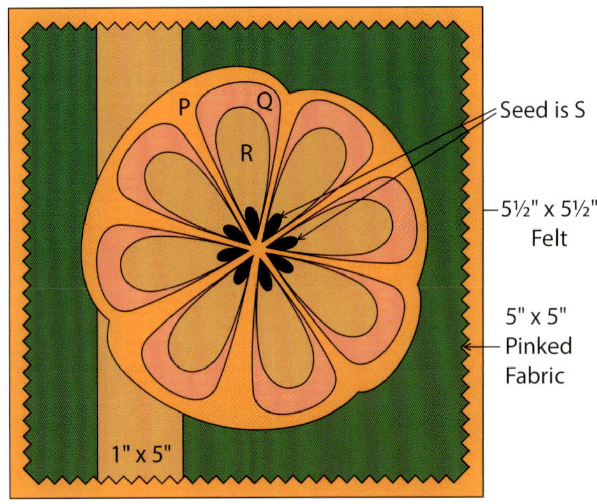

5. Press (7) Pattern S black fabric in place for orange seeds.

Apple Mug Rug

1. Place (1) batting in the center of (1) 5½" x 5½" (14 x 14cm) wine felt. Pin (1) 5" x 5" (12.7 x 12.7cm) charcoal fabric RS up on top of the batting in the center of the wine felt.

2. Blanket stitch between the points of the pinked fabric.

3. Press (1) 1" x 5" (2.5 x 12.7cm) ivory fabric at 1" (2.5cm) from the left edge, vertically. Blanket stitch around this strip.

4. Press (1) Pattern A wine felt to the mug rug. Press (1) Pattern B ivory felt inside. Press (1) Pattern E ivory fabric inside. Blanket stitch around each layer before attaching the next one.

5. Press (1) Pattern F dark brown fabric in the center of the apple vertically. Blanket stitch around.

6. Press (1) Pattern D, reversed, dark brown felt in place. Blanket stitch around. Press (1) Pattern T light olive felt in place. Press (1) Pattern U dark green fabric in place. Blanket stitch around both leaf fabric and felt at once.

Pear Mug Rug

1. Place (1) batting in the center of (1) 5½" x 5½" (14 x 14cm) dark green felt. Pin (1) 5" x 5" (12.7 x 12.7cm) ivory fabric RS up on top of the batting in the center of the dark green felt.

2. Blanket stitch between the points of the pinked fabric.

3. Press (1) 1" x 5" (2.5 x 12.7cm) light green fabric at 1" (2.5cm) from the left edge, vertically. Blanket stitch around this strip.

4. Press (1) Pattern W lime green felt to the mug rug. Press (1) Pattern X ivory felt in place. Press (1) Pattern V light green fabric in place. Blanket stitch around each layer before attaching the next one.

5. Press (1) Pattern F brown fabric in the center of the pear vertically. Blanket stitch around.

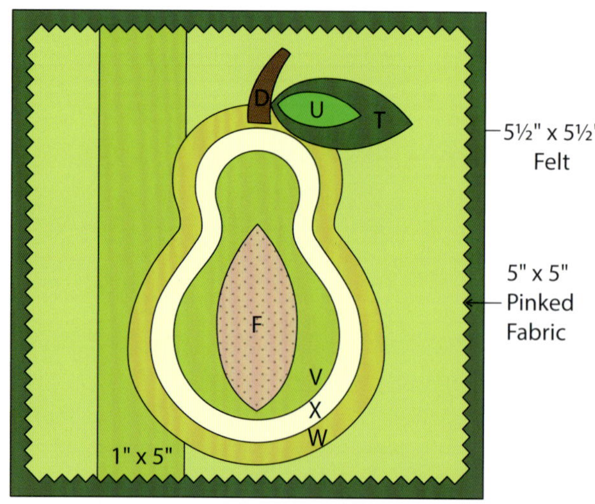

6. Press (1) Pattern D, rotated, dark brown felt in place. Blanket stitch around. Press (1) Pattern T dark green felt in place. Press (1) Pattern U dark green fabric in place. Blanket stitch around both leaf fabric and felt at once.

Felt Handbag Coasters

Finished Size: 4½" x 5¼" (11.4 x 13.3cm)

Handbags come in so many styles, colors, and sizes, and include designer handbags, vintage handbags, and recycled handbags. How many handbags do you have? If you love handbags, this set of coasters is for you. I used sewing machine embroidery stitches to embellish each, but hand embroidery would be fantastic as well.

Material Requirements

- (1) felt square of each color: purple, wine, light blue, white, burgundy, peach, olive green, rust, brown, and light brown
- Thread in colors: white, purple, gold, dark red, and brown
- Iron-on adhesive (I/O)
- HC patterns (pages 122–123)
- Basic tools (page 7)

Cutting Requirements

Purple Felt

- (2) Pattern HC-A, (1) with I/O
- (2) Pattern HC-B, (1) with I/O
- (1) Pattern HC-D with I/O

Wine Felt

- (5) ½" x 3¾" (1.2 x 9.5cm) with I/O

Light Blue Felt

- (2) Pattern HC-A, (1) with I/O
- (2) Pattern HC-B, (1) with I/O
- (1) Pattern HC-G with I/O
- (1) Pattern HC-H with I/O
- (1) Pattern HC-I with I/O

White Felt

- (1) Pattern HC-E with I/O
- (1) Pattern HC-F with I/O

Burgundy Felt

- (1) 3" x 3" (7.6cm 7.6cm) with I/O, cut in half diagonally for two triangles

Peach Felt

- (2) Pattern HC-A, (1) with I/O
- (2) Pattern HC-B, (1) with I/O
- (1) Pattern HC-J with I/O

Olive Green Felt

- (2) Pattern HC-A, (1) with I/O
- (2) Pattern HC-B, (1) with I/O
- (2) 1⅜" x 1⅝" (3.5 x 4.1cm) with I/O

Rust Felt

- (2) Pattern HC-A, (1) with I/O
- (2) Pattern HC-B, (1) with I/O
- (1) Pattern HC-C, (1) with I/O
- (2) 1¾" x 2" (4.4 x 5.1cm) with I/O
- (5) ½" (1.3cm) diameter with I/O

Brown Felt

- (2) Pattern HC-A, (1) with I/O
- (2) Pattern HC-B, (1) with I/O
- (1) Pattern HC-K with I/O

Light Brown Felt

- (3) 1" x 3½" (2.5 x 8.9cm) with I/O

Olive Coaster

1. Press (2) Pattern HC-A olive green felt together for double thickness. Press (2) Pattern HC-B olive green felt together too.

2. Press (1) Pattern HC-C rust felt to the front of the bag body, along the top edge.

3. Press (2) 1¾" x 2" (4.4 x 5.1cm) rust felt evenly on the front of the bag body.

4. Press (2) 1⅜" x 1⅝" (3.5 x 4.1cm) olive green felt evenly in the center of each of the rust squares.

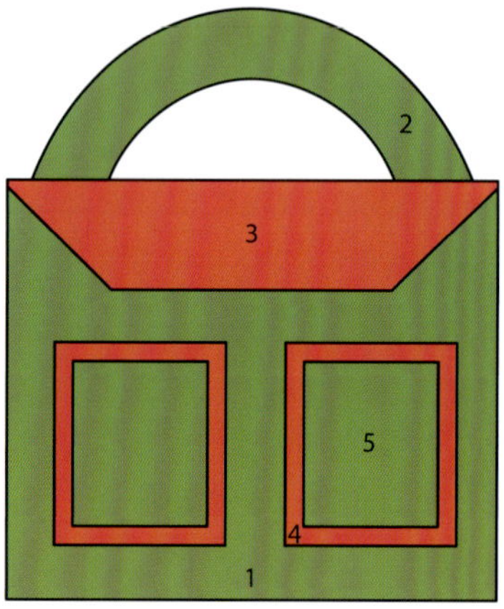

5. Stitch ⅛" (3.2mm) seam along the inside arc of Pattern HC-B. Hand-stitch the handle to the bag. I used a blanket stitch that went up and down, through the handle and body alternately.

6. Stitch decorative stitches around the outside edge of the bag flap and around the outside edge of the green squares.

Purple Coaster

1. Press (2) Pattern HC-A purple felt together for double thickness. Press (2) Pattern HC-B purple felt together too.

2. Press (5) ½" x 3¾" (1.2 x 9.5cm) wine felt strips to front of the bag body evenly as vertical stripes.

3. Press (1) Pattern HC-D purple felt evenly to the front of the bag body, covering the wine strips. This piece is larger than needed, so trim to fit the bag.

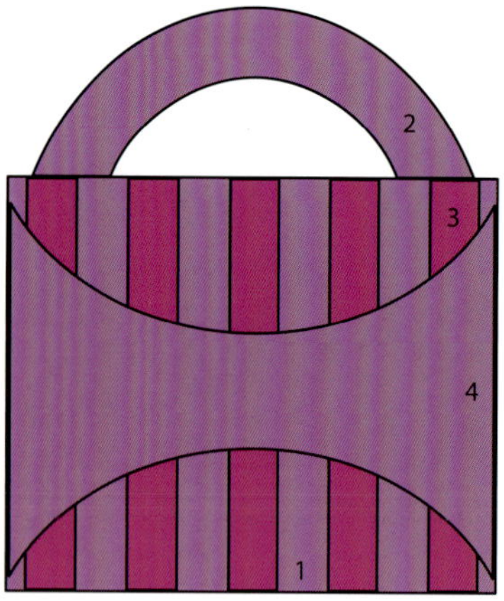

4. Stitch ⅛" (3.2mm) seam along the inside arc of Pattern HC-B. Hand-stitch the handle to the bag. I used a blanket stitch that went up and down, through the handle and body alternately.

5. Stitch decorative stitches on the top and bottom of Pattern HC-D.

Rust Coaster

1. Press (2) Pattern HC-A rust felt together for double thickness. Press (2) Pattern HC-B rust felt together too.

2. Press (1) Pattern HC-E white felt to the front of the bag body, along the top edge.

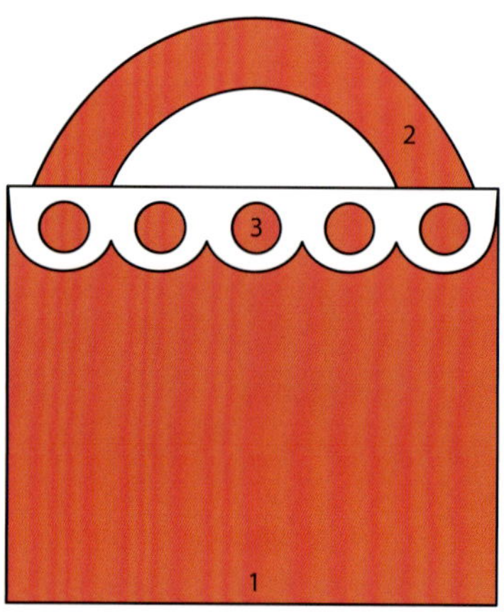

3. Stitch ⅛" (3.2mm) seam along the inside arc of Pattern HC-B. Hand-stitch the handle to the bag. I used a blanket stitch that went up and down, through the handle and body alternately.

4. Stitch vertical decorative stitches from the scallops to the bottom of the bag.

5. Press (5) rust circles to the Pattern HC-E piece, (1) in each scallop shape.

Light Blue Coaster

1. Press (2) Pattern HC-A light blue felt together for double thickness. Press (2) Pattern HC-B light blue felt together too.

2. Press (1) Pattern HC-F white felt to the front of the bag body, along the top and right edges.

3. Press (1) Pattern HC-G, (1) Pattern HC-H, and (1) Pattern HC-I light blue felt to the white triangle on the bag. Leave ⅜" (1cm) between HC-G and HC-H, and leave ½" (1.3cm) between HC-H and HC-I.

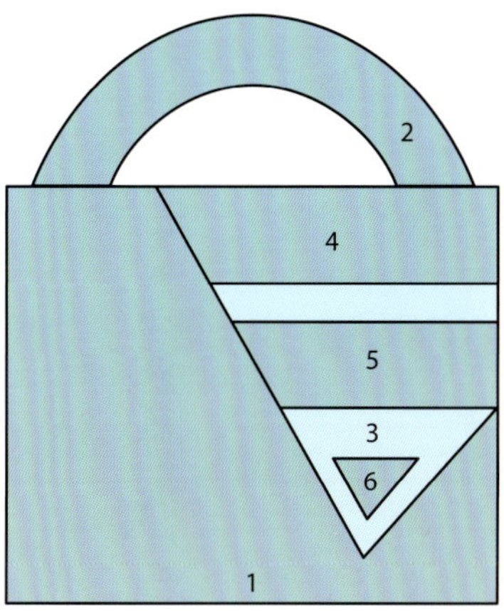

4. Stitch ⅛" (3.2mm) seam along the inside arc of Pattern HC-B. Hand-stitch the handle to the bag. I used a blanket stitch that went up and down, through the handle and body alternately.

5. Stitch decorative stitches on the (2) light blue strips. Along the left edge, stitch (3) vertical straight stitches, ⅛" (3.2mm) apart, from the bottom of the bag to around the handle.

Peach Coaster

1. Press (2) Pattern HC-A peach felt together for double thickness. Press (2) Pattern HC-B peach felt together too.

2. Press (1) burgundy triangle to the top-right corner of the bag body. Press (1) burgundy triangle to the top-left corner of the bag body, overlapping the first triangle.

3. Press (1) Pattern HC-J peach felt to the top-left triangle.

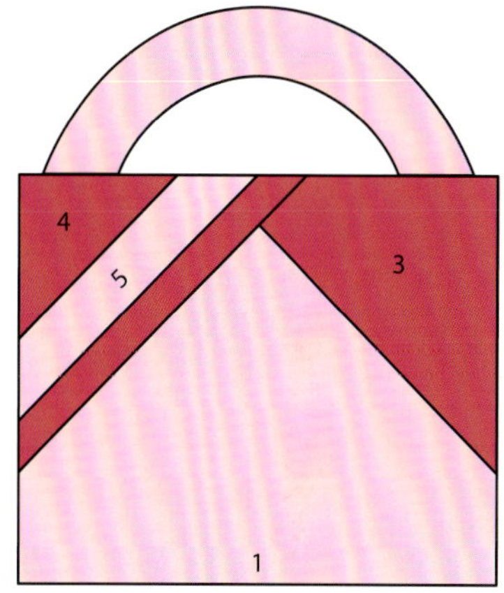

4. Stitch ⅛" (3.2mm) seam along the inside arc of Pattern HC-B. Hand-stitch the handle to the bag. I used a blanket stitch that went up and down, through the handle and body alternately.

5. Stitch decorative stitches along the edges of the peach strip.

Brown Coaster

1. Press (2) Pattern HC-A brown felt together for double thickness. Press (2) Pattern HC-B brown felt together too.

2. Press (3) 1" x 3½" (2.5 x 8.9cm) light brown felt strips to the front of the bag body vertically, spacing them evenly across the bag.

3. Stitch ⅛" (3.2mm) seam along the inside arc of Pattern HC-B. Hand-stitch the handle to the bag. I used a blanket stitch that went up and down, through the handle and body alternately.

4. Stitch decorative stitches from top to bottom on the light brown strips.

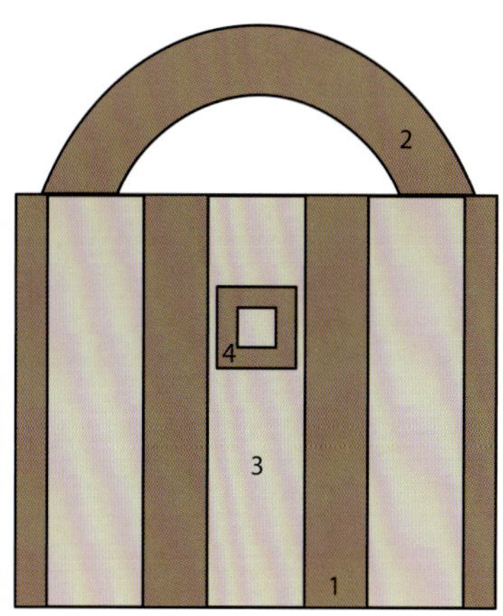

5. Press (1) Pattern HC-K brown felt to the center light brown strip.

BIAS TAPE
Projects

Bias tape is commonly used to finish raw edges on projects. This creates a finished look and hides any issues of the fabric edges. Bias tape can also be used as an embellishment.

The **Bias Tape Batik Mug Rugs** incorporate fussy cut dragonflies and bias tape embellishments. They are finished with matching bias tape on the edges.

The **Lavender Floral Striped Coasters** are made with bias tape lengths that are sewn together side by side. The stripes are cut diagonally, then the two sides are sewn together in two different directions.

Bias Tape Batik Mug Rugs

Finished Size: 5" x 8" (12.7 x 20.3cm)

I love batiks and how easy they are to work with. Rarely is there a distinct right and wrong side, so there is no need to worry about sewing the incorrect sides together! This particular dragonfly-print fabric jumped right off the shelf and matched the batiks I used. I think you'll enjoy everything about making these mug rugs as well.

Material Requirements

- Fat Quarter or (1) 9" x 44" (22.9 x 111.8cm) lime green batik fabric
- Fat Quarter or (1) 9" x 44" (22.9 x 111.8cm) light blue batik fabric
- Fat Quarter or (1) 9" x 44" (22.9 x 111.8cm) brown batik fabric
- Fat Quarter or (1) 9" x 44" (22.9 x 111.8cm) gold batik fabric
- Fat Quarter or (1) 9" x 44" (22.9 x 111.8cm) burgundy batik fabric
- Fat Quarter or (1) 9" x 44" (22.9 x 111.8cm) green batik fabric
- (1) 12" x 44" (30.5 x 111.8cm) dragonfly or butterfly fabric
- (1) 12" x 26" (30.5 x 66cm) needled cotton batting
- (1) 12" x 12" (30.5 x 30.5cm) iron-on adhesive (I/O)
- Color-coordinating threads
- Basic tools (page 7)

Cutting Requirements

Lime Green Batik Fabric
- (2) 5" x 8" (12.7 x 20.3cm)
- (3) 2" x 20" (5.1 x 50.8cm)

Light Blue Batik Fabric
- (2) 5" x 8" (12.7 x 20.3cm)
- (3) 2" x 20" (5.1 x 50.8cm)

Brown Batik Fabric
- (2) 5" x 8" (12.7 x 20.3cm)
- (3) 2" x 20" (5.1 x 50.8cm)

Gold Batik Fabric
- (2) 5" x 8" (12.7 x 20.3cm)
- (3) 2" x 20" (5.1 x 50.8cm)

Burgundy Batik Fabric
- (2) 5" x 8" (12.7 x 20.3cm)
- (3) 2" x 20" (5.1 x 50.8cm)

Green Batik Fabric
- (2) 5" x 8" (12.7 x 20.3cm)
- (3) 2" x 20" (5.1 x 50.8cm)

Dragonfly or Butterfly Fabric
- (6) 4" (10.2cm) dragonflies or butterflies with I/O, fussy cut

Needled Cotton Batting
- (6) 5" x 8" (12.7 x 20.3cm)

Note

Make sure the dragonfly or butterfly fabric has at least six dragonflies, butterflies, or another motif that are 4" (10.2cm) long. If it doesn't, you need to cut larger piece of fabric than indicated here.

Green Mug Rug

1. Use (1) 2" x 20" (5.1 x 50.8cm) burgundy strip to make (1) ½" (1.3cm) double-fold bias tape strip.

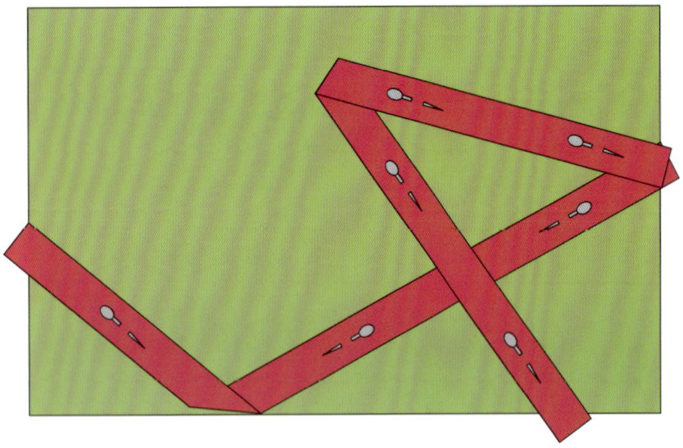

2. Pin the burgundy bias tape to (1) 5" x 8" (12.7 x 20.3cm) green rectangle as shown.

3. Press (1) dragonfly to the same green fabric as shown. The dragonfly can be covered slightly with bias tape if desired for more dimensionality.

4. With colorful thread, stitch the bias tape to the mug rug front close to each edge.

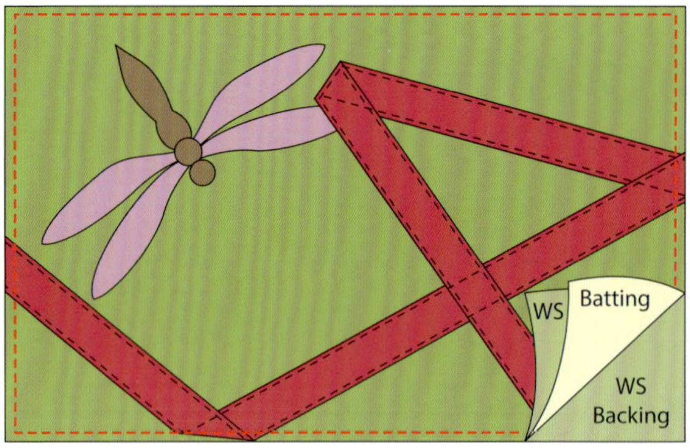

5. Make a quilt sandwich as follows: Lay (1) 5" x 8" (12.7 x 20.3cm) green rectangle RS down. Lay (1) 5" x 8" (12.7 x 20.3cm) batting on top of the fabric. Lay the mug rug front on top of the batting RS up. Stitch around the quilt sandwich as close to the edge as possible.

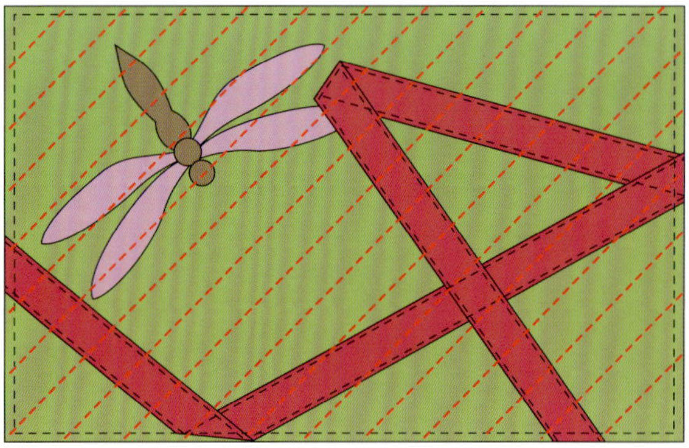

6. Quilt the mug rug with colorful thread in ½" (1.3cm) increments as shown, or quilt as desired.

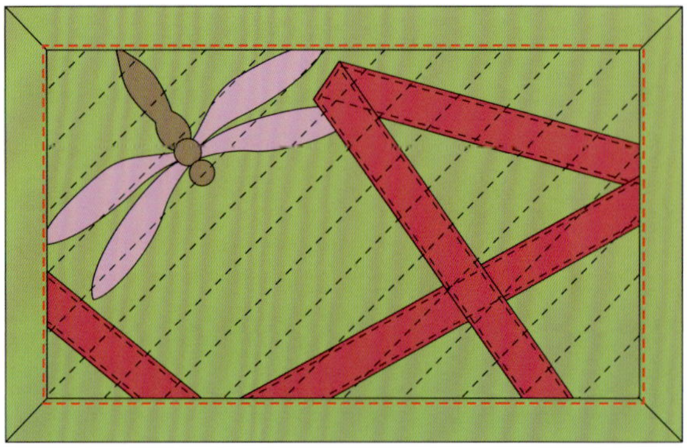

7. Stitch (2) lime green strips together end to end RST. Stitch to the front of the mug rug, flip it over the edge, and hand stitch to the back, as explained on page 10.

Light Blue Mug Rug

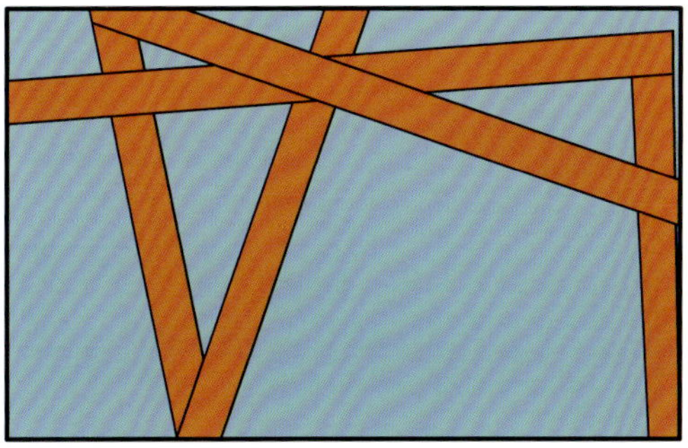

1. Repeat steps 1–7 of the Green Mug Rug. Use a brown strip for the decoration. Use the light blue fabric for the front and backing and matching bias tape for the binding.

Gold Mug Rug

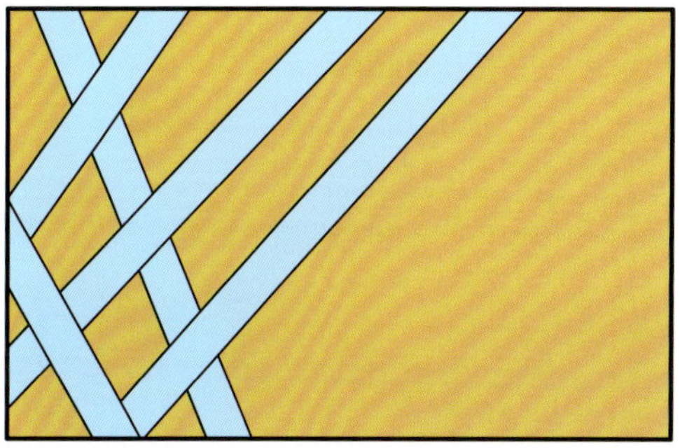

1. Repeat steps 1–7 of the Green Mug Rug. Use a light blue strip for the decoration. Use the gold fabric for the front and backing and matching bias tape for the binding.

Burgundy Mug Rug

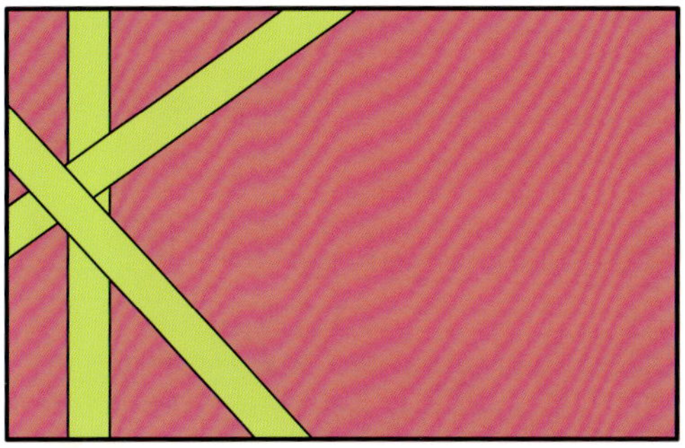

1. Repeat steps 1–7 of the Green Mug Rug. Use a lime green strip for the decoration. Use the burgundy fabric for the front and backing and matching bias tape for the binding.

Lime Green Mug Rug

1. Repeat steps 1–7 of the Green Mug Rug. Use a gold strips for the decoration. Use the lime green fabric for the front and backing and matching bias tape for the binding.

Brown Mug Rug

1. Use (1) 2" x 20" (5.1 x 50.8cm) green strip to make (1) ½" (1.3cm) double-fold bias tape strip.

2. Pin (2) ½" (1.3cm) green bias strips, side by side, to the top edge of (1) 5" x 8" (12.7 x 20.3cm) brown rectangle. Place 1" (2.5cm) from the left edge. Repeat on the right edge.

3. Measure 1" (2.5cm) from the top edge, lift (1) bias tape, and cut a ½" (1.3cm) wide horizontal slit just under the bias tape. Cut another slit 1" (2.5cm) below that. Repeat every 1" (2.5cm) until the bottom edge. Weave the bias tape through these slits.

4. With the second bias tape in the pair, measure ½" (1.3cm) from the top edge and cut a slit. Repeat every 1" (2.5cm) until the bottom edge, which should offset the slits. Weave the bias tape through the slits.

5. Repeat steps 3 and 4 for the other (2) bias strips.

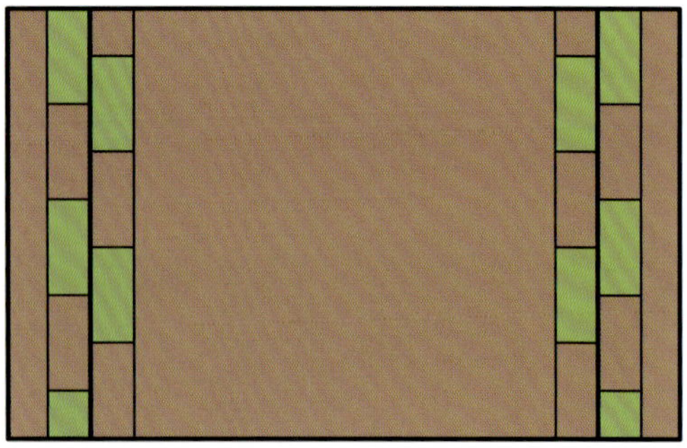

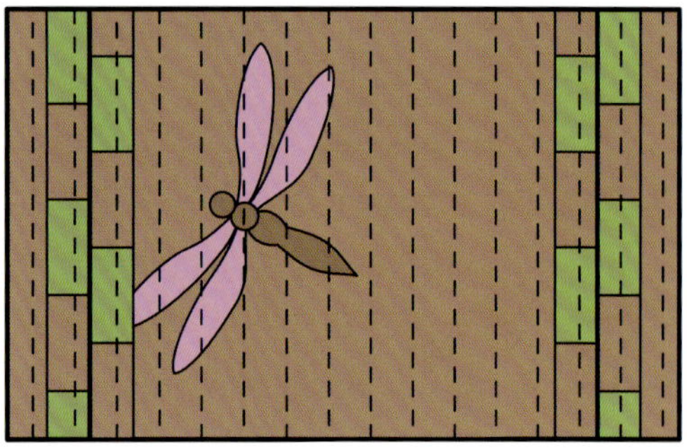

6. Repeat steps 3–7 of the Green Mug Rug. Use the brown fabric for the backing and matching bias tape for the binding.

Lavender Floral Stripe Coasters

Finished Size: 5" x 5" (12.7 x 12.7cm)

These coasters are made of bias strips, which means they come together quickly. This color combination made me think of gifts for hostesses or women who have done something wonderful in your life. Simply tie the set together with lavender ribbons.

Material Requirements

- (1) 18" x 30" (45.7 x 111.8cm) lavender floral fabric
- (1) 18" x 30" (45.7 x 111.8cm) lavender muted print fabric
- Fat Quarter or (1) 9" x 44" (22.9 x 111.8cm) gold solid fabric
- (1) 12" x 18" (30.5 x 45.7cm) needled cotton batting
- White thread
- Basic tools (page 7)

Cutting Requirements

Lavender Floral Fabric

- (1) 18" x 24" (45.7 x 61cm) for bias tape
- (3) 2" x 24" (5.1 x 61cm) for binding

Lavender Muted Print Fabric

- (1) 18" x 24" (45.7 x 61cm) for bias tape
- (3) 2" x 24" (5.1 x 61cm) for binding

Gold Solid Fabric

- (6) 5" x 5" (12.7 x 12.7cm)

Needled Cotton Batting

- (6) 5" x 5" (12.7 x 12.7cm)

Instructions

1. Use both 18" x 24" (45.7 x 61cm) pieces to make ½" (1.3cm) double-fold bias tape. Cut into (30) 6" (15.2cm) strips.

2. Lay (1) 6" (15.2cm) lavender floral bias strip side by side with (1) 6" (15.2cm) lavender muted print bias strip. Repeat for (5) strips of each, alternating fabrics. Zigzag stitch them together using ⅛" (3.2mm) wide stitch to catch both pieces of fabric pushed together.

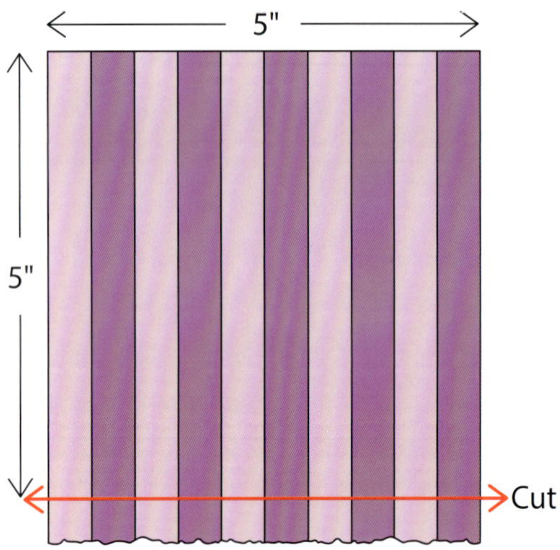

3. Trim the block of bias strips to 5" x 5" (12.7 x 12.7cm).

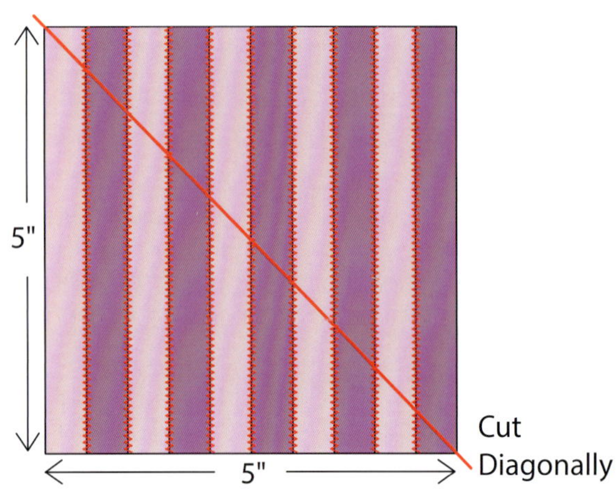

4. Cut in a diagonal from one corner of the block to the opposite corner for (2) triangles.

5. Flip one triangle over and line up the cut edges to make a square again. The stripes will match up, but the fabrics should alternate. One triangle should have vertical stripes and the other horizontal stripes.

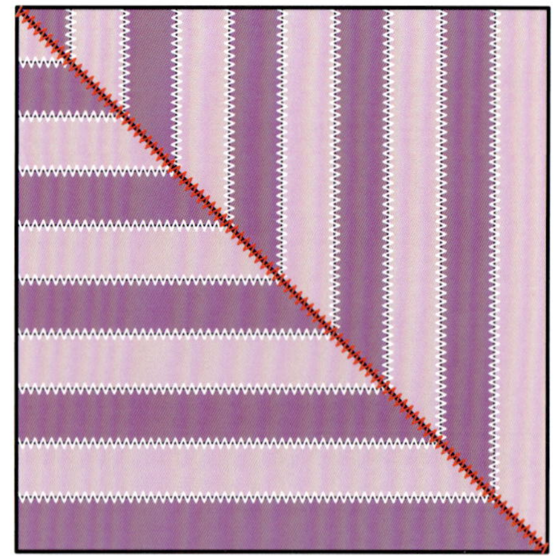

6. Zigzag stitch the (2) triangles together with a slightly larger stitch. Stitch twice if needed.

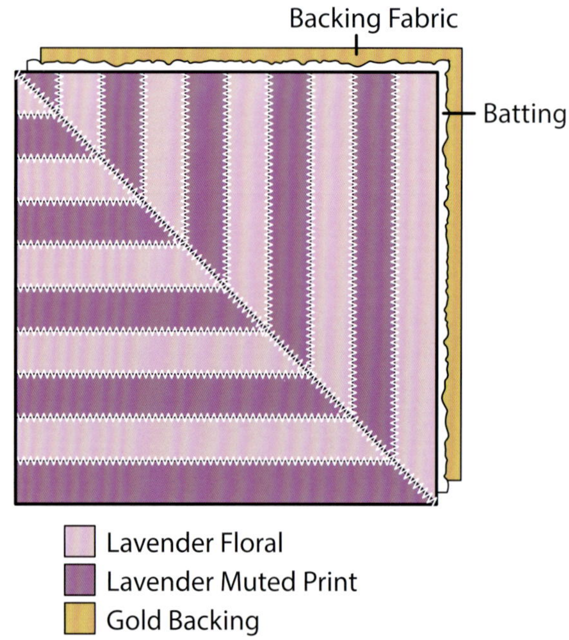

7. Make a quilt sandwich as follows: Lay (1) 5" x 5" (12.7 x 12.7cm) gold fabric RS down. Lay (1) 5" x 5" (12.7 x 12.7cm) batting on top of the fabric. Lay the mug rug front on top of the batting RS up. Pin together.

8. Stitch around the quilt sandwich as close to the edge as possible to keep all layers together.

9. Sew (1) 2" x 24" (5.1 x 61cm) lavender floral bias tape to the front of the coaster, fold it over the edge, and hand stitch to the back.

10. Repeat steps 1–9 for (5) more mug rugs. For the binding in step 9, use lavender floral bias tape for (2) coasters and lavender muted print for (3) coasters.

FUSSY CUT
Projects

Fussy cutting is a technique in which fabric is cut strategically to highlight a particular design in the fabric, whether it be a character, animal, floral, or other noticeable feature. This technique creates a focal point in the finished project that originates in the fabric itself. Often, a clear template is used to cut a design from the fabric. The design can also be cut along its edges to be used on a specific project.

When I saw the cat fabric used in **Classy Cat Coasters**, I had to use it in this book. The coaster background is geometric block colors that make the cat motif the center of attention.

The main fabric used in **Fussy Cut Window Coasters** is one of those fabulous Tula Pink prints. It's ideal for picking out motifs to frame, and here it's paired with a solid and coordinate print. The coaster windows were made in four different shapes: circle, square, hexagon, and heart. Mix and match or make your set using a single shape. The bindings and backgrounds were mixed and matched for interest, but keep them all the same if you prefer. Just make sure you have enough fabric for both the bases and bindings.

Classy Cat Coasters

Finished Size: 4" (10.2cm) diameter

This fabric has so many distinct colors that I could immediately imagine creating a geometric background that would be embellished with silly cats. There are many fabric choices when you walk into a quilt store, making it easy for you to also get inspired and create countless coasters and mug rugs. There are lots of wonderful motifs that would make great personal gifts!

Material Requirements

- (1) 9" x 12" (22.9 x 30.5cm) red solid fabric
- (1) 9" x 12" (22.9 x 30.5cm) yellow solid fabric
- (1) 9" x 12" (22.9 x 30.5cm) lime green solid fabric
- (1) 9" x 12" (22.9 x 30.5cm) purple solid fabric
- (1) 9" x 12" (22.9 x 30.5cm) turquoise solid fabric
- (1) 9" x 12" (22.9 x 30.5cm) orange solid fabric
- ⅓ yard (30.5cm) cat motif fabric
- (6) 4" x 4" (10.2 x 10.2cm) needled cotton batting
- (1) 12" x 18" (30.5 x 45.7cm) iron-on adhesive (I/O)
- 2 yards (182.9cm) red embroidery floss
- 2 yards (182.9cm) orange embroidery floss
- 2 yards (182.9cm) blue embroidery floss
- 2 yards (182.9cm) green embroidery floss
- 2 yards (182.9cm) yellow embroidery floss
- 2 yards (182.9cm) purple embroidery floss
- Hand-sewing needle
- White thread
- CC patterns (page 123)
- Basic tools (page 7)

Cutting Requirements

Red Solid Fabric

- (1) Pattern CC-A
- (1) Pattern CC-C
- (1) Pattern CC-D
- (1) Pattern CC-E

Yellow Solid Fabric

- (1) Pattern CC-A
- (2) Pattern CC-B
- (1) Pattern CC-D
- (1) Pattern CC-E

Lime Green Solid Fabric

- (1) Pattern CC-A
- (1) Pattern CC-C
- (1) Pattern CC-D
- (1) Pattern CC-E

Purple Solid Fabric

- (1) Pattern CC-A
- (2) Pattern CC-C
- (1) Pattern CC-E

Turquoise Solid Fabric

- (1) Pattern CC-A
- (2) Pattern CC-B
- (1) Pattern CC-C
- (1) Pattern CC-E

Orange Solid Fabric

- (2) Pattern CC-A
- (1) Pattern CC-C
- (1) Pattern CC-D
- (1) Pattern CC-E

Cat Motif Fabric

- (6) cats with I/O, fussy cut
- (6) flowers with I/O, fussy cut

Batting

- (6) Pattern CC-A

Note

Make sure the cat motif fabric has at least six cats or another motif that fits inside Pattern CC-A (about 4" [10.2cm] diameter). If it doesn't, you need to cut a larger piece of fabric than indicated here.

Coaster 1

1. Make a quilt sandwich as follows: Lay (1) Pattern CC-A orange RS down. Lay (1) batting on top of the fabric. Lay (1) Pattern CC-A orange RS up.

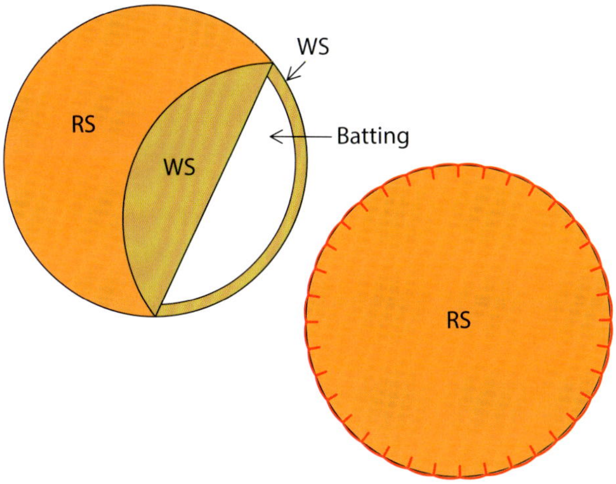

2. With (2) strands of yellow embroidery floss, blanket stitch (see page 11) around the perimeter of the coaster through all three layers. Keep thread taut so the batting does not show.

3. Press (1) cat motif in place on the front. Press (1) flower motif on the back where desired.

Coaster 2

1. Stitch (1) Pattern CC-B turquoise RST with (1) Pattern CC-B yellow using a ¼" (6.4mm) seam. Press toward darker fabric.

2. Make a quilt sandwich as follows: Lay (1) Pattern CC-A yellow RS down. Lay (1) batting on top of the fabric. Lay the front from step 1 RS up.

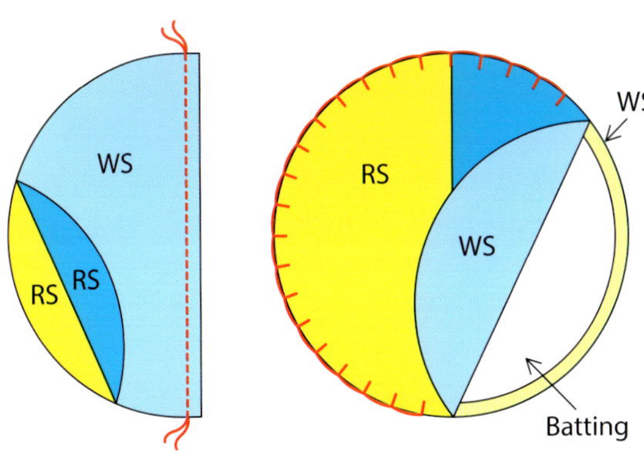

3. With (2) strands of turquoise embroidery floss, blanket stitch around the perimeter of the coaster through all three layers. Keep thread taut so the batting does not show.

4. Press (1) cat motif in place on the front. Press (1) flower motif on the back where desired.

Coaster 3

1. Stitch (1) Pattern CC-C orange RST with (1) Pattern CC-C purple to create a half circle. Stitch the unit RST with (1) Pattern CC-B yellow. Use ¼" (6.4mm) seams. Press toward the darkest fabric after each seam is made.

2. Make a quilt sandwich as follows: Lay (1) Pattern CC-A purple RS down. Lay (1) batting on top of the fabric. Lay the front from step 1 RS up.

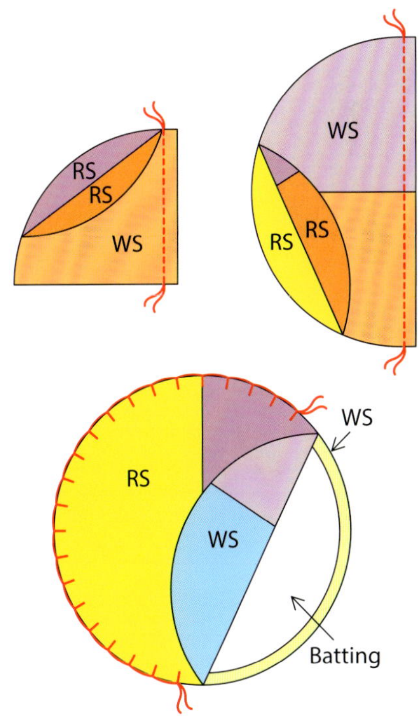

3. With (2) strands of orange embroidery floss, blanket stitch around the perimeter of the coaster through all three layers. Keep thread taut so the batting does not show.

4. Press (1) cat motif in place on the front. Press (1) flower motif on the back where desired.

Coaster 4

1. Stitch (1) Pattern CC-C turquoise RST with (1) Pattern CC-C red to create a half circle. Stitch (1) Pattern CC-C purple RST with (1) Pattern CC-C lime green to create a half circle. Use ¼" (6.4mm) seams. Press toward the darker fabric.

2. Stitch the (2) half-circle units RST using a ¼" (6.4mm) seam. Press toward the darker fabrics.

3. Make a quilt sandwich as follows: Lay (1) Pattern CC-A turquoise RS down. Lay (1) batting on top of the fabric. Lay the front from step 2 RS up.

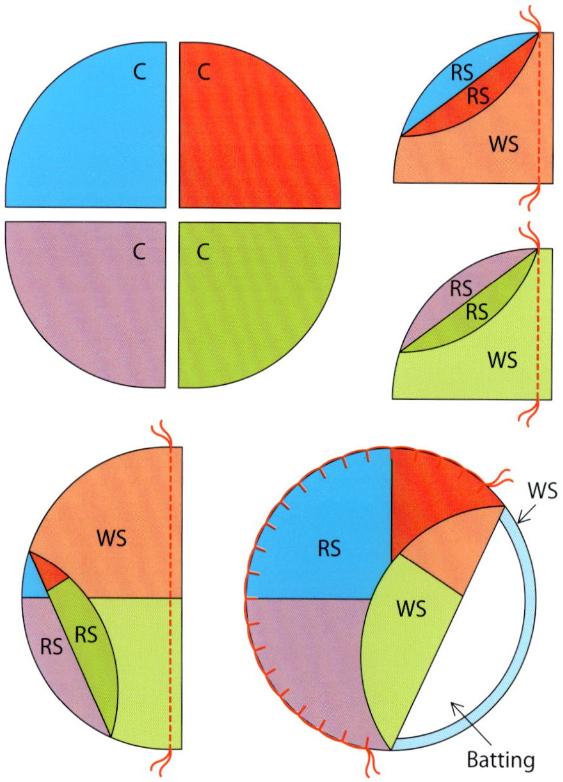

4. With (2) strands of turquoise embroidery floss, blanket stitch around the perimeter of the coaster through all three layers. Keep thread taut so the batting does not show.

5. Press (1) cat motif in place on the front. Press (1) flower motif on the back where desired.

Coaster 5

1. Stitch (1) Pattern CC-D yellow RST with (1) Pattern CC-D lime green to create a quarter circle. Stitch (1) Pattern CC-D orange RST with (1) Pattern CC-D red to create a quarter circle. Use ¼" (6.4mm) seams. Press toward the darker fabric.

2. Stitch the (2) quarter-circle units RST using a ¼" (6.4mm) seam to create a half circle. Press toward the darker fabric.

3. Stitch (1) Pattern CC-B turquoise RST with (1) half-circle unit using a ¼" (6.4mm) seam. Press toward darker fabrics.

4. Make a quilt sandwich as follows: Lay (1) Pattern CC-A red RS down. Lay (1) batting on top of the fabric. Lay the front from step 3 RS up.

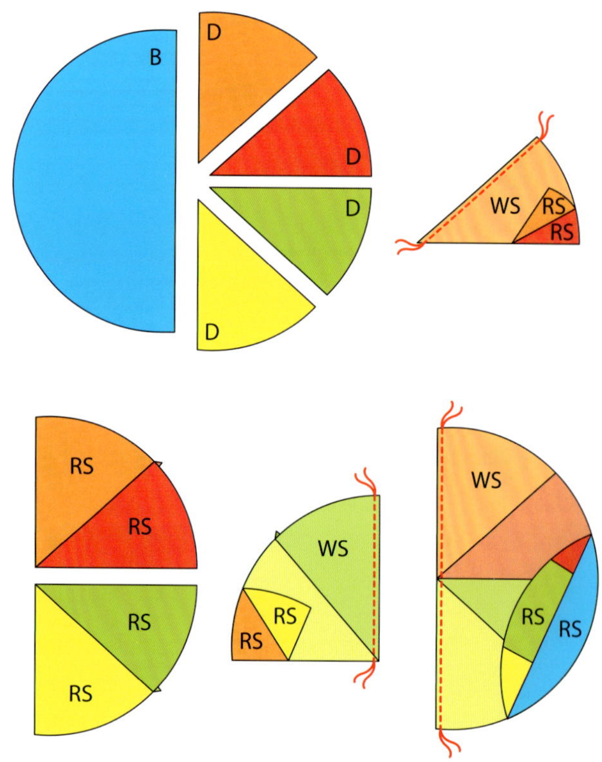

5. With (2) strands of red embroidery floss, blanket stitch around the perimeter of the coaster through all three layers. Keep thread taut so the batting does not show.

6. Press (1) cat motif in place on the front. Press (1) flower motif on the back where desired.

Coaster 6

1. Stitch (1) Pattern CC-E red RST with (1) Pattern CC-E turquoise. Open then stitch (1) Pattern CC-E yellow RST with the unit to create a half circle. Use ¼" (6.4mm) seams. Press toward the darker fabric.

2. Stitch (1) Pattern CC-E orange RST with (1) Pattern CC-E lime green. Open then stitch (1) Pattern CC-E purple RST with the unit to create a half circle. Use ¼" (6.4mm) seams. Press toward the darker fabric.

3. Stitch the (2) half-circle units RST using a ¼" (6.4mm) seam. Press toward the darker fabrics.

4. Make a quilt sandwich as follows: Lay (1) Pattern CC-A lime green RS down. Lay (1) batting on top of the fabric. Lay the front from step 3 RS up.

5. With (2) strands of purple embroidery floss, blanket stitch around the perimeter of the coaster through all three layers. Keep thread taut so the batting does not show.

6. Press (1) cat motif in place on the front. Press (1) flower motif on the back where desired.

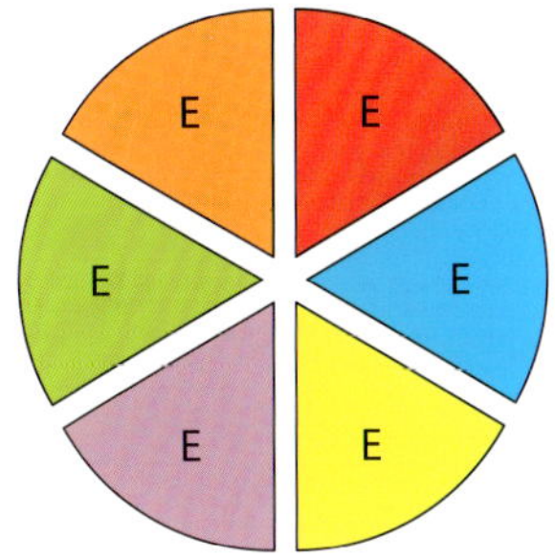

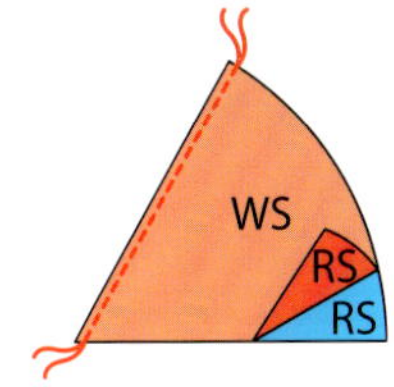

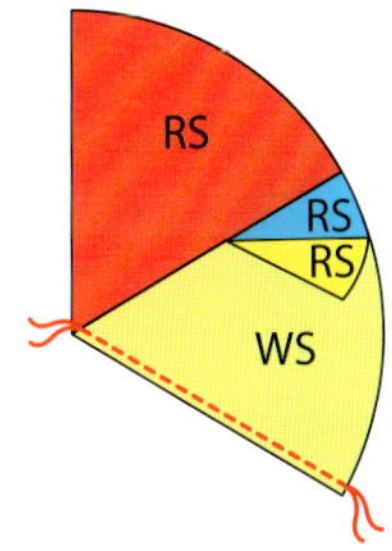

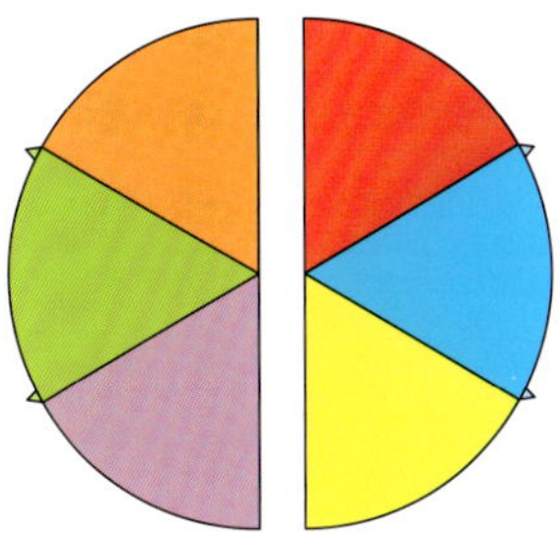

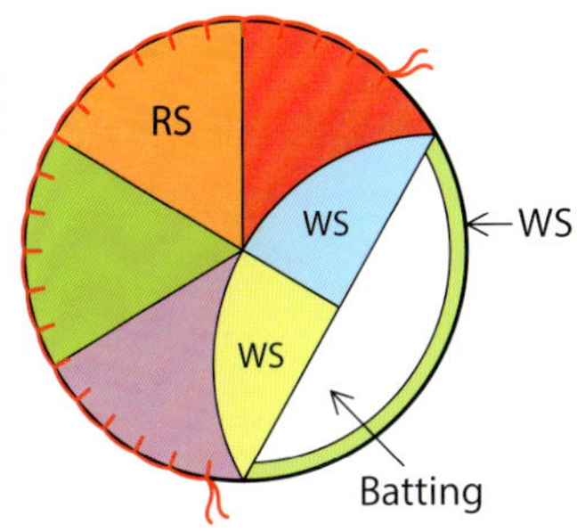

Fussy Cut Window Coasters

Finished Size: 5" x 5" (12.7 x 12.7cm)

Fussy cutting paired with shaped windows is such a fun way to use up scraps of your favorite novelty fabrics. This set uses a heart, square, hexagon, and circle for the openings, but you can play with any simple shape you choose. Novelty print fabric collections are ideal for a colorful coaster set.

Material Requirements

- (1) 9" x 44" (22.9 x 111.8cm) motif print fabric
- (1) 9" x 44" (22.9 x 111.8cm) coordinate print fabric
- (1) 9" x 44" (22.9 x 111.8cm) cotton batting
- (1) 9" x 44" (22.9 x 111.8cm) fusible interfacing
- Color-coordinating threads
- Wash-away marking pen or chalk marker
- Spray adhesive, optional
- FCW patterns (page 124)
- Basic tools (page 7)

Cutting Requirements

Motif Print Fabric

- (2) 1½" x 30" (3.8 x 76.2cm) for binding

Coordinate Print Fabric

- (12) 7" x 7" (17.8 x 17.8cm)
- (2) 1½" x 30" (3.8 x 76.2cm) for binding

Batting

- (4) 7" x 7" (17.8 x 17.8cm)

Fusible Interfacing

- (4) 7" x 7" (17.8 x 17.8cm)

Note

Make sure the motifs in the print fabric can fit in approximately 3½" x 3½" (8.9 x 8.9cm) windows.

Instructions

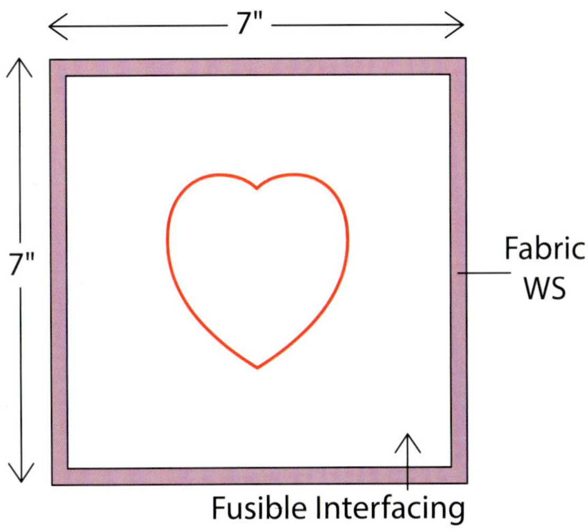

1. Prepare (1) 7" x 7" (17.8 x 17.8cm) coordinate fabric with fusible interfacing on the WS, according to the manufacturer's instructions. Trace either the heart, hexagon, square, or circle pattern in the center.

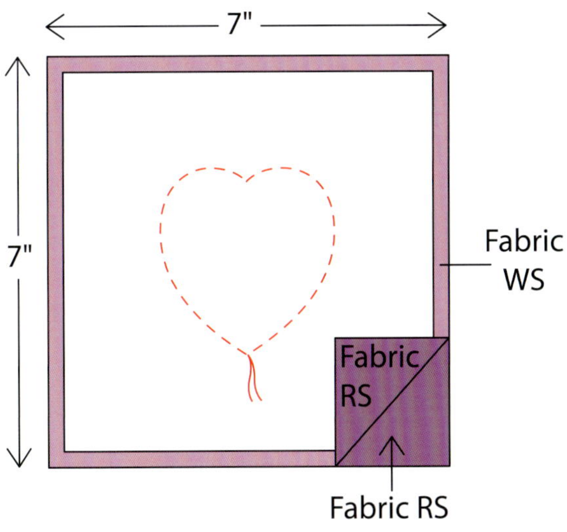

2. Lay the fabric RST with a second coordinate fabric. Machine stitch (L=2.0) directly onto the traced shape outline.

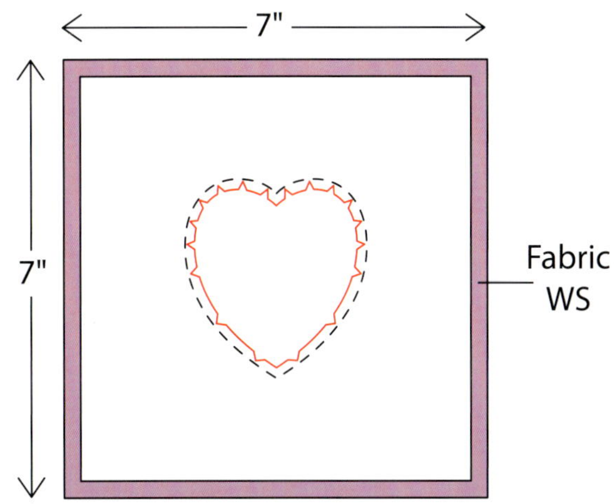

3. Using sharp scissors, cut out the inside of the shape through both layers, stopping ¼" (6.4mm) from the stitched line. If making the heart or circle, clip the seam allowance around the curves and to the points. If making the hexagon or square, clip to the corners. Do not clip through the stitch line.

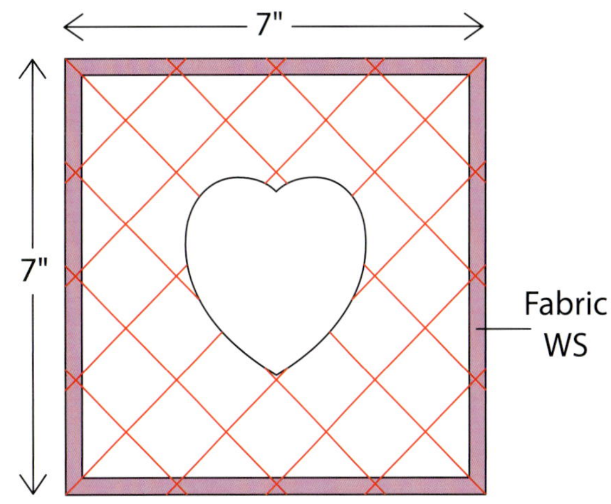

4. Turn the fabric squares RS out. Press to create a flat window opening. Using a wash-away marker or chalk marker, draw a diagonal grid pattern on the window piece by lining up a ruler from corner to corner. You can also choose to free-motion quilt.

5. Lay the window over the motif print fabric, positioning the motif inside as desired. Following around the edge of the window square, cut the fabric; all should be approximately 7" x 7" (17.8 x 17.8cm).

6. Make a quilt sandwich as follows: Lay (1) 7" x 7" (17.8 x 17.8cm) coordinate fabric RS down. Lay (1) batting on top of the fabric. Lay the motif square from step 5 RS up. Lay the window from step 4 RS up. Pin or use a spray adhesive to secure the layers.

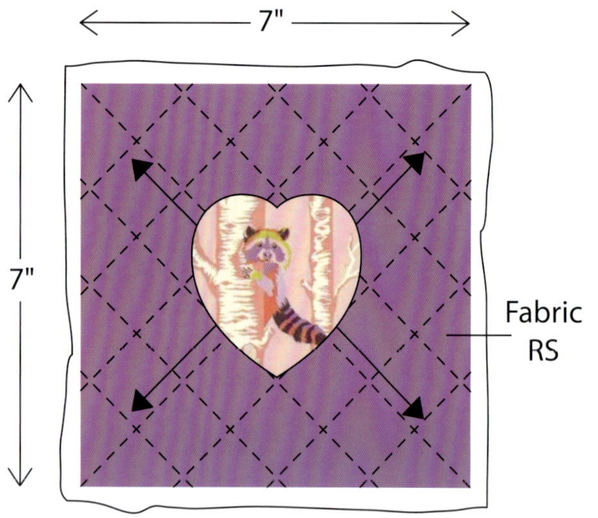

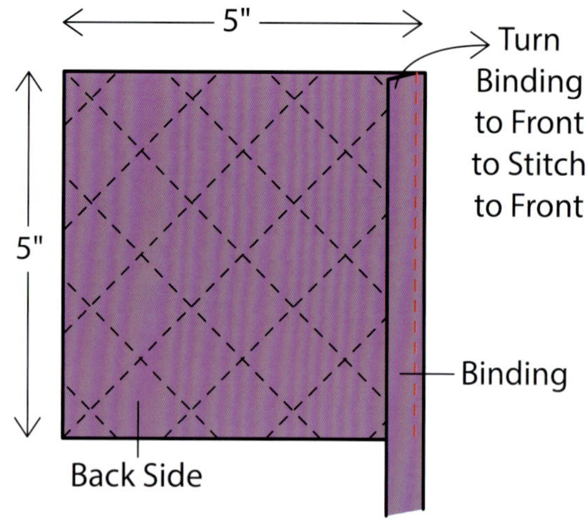

7. Starting with a fix stitch at the edge of the window opening, quilt through all layers. Work from the center out to not distort the window opening.

8. Center the window and trim the coaster to 5" x 5" (12.7 x 12.7cm) or 5½" x 5½" (14 x 14cm) if you prefer a slightly larger coaster.

9. For these square coasters, I followed the traditional binding (see page 10), but rather than stitch the binding on the front first then hand stitch to the back, I stitched the binding to the back then folded it over and machine stitched to the front for a nice edgestitch finish.

10. Repeat steps 1–9 for the remaining (3) coasters, choosing a different window shape if desired.

SHAPED Projects

Coasters are usually sold in a round or square shape. This is because they are the most basic shapes and easiest to manufacture. When you are creating your own coasters, you have the opportunity to use your creativity and design whatever you want.

The **Orange Slice Table Mat with Coasters** project was designed as something slightly comical yet useful in many ways. The coasters are orange slices that are attached to the orange table mat by clothing snaps. With or without the coasters in place, the orange base is great for a table centerpiece.

The **Snowman Hot Chocolate Coasters** are fun winter coasters that are packed with hot chocolate fun! This is another pocket-type coaster that is easy to make with just a few color changes in the collection. Don't forget the marshmallows!

Orange Slice Table Mat & Coasters

- **Table Mat Finished Size: 17" (43.2cm) diameter**
- **Coaster Finished Size: 3½" x 6½" (8.9 x 16.5cm)**

Looking for a clever way to make and display coasters for your dining room or kitchen? Look no further; these orange slice coasters snap on and off the table mat when needed. These coasters are shaped, meaning they are not traditional square, rectangle, or circular coasters. This is a unique and colorful gift that can be used all year long.

Material Requirements

- ⅔ yard (61cm) orange polka-dot fabric
- Fat Quarter or ½ yard (45.7cm) melon mottled print fabric
- (2) Fat Quarters or (1) ½ yard (45.7cm) yellow/orange mottled print fabric
- 2 yards (182.9cm) white jumbo-size rickrack
- 2½ yards (228.6cm) white large-size rickrack
- 54" x 36" (137.2 x 91.4cm) needled cotton batting
- White thread
- Orange thread
- (8) large sewing snaps sets
- Chalk marker
- OSC pattern (page 126)
- Basic tools (page 7)

Cutting Requirements

Orange Polka-Dot Fabric

- (2) 17½" (44.5cm) diameter
- (8) 1" x 14" (2.5 x 35.6cm)

Melon Mottled Print Fabric

- (1) 16" (40.6cm) diameter

Yellow/Orange Mottled Print Fabric

- (16) Pattern OSC-A

White Large-Size Rickrack

- (4) 15" (38.1cm)

Batting

- (1) 17" (43.2cm) diameter
- (1) 15" (38.1cm) diameter
- (8) Pattern OSC-A

Table Mat

1. Make a quilt sandwich as follows: Lay (2) 17½" (44.5cm) orange polka-dot circles RST. Lay (1) 17" (43.2cm) batting on top and centered.

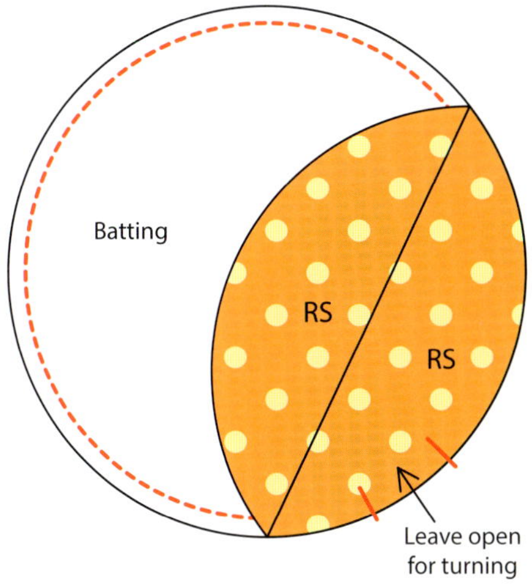

2. Stitch around the quilt sandwich as close to the edge of the batting as possible. Leave a 3" (7.6cm) opening so the piece can be turned.

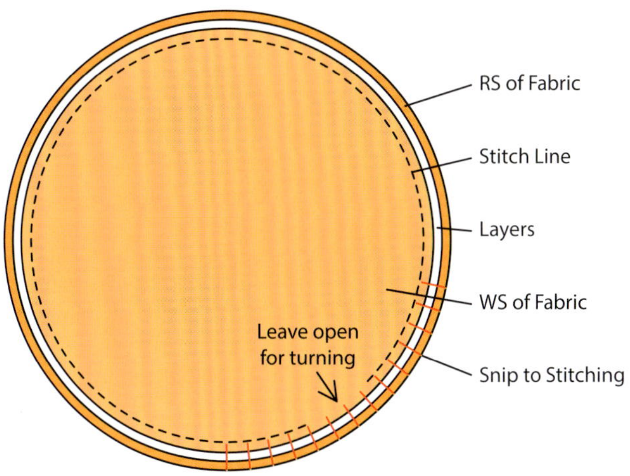

3. Clip the seam allowance around the curves, including the opening. Do not clip through the stitch line.

4. Turn the fabric and batting RS out. The batting should be inside the sandwich. Hand stitch the 3" (7.6cm) opening closed. Press and set aside.

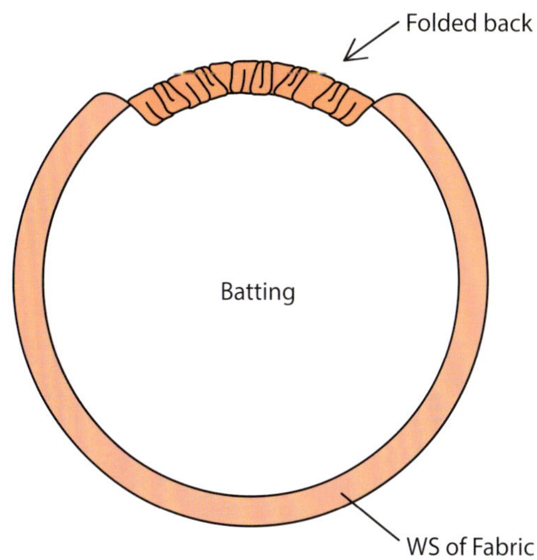

5. Lay (1) 16" (40.6cm) melon circle RS down. Lay (1) 15" (38.1cm) batting on top and centered. Fold and pin the extra width of the fabric over the edge of the batting all around. Sew them together around the outside for stability.

6. Lay the melon fabric/batting RS down. Pin the jumbo rickrack around the outside of the circle and stitch in place on the WS. The rickrack should be evenly exposed and layered to the fabric.

7. Lay the polka-dot circle RS up. Lay the melon fabric/batting on top, RS up and centered. Pin in place and zigzag stitch around the melon perimeter, close to the edge.

8. With a chalk marker, split the melon circle into (8) equal sections. Sew the large rickrack strips over the lines, from one side to the other, with a zigzag stitch using white thread.

Coasters

1. Make a quilt sandwich as follows: Lay (1) Pattern OSC-A yellow/orange fabric RS down. Lay (1) Pattern OSC-A batting on top of the fabric. Lay (1) Pattern OSC-A yellow/orange fabric on top of the batting RS up. Stitch around the perimeter. Repeat for (7) more "orange slices."

2. Make ½" (1.3cm) double-fold bias tape from (1) 1" x 14" (2.5 x 35.6cm) orange polka-dot strip, as explained on page 9. Repeat for (7) more strips.

3. Machine stitch the bias tape to the front of (1) orange slice as explained on page 10. Fold the bias tape over the edge and hand sew to the back. Repeat for (7) more coasters.

4. Place the coasters in the orange sections from step 8 of the Table Mat. With a chalk marker, make a dot on the back of the coaster, 1½" (3.8cm) from the narrow end. Mark the matching spot on the mat.

5. Stitch the snaps where marked to easily remove the slices from the centerpiece.

Snowman Hot Chocolate Coasters

Finished Size: 4" x 5" (10.2 x 12.7cm)

What is better than hot chocolate on a chilly day or in the evening? Celebrate this delicious treat by making these snowman pocket coasters that are shaped like a house. You can stick a hot chocolate packet in the pocket, give them away as ornaments, or make six for use at your own home.

Material Requirements

- Fat Quarter or (1) 9" x 44" (22.9 x 111.8cm) red snowflake print fabric
- Fat Quarter or (1) 9" x 44" (22.9 x 111.8cm) green snowflake print fabric
- Fat Quarter or (1) 9" x 44" (22.9 x 111.8cm) blue snowflake print fabric
- Fat Quarter or (1) 9" x 44" (22.9 x 111.8cm) orange solid fabric
- Scraps or (1) 6" x 6" (15.2 x 15.2cm) holly print fabric
- (6) 4" x 5" (10.2 x 12.7cm) needled cotton batting
- (1) 12" x 18" (30.5 x 45.7cm) iron-on adhesive (I/O)
- White embroidery thread
- (18) 8mm red sequins
- SHC patterns (page 125)
- Basic tools (page 7)

Cutting Requirements

Red Snowflake Print Fabric

- (6) Pattern SHC-A
- (2) Pattern SHC-B with I/O
- (2) Pattern SHC-C with I/O
- (2) ¼" x 6" (6.4 x 15.2cm) with I/O
- (2) ¼" x 1½" (6.4 x 3.8cm) with I/O

Green Snowflake Print Fabric

- (6) Pattern SHC-A
- (2) Pattern SHC-B with I/O
- (2) Pattern SHC-C with I/O
- (2) ¼" x 6" (6.4 x 15.2cm) with I/O
- (2) ¼" x 1½" (6.4 x 3.8cm) with I/O

Blue Snowflake Print Fabric

- (6) Pattern SHC-A
- (2) Pattern SHC-B with I/O
- (2) Pattern SHC-C with I/O
- (2) ¼" x 6" (6.4 x 15.2cm) with I/O
- (2) ¼" x 1½" (6.4 x 3.8cm) with I/O

Orange Solid Fabric

- (6) Pattern SHC-D with I/O
- (6) 1" x 20" (2.5 x 50.8cm) for bias tape

Holly Print Fabric

- (36) Pattern SHC-E with I/O

Batting

- (6) Pattern SHC-A
- (6) Pattern SHC-F

Green/Red Coaster

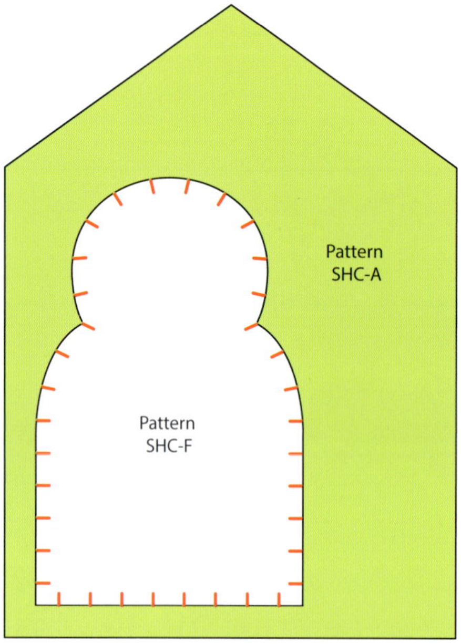

1. Pin (1) Pattern SHC-F batting onto (1) Pattern SHC-A green snowflake fabric as shown. Blanket stitch around the outside of the snowman body with (2) strands of white embroidery floss.

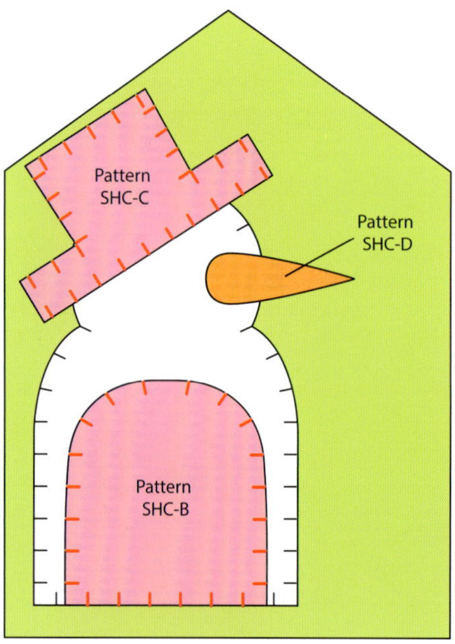

2. Press (1) Pattern SHC-C red snowflake fabric, (1) Pattern SHC-B red snowflake fabric, and (1) Pattern SHC-D orange fabric in place on the snowman as shown. Blanket stitch around the hat and tummy.

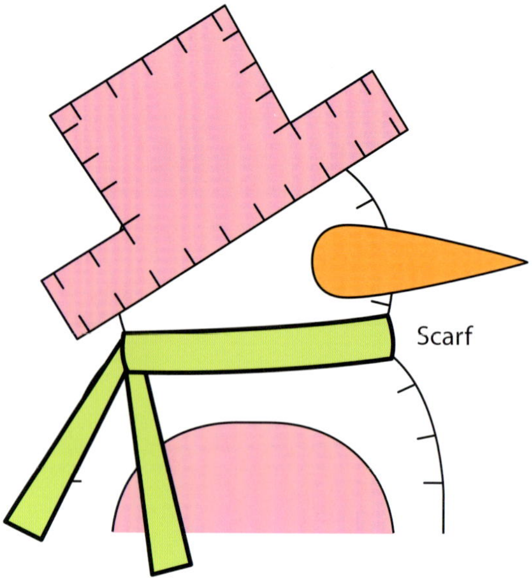

3. Press (1) ¼" x 6" (6.4 x 15.2cm) green snowflake fabric to the neck. Fold the ends over as shown to make the tails of the scarf.

4. Press (1) ¼" x 1½" (6.4 x 3.8cm) green snowflake fabric to the hat for a hatband.

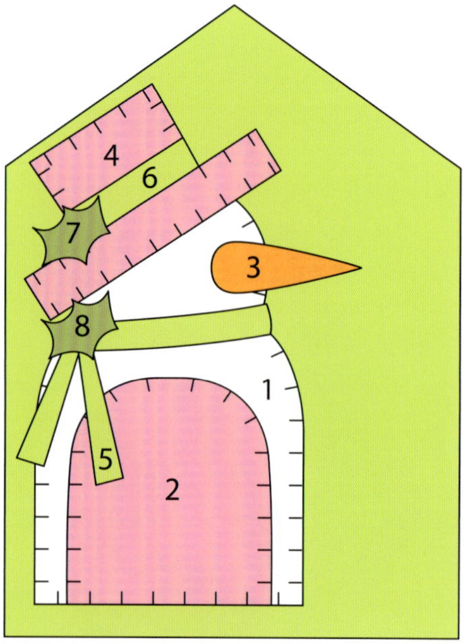

5. Press (1) holly leaf to the hat and (2) leaves to the scarf as shown. Stitch (2) red sequins, placing in the center of the leaves.

6. Make a quilt sandwich as follows: Lay (2) Pattern SHC-A green snowflake fabrics RS down. Lay (1) Pattern SHC-A batting on top of the fabric. Lay the mug rug front from step 5 on top of the batting RS up.

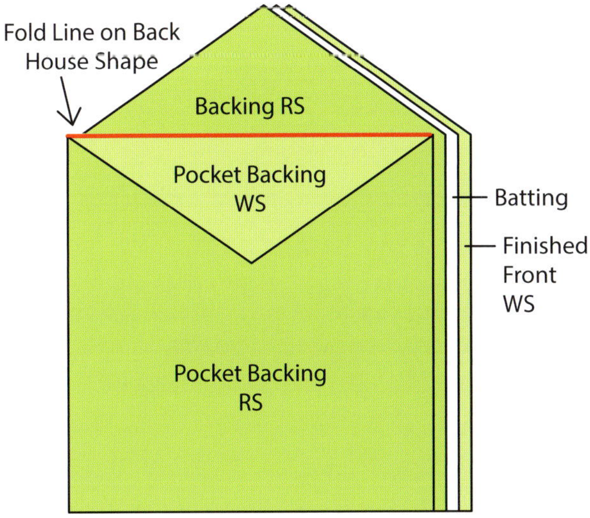

7. Flip the entire unit so the backing is RS up. The top Pattern SHC-A is the pocket piece. Fold it down to the top of the sides, along the "roofline" of the house. Blanket stitch the flap down.

8. Stitch around the quilt sandwich as close to the edge as possible to keep all layers together.

9. Press (3) holly leaves along the edge of the pocket flap. Stitch (1) red sequin in the center of the leaves.

10. Make ¼" (6.4mm) double-fold bias tape from (1) 1" x 20" (2.5 x 50.8cm) orange fabric. Stitch the bias tape around the outside edge. Flip it over the edge and hand stitch to the back.

Green/Blue Coaster

1. Repeat steps 1–10 of the Green/Red Coaster, using blue snowflake fabric for the hat and tummy.

Blue/Green Coaster

1. Repeat steps 1–10 of the Green/Red Coaster. Use blue snowflake fabric for the scarf, hatband, front, backing, and pocket. Use green snowflake fabric for the hat and tummy.

Blue/Red Coaster

1. Repeat steps 1–10 of the Green/Red Coaster, using blue snowflake fabric for the scarf, hatband, front, backing, and pocket.

Red/Blue Coaster

1. Repeat steps 1–10 of the Green/Red Coaster. Use red snowflake fabric for the scarf, hatband, front, backing, and pocket. Use blue snowflake fabric for the hat and tummy.

Red/Green Coaster

1. Repeat steps 1–10 of the Green/Red Coaster. Use red snowflake fabric for the scarf, hatband, front, backing, and pocket. Use green snowflake fabric for the hat and tummy.

FOLDED
Projects

“Fabric folding” can involve folding, pleating, gathering, and twisting. These techniques are used to alter the texture and volume of fabric, creating a three-dimensional appearance. It can also be referred to as fabric manipulation.

The **Folded Star Mug Rugs** are created by overlapping edges to create a cone shape. For mug rugs, the cones are pressed flat in the design. This simple technique has been used with ribbons, paper, and other mediums for holiday decor.

In the **Folded Pocket Coasters**, we use a little origami influence to fold the sides together, creating a small pouch or pocket to hold a gift for your guest. Pocket coasters can also be used to give a gift—stuff $5 in the pocket for a small treat!

Folded Star Mug Rugs

Finished Size: 8" (20.3cm) diameter

These mug rugs are fashioned after a vintage design used for Christmas tree décor, often made with paper. Each "petal" of the star is formed of folded fabric that is then pressed and fit together with seven other pieces. These are relaxing to make and then adorned with small wooden beads. The dimensional appearance of these mug rugs adds interest and texture to your table surface.

Material Requirements

- (2) Fat Quarters or (1) 18" x 44" (45.7 x 111.8cm) blue print fabric
- (2) Fat Quarters or (1) 18" x 44" (45.7 x 111.8cm) light green fabric
- (3) Fat Quarters or (1) 24" x 44" (61 x 111.8cm) orange fabric
- Green thread
- Orange thread
- (48) ¼" (6.4mm) wooden beads
- Basic tools (page 7)

Cutting Requirements

Blue Print Fabric

- (32) 3½" x 3½" (8.9 x 8.9cm)

Light Green Fabric

- (24) 3½" x 3½" (8.9 x 8.9cm)

Orange Fabric

- (48) 3½" x 3½" (8.9 x 8.9cm)

Mug Rug 1

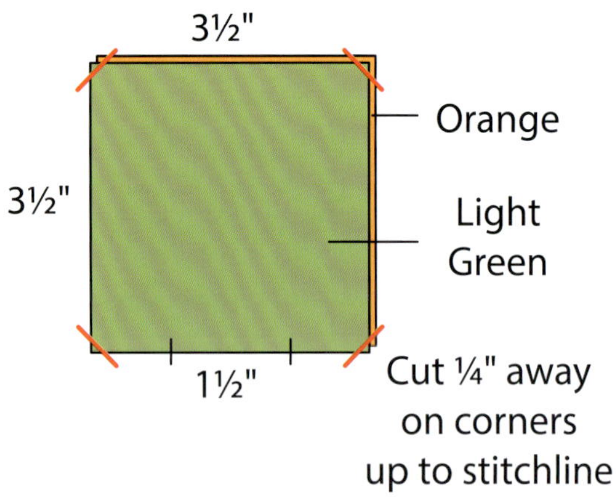

1. Sew (1) 3½" x 3½" (8.9 x 8.9cm) light green fabric RST with (1) 3½" x 3½" (8.9 x 8.9cm) orange fabric. Leave a 1½" (3.8cm) opening for turning. Clip corners diagonally; do not go past the stitching.

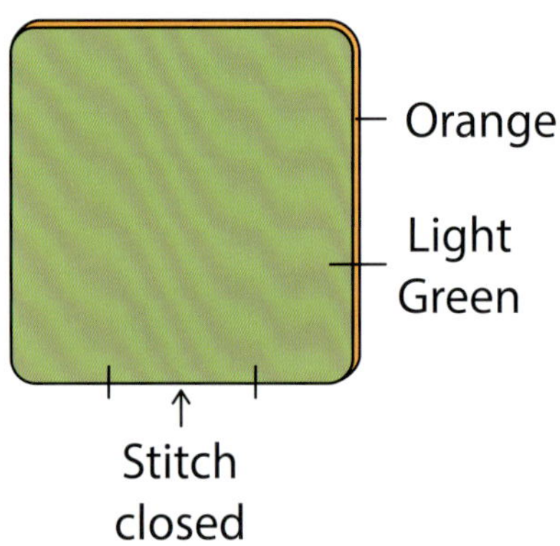

2. Turn the squares RS out through the opening. Be sure to push the corners out. Press the square flat. Stitch the opening closed with a needle and thread.

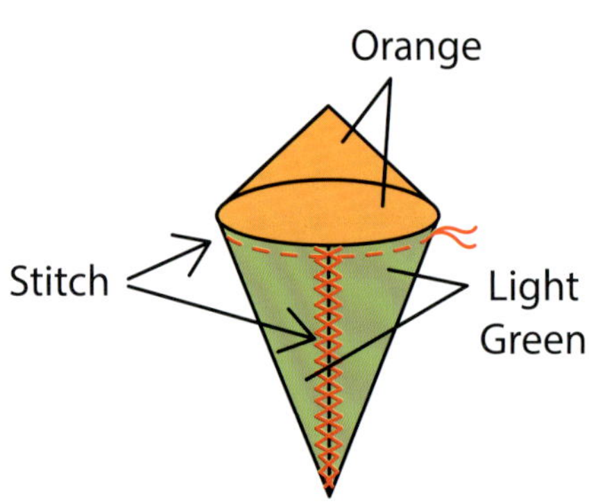

3. Lay the square so the orange side is facing up. Fold (2) opposite corners together in the center of the square. Press the diamond flat. Sew a straight stitch across the top of the matching pieces. Zigzag stitch in front, along the two folded pieces.

4. Repeat steps 1–3 for (7) more cones.

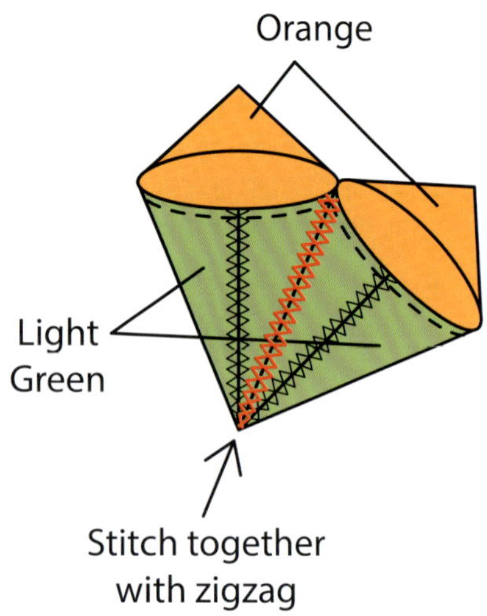

5. Set (2) cones next to each other. Zigzag stitch them together from the folded edge to the end of the point. Repeat, adding a new cone each time until the (8) cones are all attached.

6. The (8) cones will form a star shape. Stitch through the center to be sure all are attached. Press the star flat.

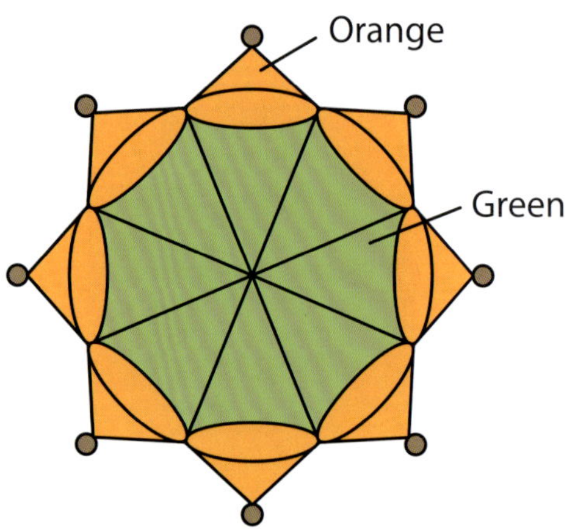

7. Stitch (1) bead onto each point with matching thread. Hide knots inside the beads or fabric seams.

Mug Rug 2

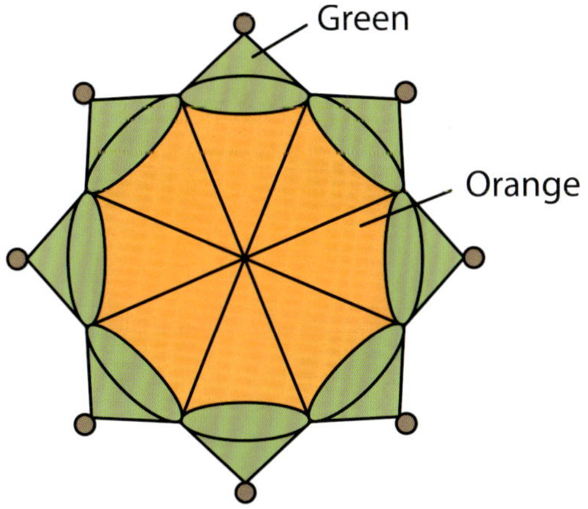

1. Repeat steps 1–7 of Mug Rug 1. In step 3, lay the square so the green side is facing up.

Mug Rug 3

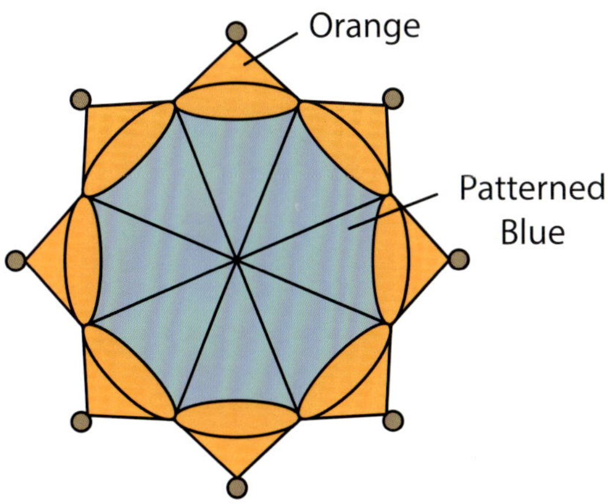

1. Repeat steps 1–7 of Mug Rug 1, using blue fabric instead of green.

Mug Rug 4

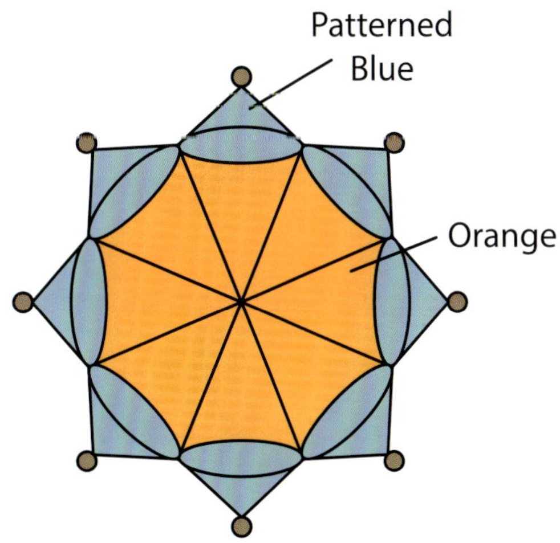

1. Repeat steps 1–7 of Mug Rug 1, using blue fabric instead of green. In step 3, lay the square so the blue side is facing up.

Mug Rug 5

1. Repeat steps 1–4 of Mug Rug 1, using blue fabric instead of orange.

2. Set (2) cones next to each other. Flip one so the all-green back is facing up. Zigzag stitch them together from the folded edge to the end of the point. Repeat, adding a new cone each time and alternating the direction until the (8) cones are all attached.

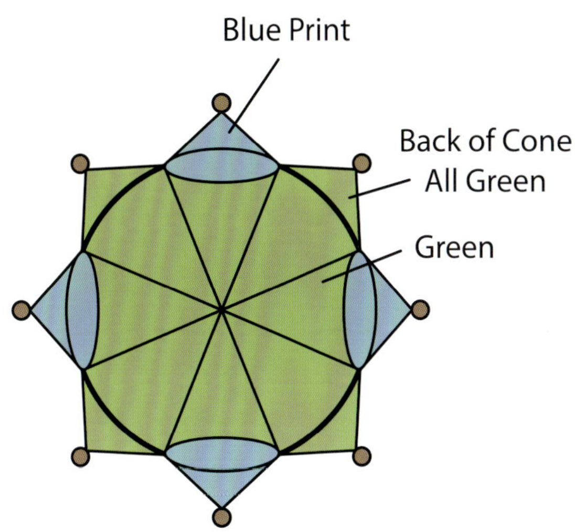

3. Repeat steps 6 and 7 of Mug Rug 1.

Mug Rug 6

1. Repeat steps 1 and 2 of Mug Rug 1, using blue fabric instead of green.

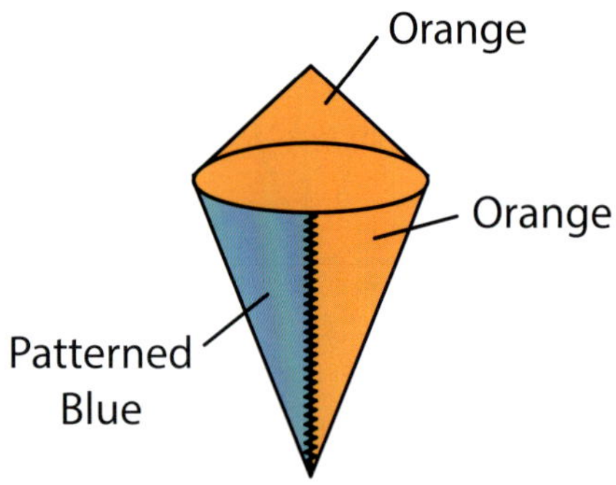

2. Lay the square so the orange side is facing up. Fold (1) corner on the front in the center of the square. Fold the opposite corner on the back in the center of the square. Press the diamond flat. Zigzag stitch down the center.

3. Repeat step 1 and 2 for (7) more cones.

> **Tip**
>
> Make sure to place the edge of both folds in the same place on the front and back, so when they are sewn, the edges are sewn together.

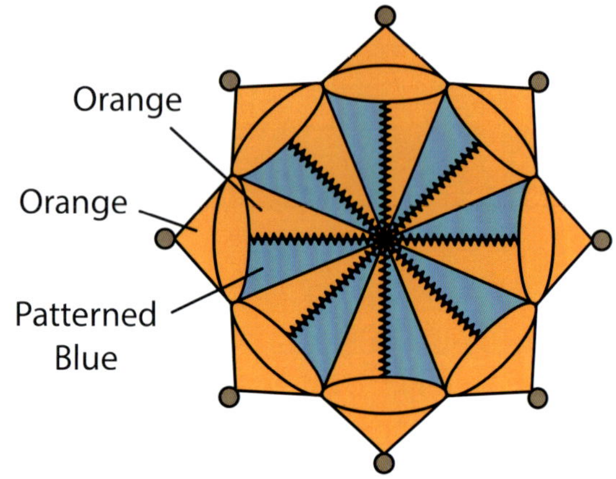

4. Repeat steps 5–7 of Mug Rug 1. This will create a pinwheel effect when the cones are sewn together.

Folded Pocket Coasters

Finished Size: 4" x 4" (10.2 x 10.2cm)

I've always been interested in origami—the art of paper folding—and thought a pocket coaster to hold a tea bag would be fun for entertaining or gifting. Folding fabric is different than folding paper, so be sure to press between all steps for a nicely finished coaster.

Material Requirements

- (1) 18" x 44" (45.7 x 111.8cm) large flower blue fabric
- (1) 18" x 44" (45.7 x 111.8cm) small flower blue fabric
- (1) 18" x 44" (45.7 x 111.8cm) gridwork purple fabric
- (6) 4" x 4" (10.2 x 10.2cm) cotton needled batting
- Blue thread
- Off-white thread
- FP pattern (page 126)
- Basic tools (page 7)

Cutting Requirements

Large Flower Blue Fabric

- (2) Pattern FP-A
- (2) 1½" x 30" (3.8 x 76.2cm)

Small Flower Blue Fabric

- (2) Pattern FP-A
- (2) 1½" x 30" (3.8 x 76.2cm)

Gridwork Purple Fabric

- (2) Pattern FP-A
- (2) 1½" x 30" (3.8 x 76.2cm)

Note

For Pattern FP-A, cut the two pieces out first. Then glue or tape them together to match what is shown in the steps.

Coaster 1

1. Use (1) 1½" x 30" (3.8 x 76.2cm) large flower blue fabric to make ½" (1.3cm) double-fold bias tape. Cut (2) 4" (10.2cm) lengths from the bias tape. Set the excess bias tape aside.

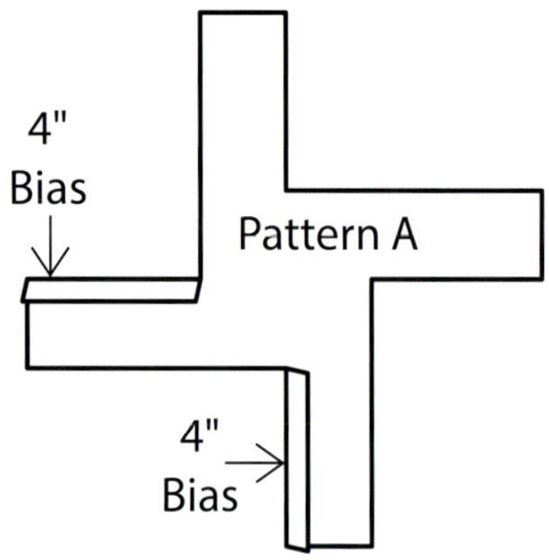

2. Lay (1) Pattern FP-A small flower blue fabric RS down. Sew (2) 4" (10.2cm) bias tapes onto the (2) edges shown.

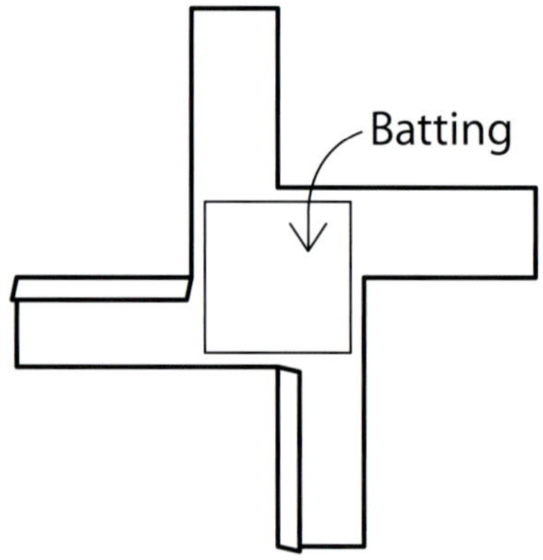

3. Lay (1) batting on the WS of the small flower blue fabric, centered. Quilt straight lines from corner to corner, top to bottom, and side to side.

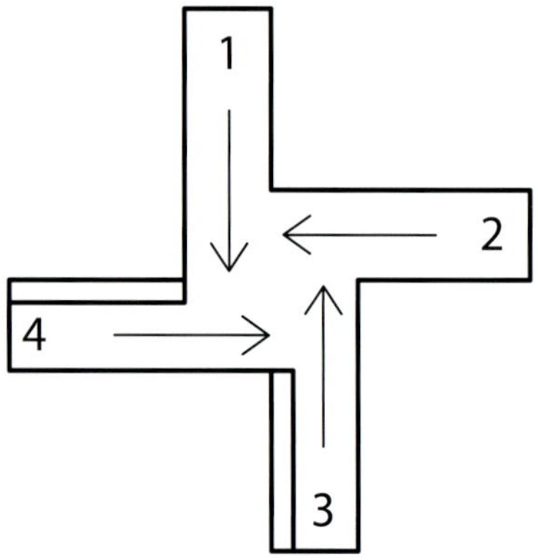

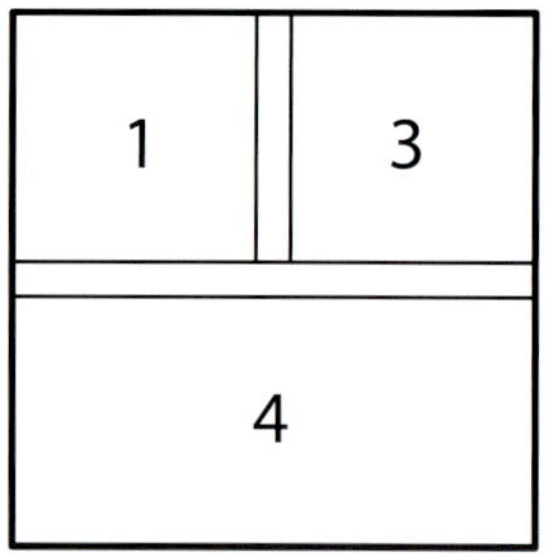

4. Fold the legs of the small flower fabric across the square in the order shown. This creates a pocket that can hold special messages or an aromatic tea bag.

5. Sew the remaining bias tape from step 1 around the outside of the square to hold all pieces in place.

Mug Rug 2

1. Repeat steps 1–5 of Mug Rug 1, using Pattern FP-A gridwork purple fabric.

Mug Rug 3

1. Repeat steps 1–5 of Mug Rug 1. Use Pattern FP-A large flower blue fabric. Use small flower blue fabric for the bias tape.

Mug Rug 4

1. Repeat steps 1–5 of Mug Rug 1. Use Pattern FP-A gridwork purple fabric. Use small flower blue fabric for the bias tape.

Mug Rug 5

1. Repeat steps 1–5 of Mug Rug 1. Use Pattern FP-A large flower blue fabric. Use gridwork purple fabric for the bias tape.

Mug Rug 6

1. Repeat steps 1–5 of Mug Rug 1, using gridwork purple fabric for the bias tape.

Patterns

Crazy Quilt Tasseled Coasters & Grandma's Quilted Mug Rugs

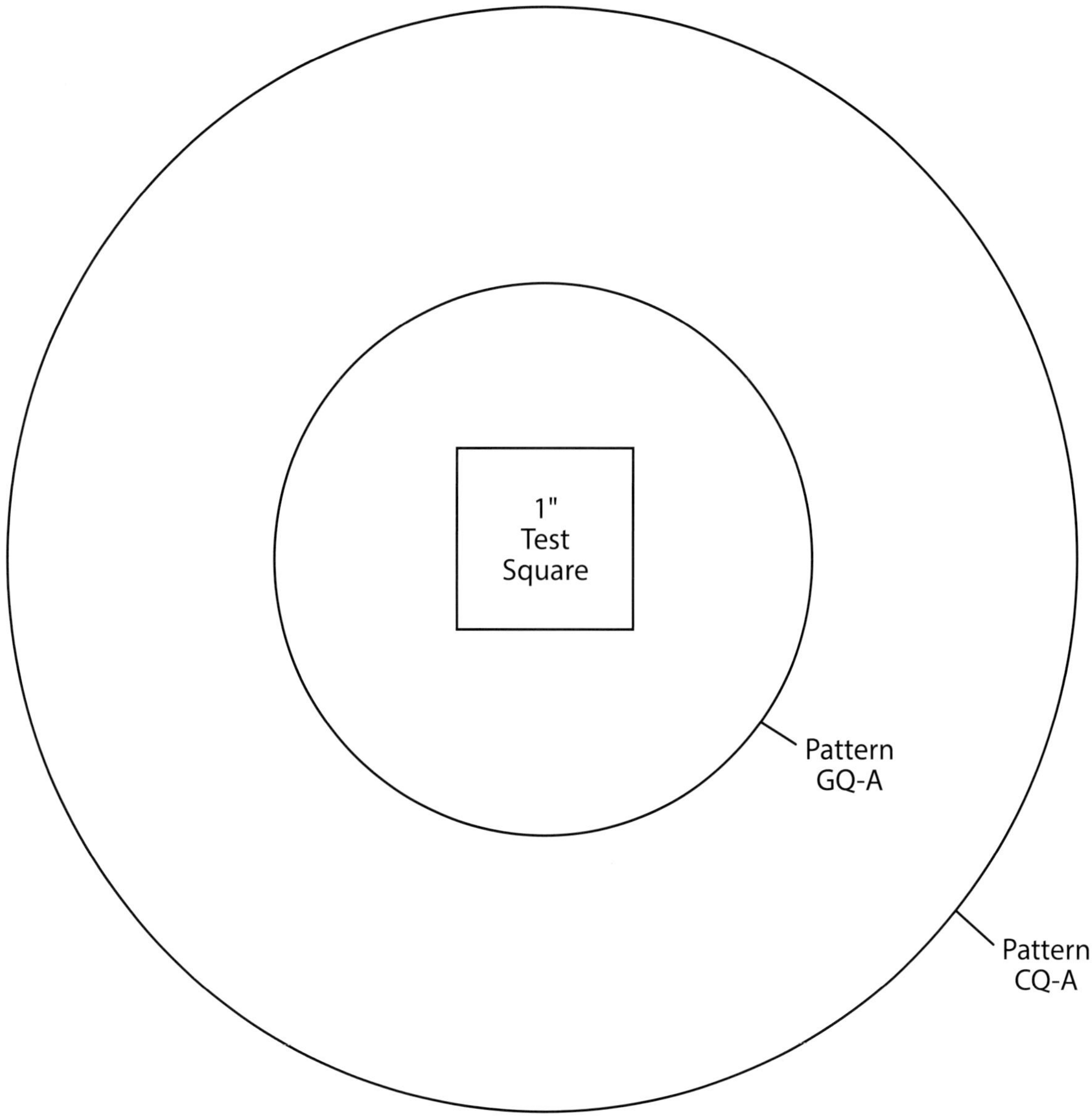

Modern "Squircles" Mug Rugs

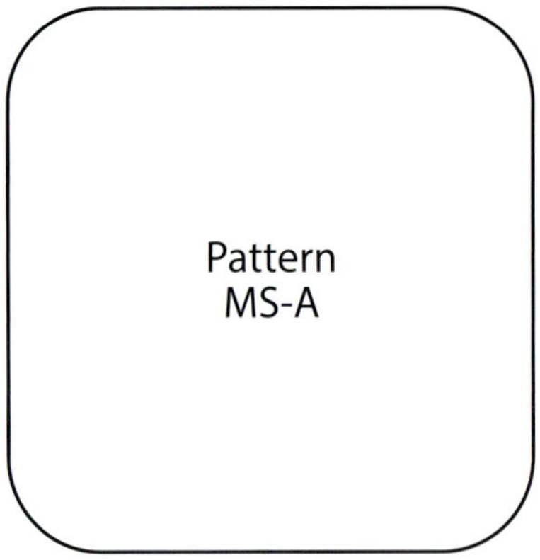

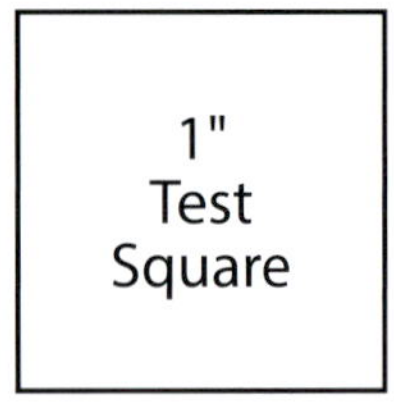

Traditional Kawandi Mug Rugs with a Twist

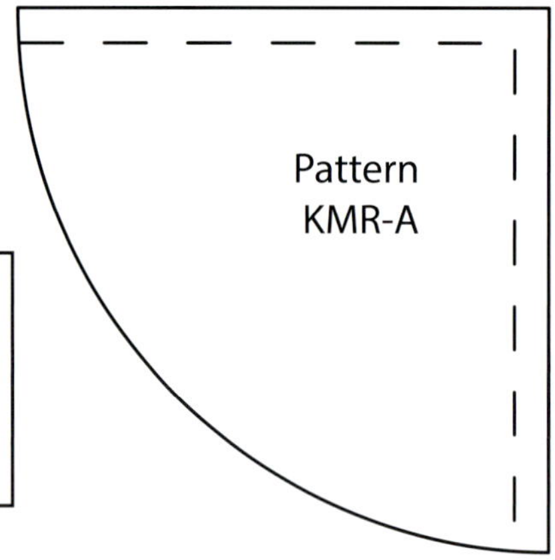

Reverse Appliqué Denim Mug Rugs

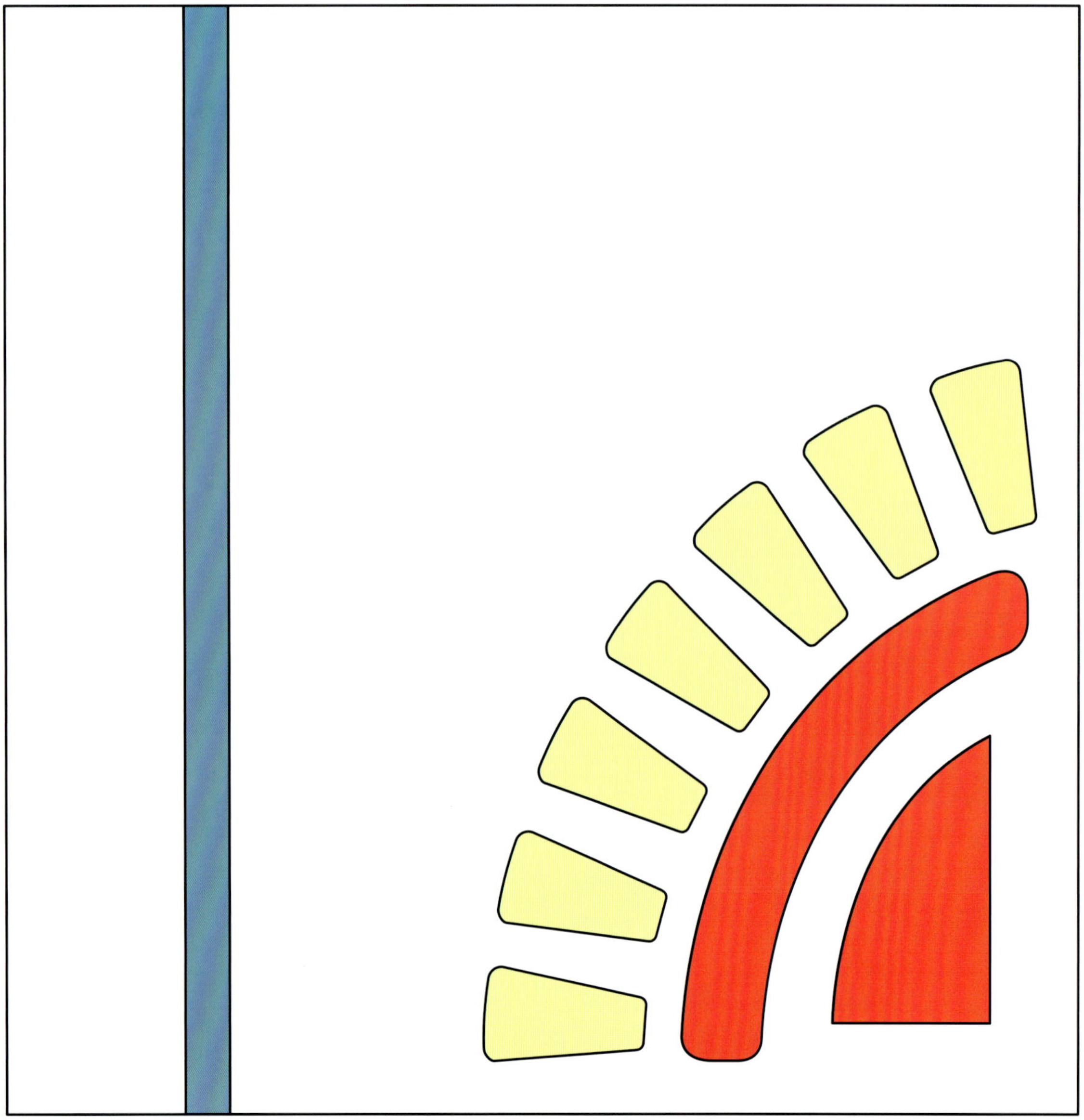

Pattern RAD-A

Pattern RAD-B

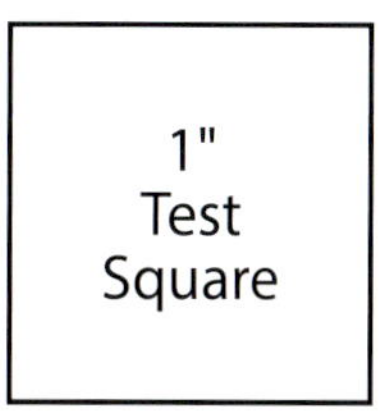

Reverse Appliqué Denim Mug Rugs

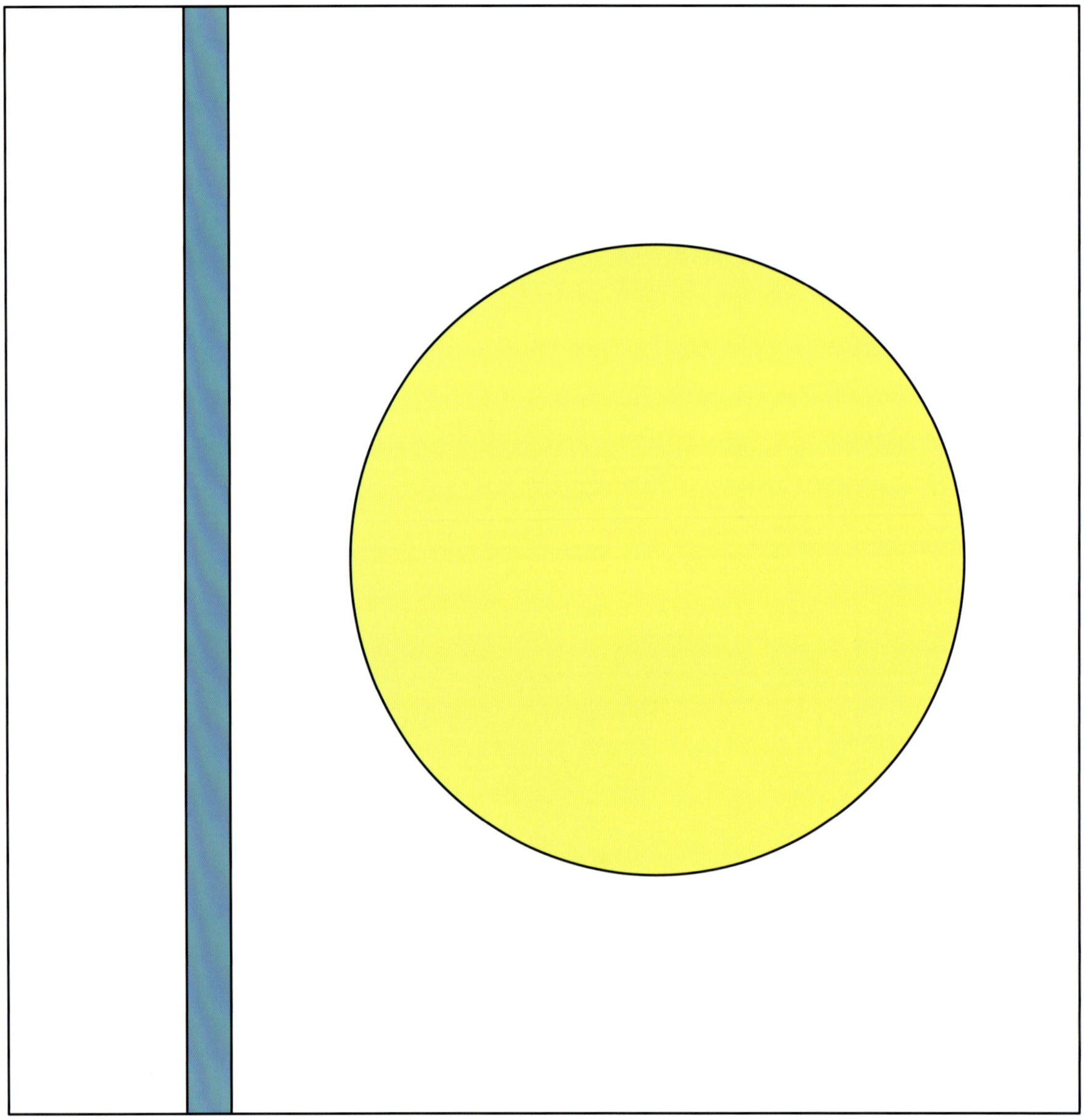

Pattern RAD-C

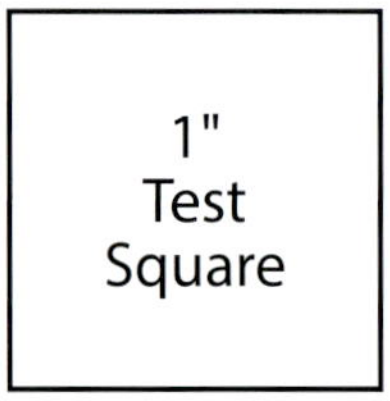

Reverse Appliqué Denim Mug Rugs

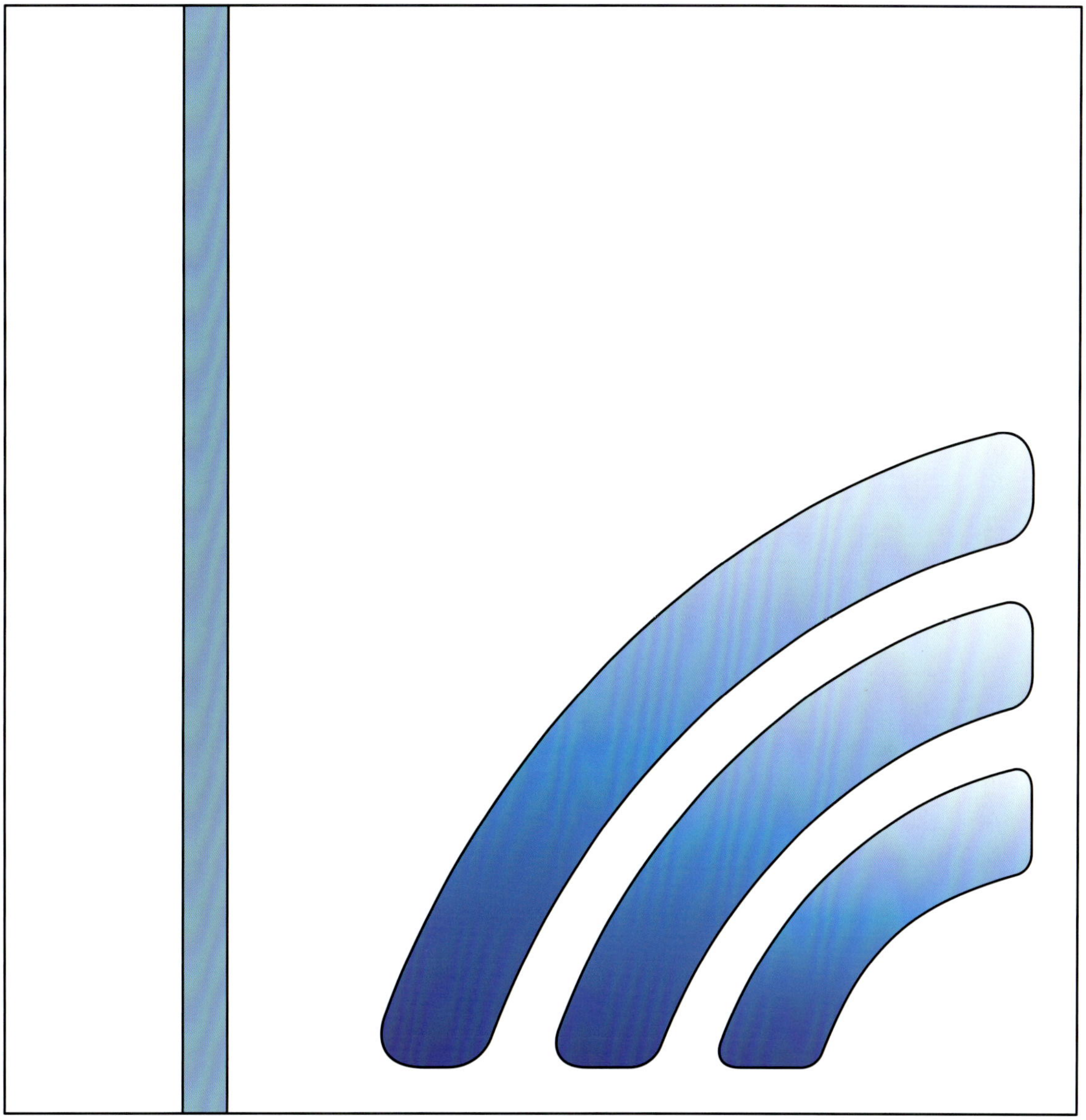

Pattern RAD-D

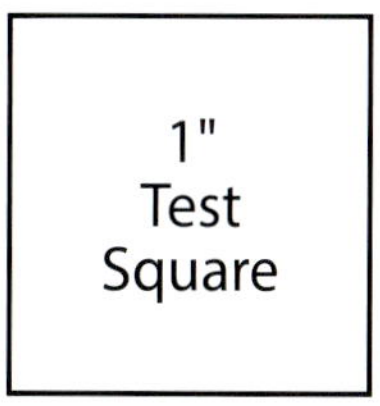

Reverse Appliqué Denim Mug Rugs

Pattern RAD-E

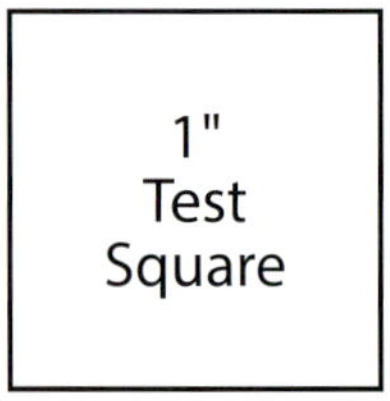

Reverse Appliqué Denim Mug Rugs

Pattern RAD-F

1" Test Square

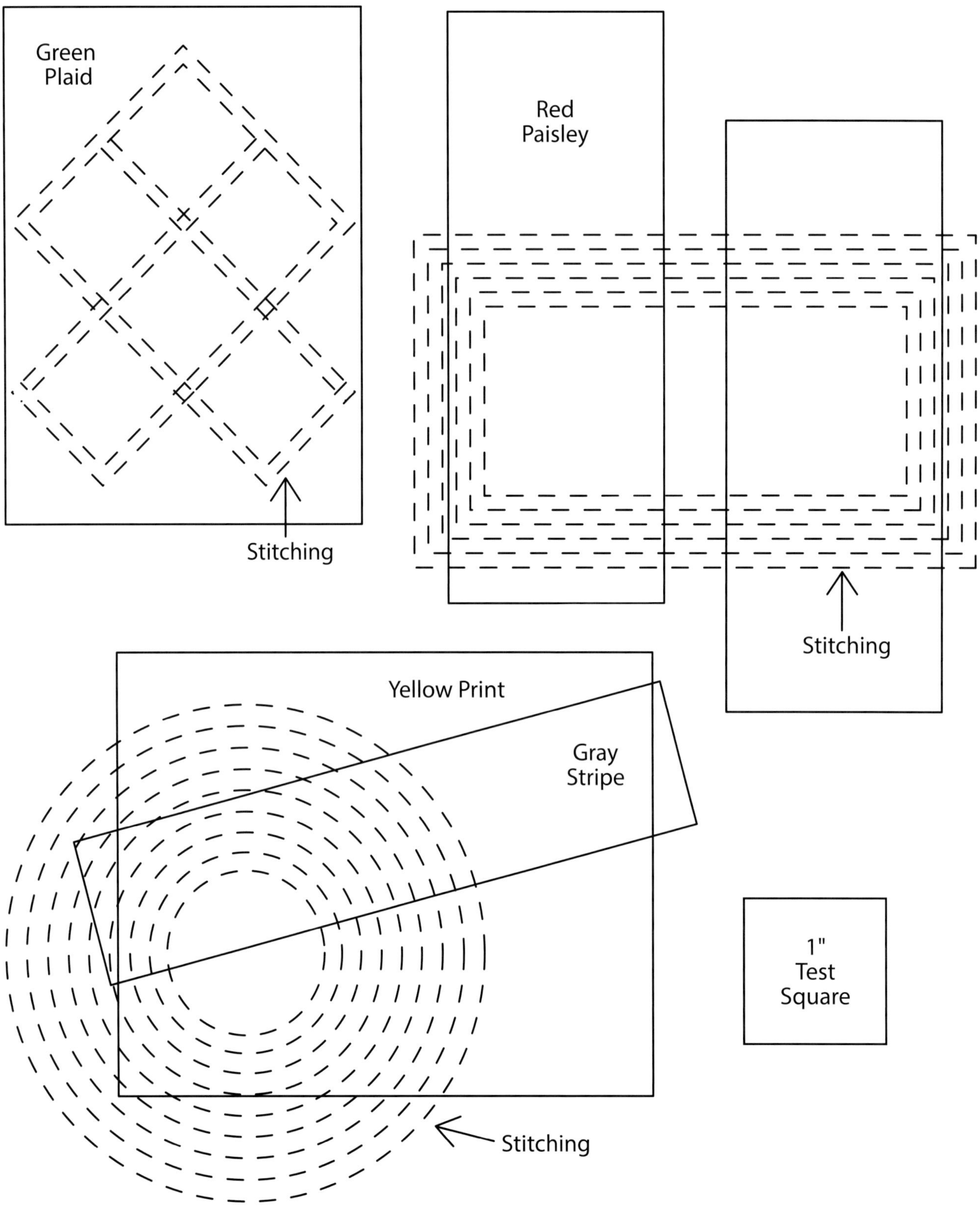
Green
Plaid
Stitching
Red
Paisley
Stitching
Yellow Print
Gray
Stripe
Stitching
1"
Test
Square

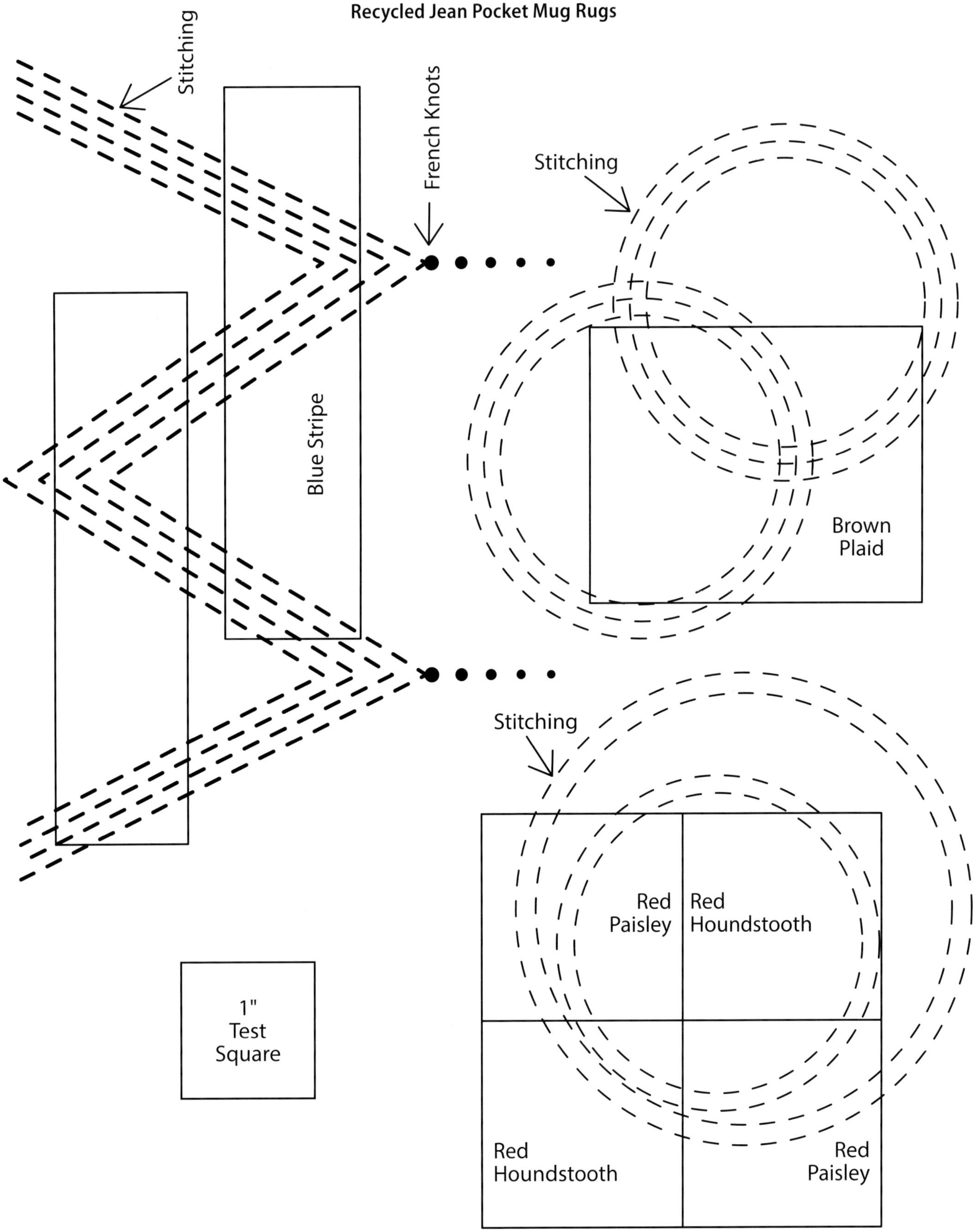

Stitching
French Knots
Stitching
Blue Stripe
Brown
Plaid
Stitching
Red
Paisley
Red
Houndstooth
1"
Test
Square
Red
Houndstooth
Red
Paisley

Blue Rope Mug Rugs

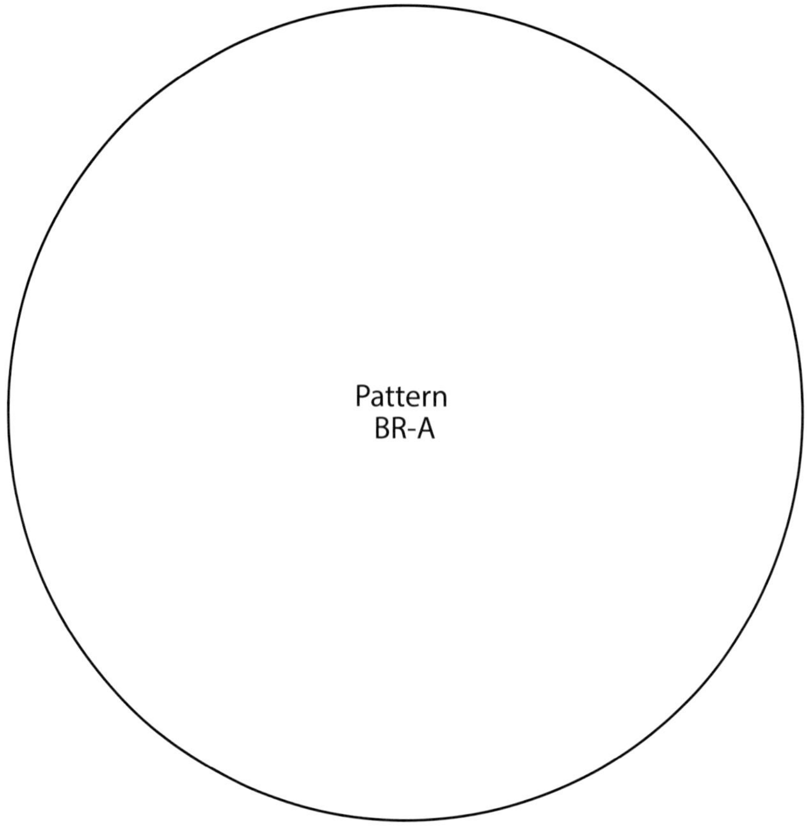

Felt Fruit Mug Rugs

¼" Increments

Felt Fruit Mug Rugs

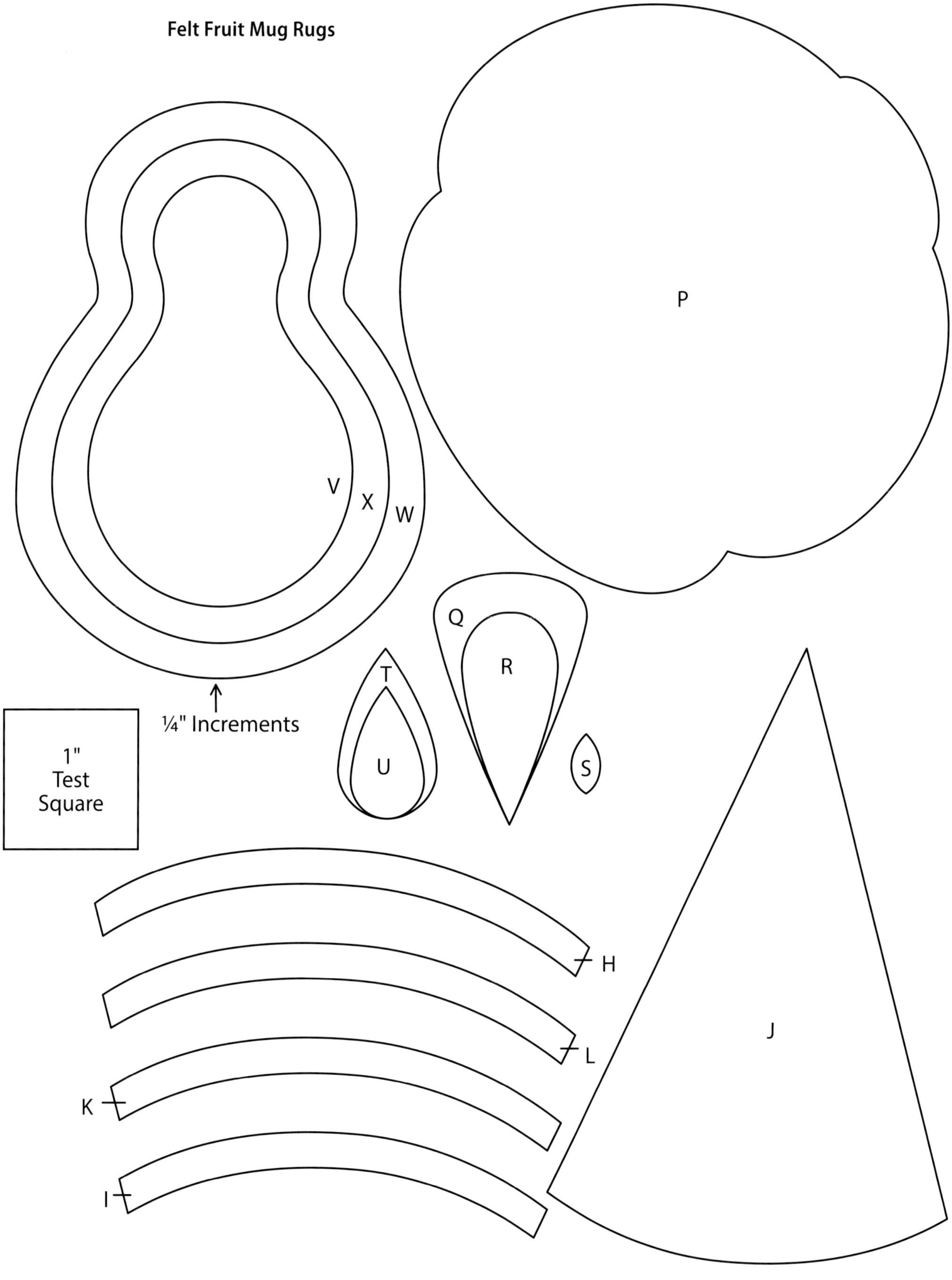

Felt Handbag Coasters

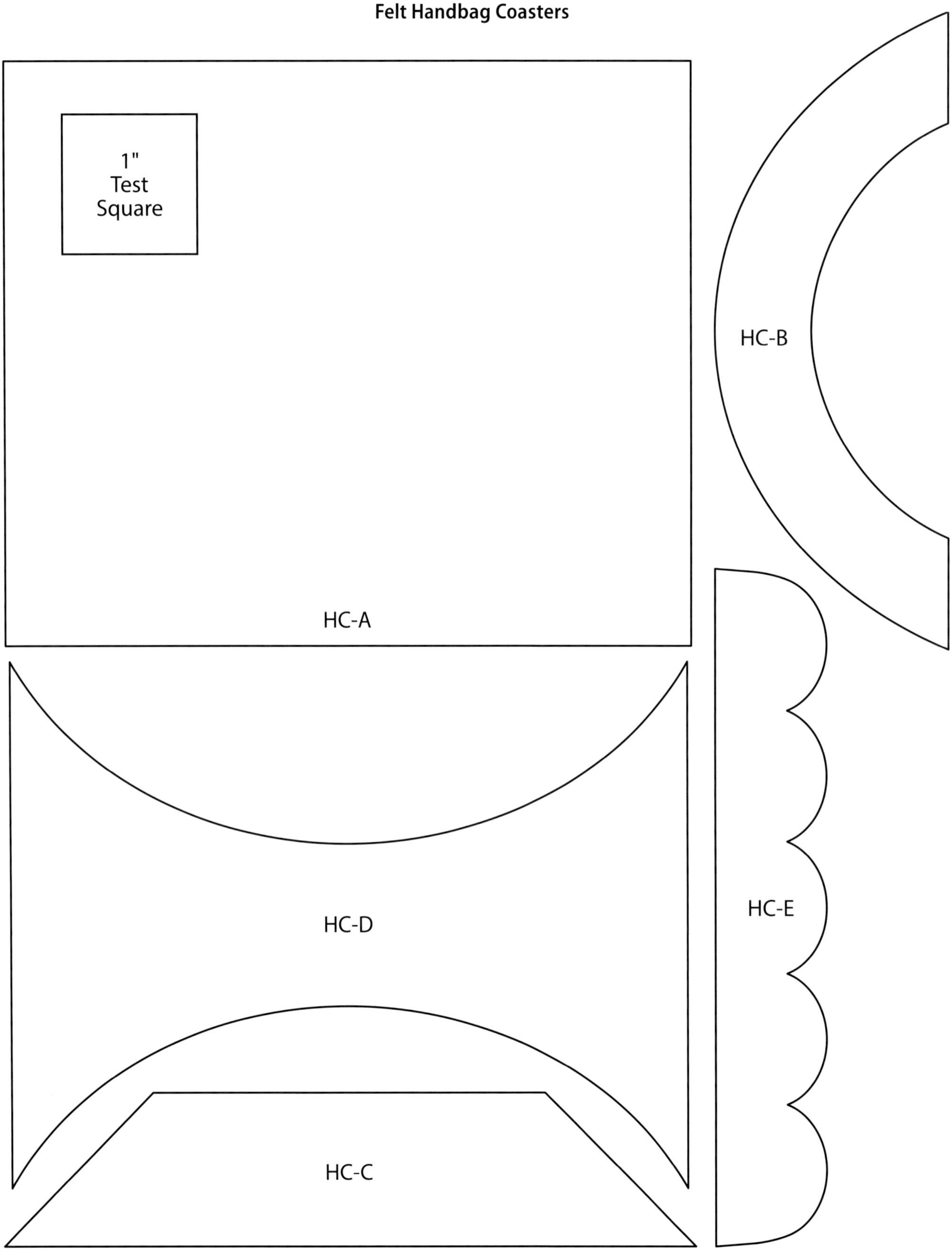

Felt Handbag Coasters

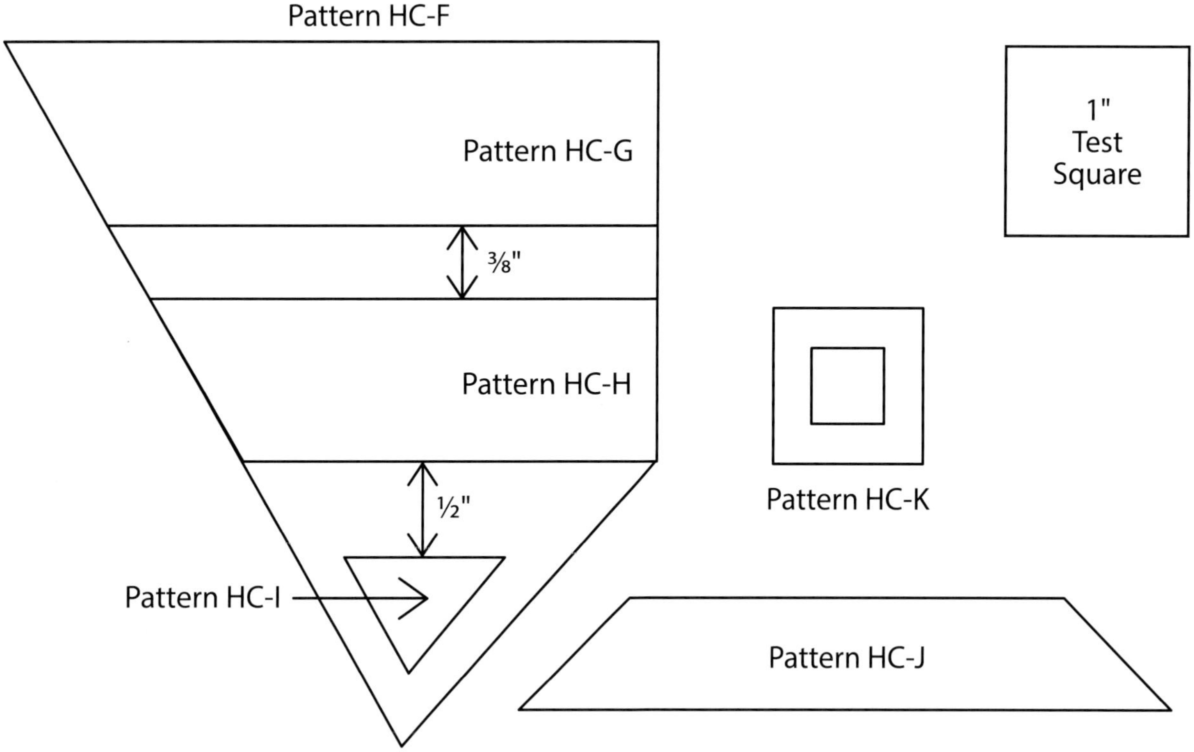

Classy Cat Coasters

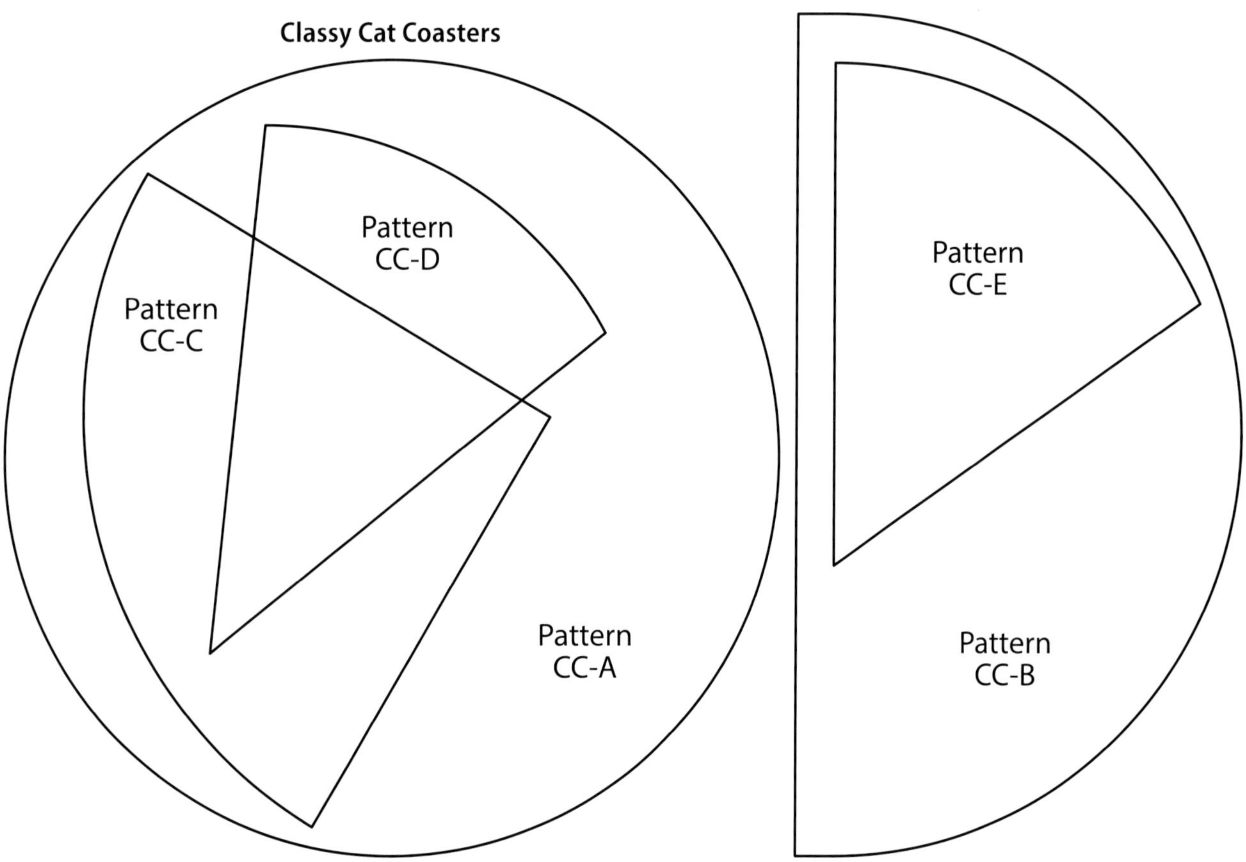

Fussy Cut Window Coaster

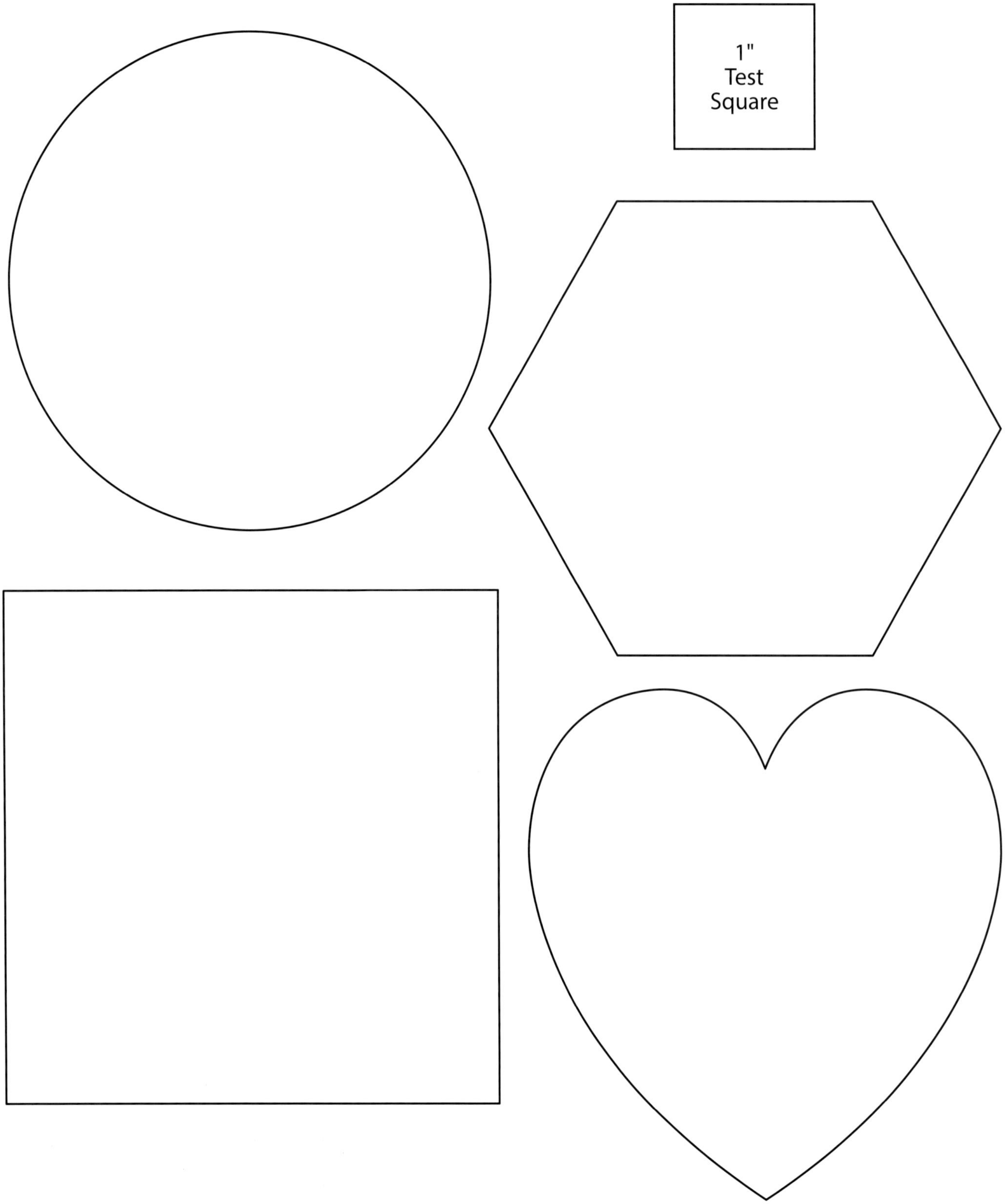

Snowman Hot Chocolate Coasters

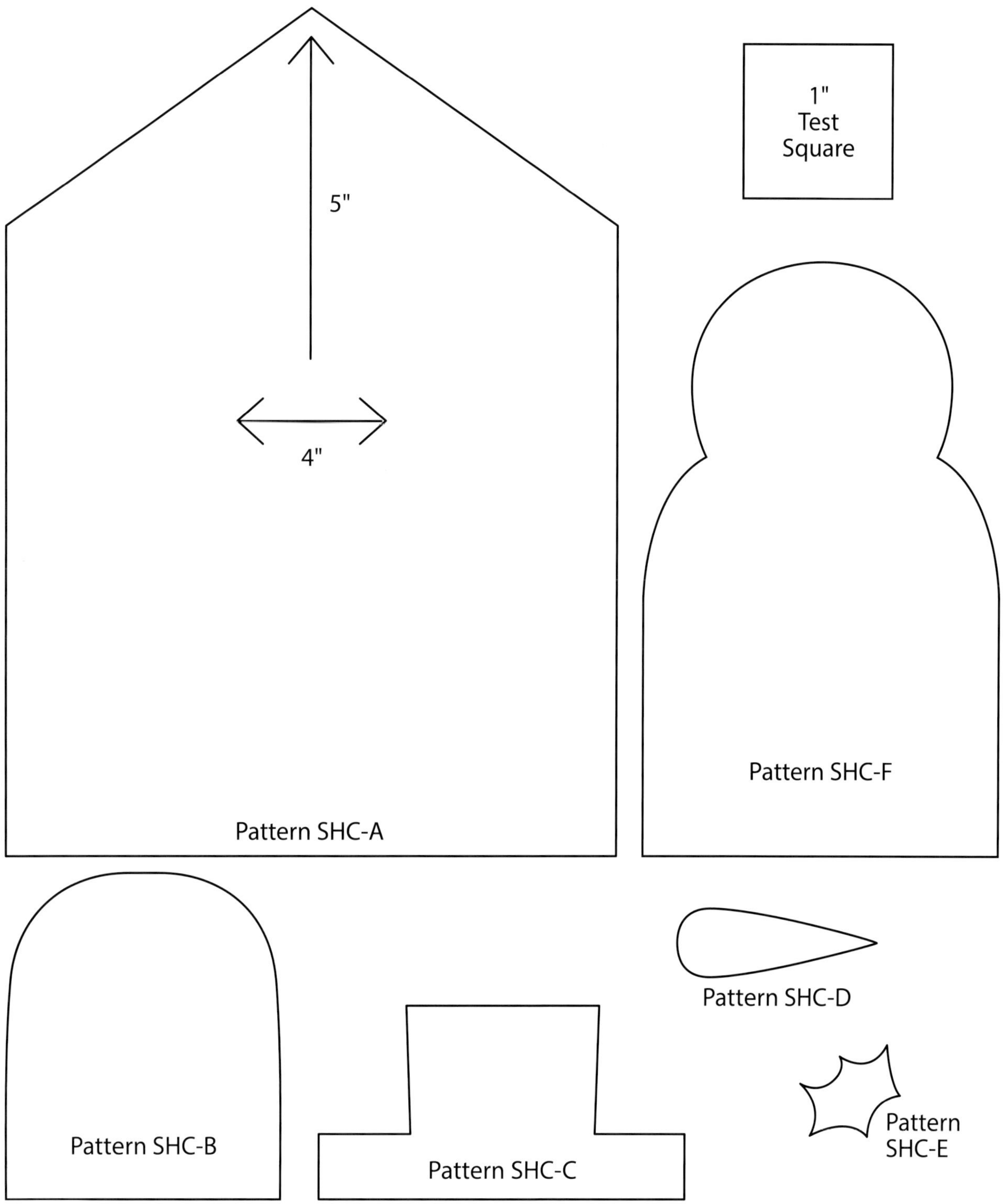

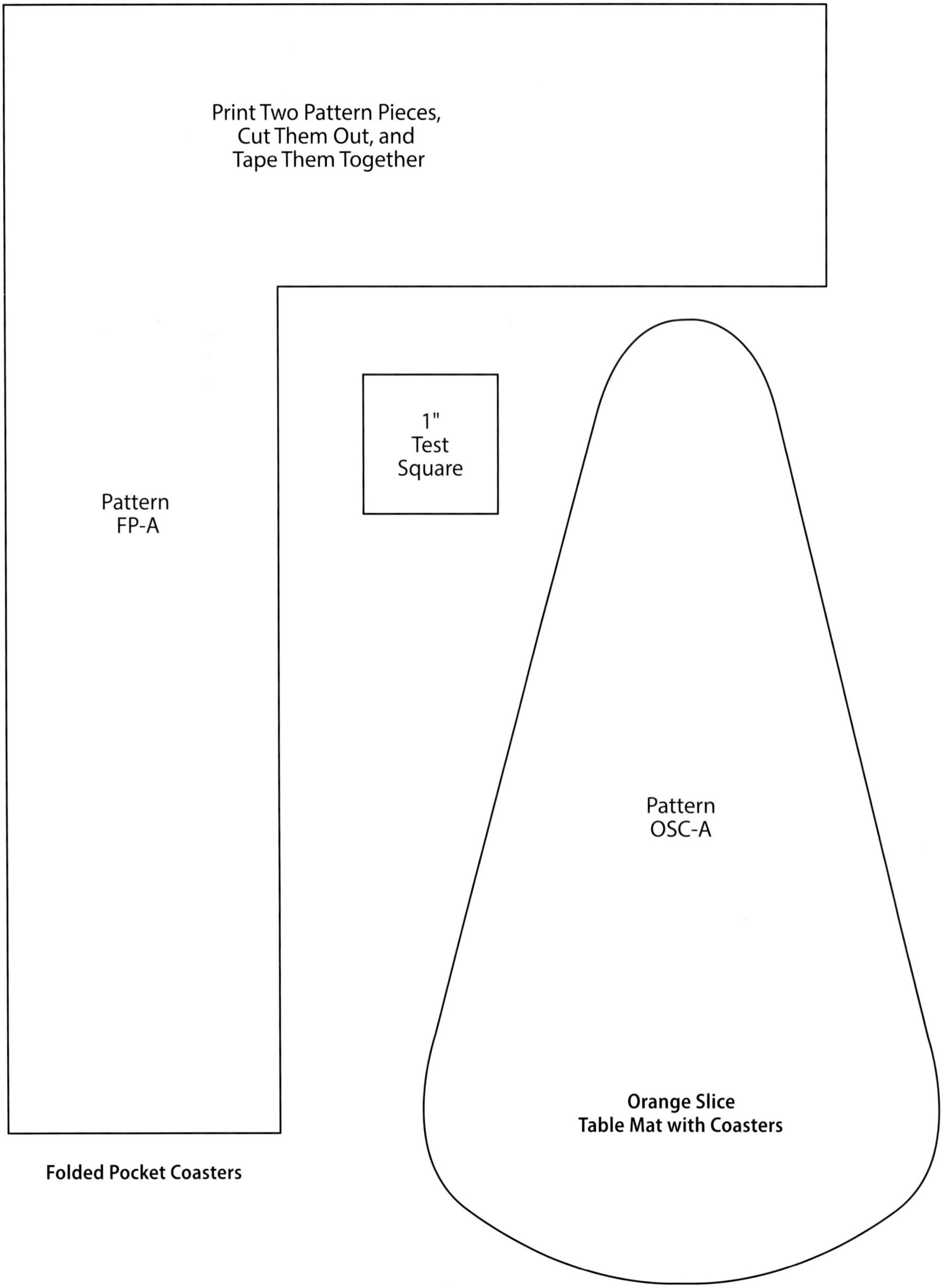
Print Two Pattern Pieces,
Cut Them Out, and
Tape Them Together
Pattern
FP-A
1"
Test
Square
Pattern
OSC-A
Orange Slice
Table Mat with Coasters
Folded Pocket Coasters

About the Author

Debi Schmitz Noriega has been a lifelong creator and a professional designer for over 35 years. With hundreds of tear sheets and magazine designs, she has also appeared on television and has authored numerous craft books.

Debi earned her stripes in the craft industry and is known as one of the "seasoned professionals." Many of her designs have been featured in online magazines, manufacturer websites, advertisements, and at multiple trade shows across the country. She fervently follows worldwide trends to introduce new products for the craft, home décor, fashion, and quilt industries.

Her first book from Landauer, *Piece and Quilt as You Go*, was published in 2024.

Special Thanks

Thank you for the following companies and products:

Belagio Enterprises, Inc.: Cork fabric and rickrack trims
Website: www.belagioenterprises.com

Crazy Redhead Quilting (Newton, Iowa): Quilt shop
I'd like to thank Laura and the staff at her store for taking the time to work with me on fabric choices, sending needed fabrics in a hurry, and supporting me in my design career!
Website: www.crazyredheadquilting.com

Mary Ellen Products: Best Press Starch and Sizing Alternative
Website: www.maryellenproducts.com

Therm O Web: Basting spray, iron-on adhesive, iron-on leather-like fabric stabilizer, and iron-on fusible interfacing
Website: www.thermoweb.com

The Warm Company: Warm & Natural® Needled Cotton Batting
Website: www.warmcompany.com

Index